W9-AEM-480

ANDREW JOHNSON:
PRESIDENT ON TRIAL

Andrew Johnson:

PRESIDENT ON TRIAL

By Milton Lomask

OCTAGON BOOKS

A DIVISION OF FARRAR, STRAUS AND GIROUX

New York   1973

Reprinted 1973

OCTAGON BOOKS

A DIVISION OF FARRAR, STRAUS & GIROUX, INC.

19 Union Square West

New York, N. Y. 10003

Library of Congress Cataloging in Publication Data

Lomask, Milton.

Andrew Johnson: President on trial. New York,

Reprint of the ed. published by Farrar, Straus, New York.

Bibliography: p.

1. Johnson, Andrew, Pres. U. S., 1808-1875—Impeachment.

[E666.L84   1973]   973.5'6'0924 [B]   73-9876

ISBN 0-374-95082-2

Printed in USA by
Thomson-Shore, Inc.
Dexter, Michigan

WITH AFFECTIONATE ESTEEM
TO RALPH GORMAN, C.P.

CONTENTS

[vii]

Part Three: THE VICTORY

PART ONE

The President

I

THE VICE PRESIDENT

On the evening of April 14, 1865, the Vice President of the United States sat down to dinner at the usual hour, five P.M., in the usual place, the dining-room of the Kirkwood House on Pennsylvania Avenue. Andrew Johnson had reached his fifty-seventh year in fair condition except for a recurrent pain owing to "gravel in the kidney." He was of stocky build, carrying one hundred and seventy-eight pounds on a five-foot-eight-inch frame. His eyes, considered his best feature, were black, deep-set and compelling, and it was his habit when speaking to fasten them hard on his listener. When he himself was listener, he usually lowered them in a scowl of concentration that knotted the heavy lines of his brow and accentuated the downward thrust of the corners of his mouth.

Charles Dickens thought Johnson's face one of the most remarkable he had ever seen. Not imaginative, according to the English novelist, but strong—or stubborn; Dickens was not sure which. It was the face, he concluded, of a man who could not "be turned or trifled with. A man (I should say) who would have to be killed to be got out of the way." Another literary man, Henry Adams, came away from his one conversation with Johnson convinced that he had met a representative Southern gentleman, an ironic reaction in view of Johnson's hatred of what he termed the "illegitimate, swaggering, bastard, scrub aristocracy" of the South.

The Vice President ate alone. His meal completed, he lost no time leaving the gaslit room, mounting the few steps at the door and hastening along a short passageway to Number 68, his two-room suite behind the hotel parlor. Because it was Good Friday, most government offices had closed. Except for a call at the White House, Johnson had spent the day in his own office in the Capitol, taking care of sundry personal affairs in preparation for a contemplated trip home to Tennessee to his invalid wife, his sons, his daughters and their children. He was tired and his plan was to read a while and retire early.

But first there were visitors. William A. Browning, his secretary, dropped by for a short time. After the young man's departure Leonard J. Farwell, inspector of inventions at the Patent Office and former Governor of Wisconsin, came in. A friend of Farwell's was in town, a Mr. J. B. Crosby of Massachusetts. Crosby, before leaving the city, wanted to have a look at Abraham Lincoln. Since it was known that the President would be attending the play at Ford's Theatre, Farwell was on his way to purchase seats. He suggested that the Vice President make it a threesome.

Johnson tempered his refusal with one of his infrequent smiles. He was no theatregoer. As a young man in the mountains of upper East Tennessee he had witnessed a circus and a minstrel show. Once he and some friends had spent an evening at a Baltimore burlesque house—a memorable evening, apparently, for Johnson in a letter home had expressed his delight in watching "forty-eight little girls performing every imagionable [sic] evolution." But these items just about measured his familiarity with the stage. All his life his spare hours had been devoted to reading and study in an effort to make up for the formal education he had never had. Somehow there had never been time to cultivate an interest in what he thought of as "frivolity."

He and Farwell talked of other things. The times were tense and there was much to talk about. On the previous April 2 there had been incredulity in Washington at rumors that Richmond, capital of the Confederacy, was about to surrender. Then the *Evening Star* had corroborated the rumors in raucous headlines: "GLORY! ! ! HAIL COLUMBIA! ! ! HALLELUJAH! ! ! RICHMOND OURS! ! !" And to the boom of 900 guns, sounding from Fourteenth and M streets and from the Navy Yard wharf, Washington had gone mad. Washington had stayed mad ever since. Lee's surrender to Grant on April 9 had brought the Civil War to a virtual standstill; the news now was that the three Confederate generals still in the field would be yielding up their forces at any moment.

For an hour or so the Vice President and his companion discussed these matters. Then Farwell left to meet Crosby, and Johnson made ready for bed.

The night into which Governor Farwell stepped was raw and gusty with a rain-wind blowing through the streets. Pennsylvania Avenue in front of the Kirkwood House was lively with pleasure-seekers and illuminated with transparencies of peace and victory that had been mounted on every building along the cobblestoned thoroughfare.

At Ford's Theatre on Tenth Street Farwell and his Massachusetts friend managed to obtain seats giving them a view on their right of the double box shortly occupied by the President, his wife and their guests. The play, *Our American Cousin,* a mediocre comedy of English origin, was somewhat redeemed by the vivacious acting of the star, Miss Laura Keene, and a competent company. Farwell's eyes were on the stage and he was laughing with the rest of the audience at a third-act witticism when the single shot from J. Wilkes Booth's brass derringer rang out. Farwell saw the murderer's lithe figure leaping to the stage from the Presidential box. He heard Booth's pathetic *"Sic semper tyrannis"* and the cry, "Assassination!" from individuals in the crowded house.

He waited to hear and see no more. Leaving Crosby behind, he bolted from the theatre without attempting to confirm his fears. He had read a recent newspaper story of a man in Selma, Alabama, who had offered to help raise a million dollars as reward to anyone who would kill the President and other key figures in the Union government and army. Leonard Farwell, a perspiring middle-aged man concerned about his friend, ran the two and a half blocks to the Kirkwood House.

Seeing one of the hotel clerks standing on the sidewalk, he shouted: "Place a guard at the door! President Lincoln is murdered!"

Inside, he called to another clerk at the desk: "Guard the stairway and Governor Johnson's room! Mr. Lincoln is assassinated!"

He rushed up the stairs and pounded once and then again on the door of Number 68. There was no response. Grabbing the moulding above, he hoisted himself and peered through the dark skylight. He could see nothing. He dropped down, mobilizing his failing breath, and called out:

"Governor Johnson, if you are in the room, I must see you!"

By this time the Vice President had awakened sufficiently to have a muddled apprehension of what was happening. He lighted his lamp, stepped into a pair of trousers and stumbled into the other room.

"Farwell? Is that you?"

"Yes. Let me in!"

Johnson opened the door and Farwell, entering, closed it behind him and gasped out his news. There was a second of immobility. Then, clasping hands, the two men fell upon each other's shoulders in a sudden and irresistible need for mutual support.

Farwell was only the first of Johnson's acquaintances to reach the hotel. Soon the lobby and the second-floor corridor were awash with people, inquiring after the Vice President and supplying further and often contradictory details of the night's events.

Lincoln had been carried from Ford's Theatre to the main floor bedroom in a lodging house belonging to William Petersen across the street. Secretary of War Edwin McMasters Stanton was taking steps to identify and capture the assassin and his accomplices, one of whom had assaulted Secretary of State William H. Seward in the bedroom of his home overlooking Lafayette Park.

Beyond these few accurate reports, all was confusion. Much that would be known shortly was not yet known at all or known only in a fragmentary way. Some time would pass before the public would hear of George B. Atzerodt, the boozy and childlike carriage-maker from Port Tobacco to whom Booth had assigned the job of murdering Vice President Johnson.

Atzerodt had registered at the Kirkwood House that morning, getting a room on the floor above Johnson's suite. He had deposited some weapons under the pillows of his bed, had gone downstairs to snoop about, have a drink; after which, suddenly unnerved, he had scuffled away, never to be seen at the Kirkwood House again.

Booth himself had visited the hotel sometime during the day. Told that Atzerodt was out, the raven-haired actor did a puzzling thing. He asked the clerk if the Vice President were in his rooms— or was it William A. Browning, Johnson's secretary, that Booth asked about? Robert R. Jones, the clerk on duty, was unable to remember afterwards. Both Johnson and Browning were out, so Booth asked for a card and scratched off a note, reading:

"Don't wish to disturb you. Are you at home? J. Wilkes Booth."

Jones put the card in Browning's box. When Browning picked it up at 5 P.M. he gave it no special thought. During the war he and Johnson had been introduced to the famous actor in Nashville, Tennessee. Later, after the assassination, a suspicion took form in Browning's mind. It was his belief that Booth had meant his note for Johnson. Realizing that Atzerodt would never get up courage enough to kill the Vice President, Booth had intended his message to suggest an intimacy with Johnson that might prove embarrassing to Lincoln's successor.

The friends swarming into the Vice President's rooms knew nothing of all this. They were not yet certain concerning the identity of Lincoln's killer, or of the man who had wounded Seward. Some said they were one and the same person; some said they were different; some said Lincoln's brilliant little Secretary of State was already dead, and some said not.

Johnson, recovering from his initial shock, requested Farwell to get the facts. "Go to the President and Seward," he ordered. "See them personally and do not credit any rumors that may be flying around the City."*

Farwell left at once. Seemingly half of Washington was in the streets. The downtown avenues and the passageways between the buildings were a mass of humanity, through which he edged his way with difficulty. There was a delay at the Petersen house while he identified himself to the guards. Then he stood in the stale air of a crowded room, looking down on the face of the tall man on the bed, needing no word from the doctors to know that the end was near. At Seward's there were further horrors: five men had been beaten or stabbed, victims of Booth's accomplice who had gained entrance by a ruse. The Secretary of State was deeply gashed about the neck. Two weeks earlier he had been thrown from his carriage and the doctors had steadied his fractured jaw with an elastic wire bandage that extended downward over his throat. This ghastly-looking contraption, deflecting the bowie knife of the assassin, had saved his life.

Working his way back to the Kirkwood, Farwell made his report. Johnson heard him out with lowered eyes. Then he put on his coat and gave notice that he would go to the President. Protests arose from friends who feared for his life in the crowded streets, but Johnson ignored them. Major James O. O'Beirne, commander of the provost guard, had arrived, bringing soldiers to replace the

---

* Johnson's remark here is a case of converting to the first person Governnor Farwell's paraphrase of the Vice President's words as given in Farwell's letter of February 8, 1866, to Senator James R. Doolittle of Wisconsin. Doolittle, as he explains in a letter of March 12, 1866, to the State Historical Society of Wisconsin, requested the letter from Farwell principally for the purpose of providing future generations with a first-hand account of Andrew Johnson's activities on the night of Lincoln's assassination. The originals of both Farwell's and Doolittle's letters, photostats of which were kindly provided the author by the Wisconsin Historical Society, are in the Doolittle papers at Madison.

guards hastily posted by the hotel proprietors. O'Beirne urged Johnson to take along a detachment of troops. The suggestion was waved aside. Buttoning his coat and pulling his hat over the upper part of his face, the Vice President, accompanied by O'Beirne and Farwell, hastened to the little room where Abraham Lincoln lay dying in a walnut bed that was too small for him.

It was now 2 A.M. Johnson remained about thirty minutes. He gave as his reason for leaving that the house was crowded and his space could be better used by the doctors and others who might do something for Mr. Lincoln. The secretary of Senator Charles Sumner of Massachusetts, who was at the bedside, recorded another reason in his diary. Sumner, he wrote, begged Johnson to go, pointing out that his presence only added to the grief of Mrs. Lincoln. It is known that Mary Lincoln could not abide the Vice President; "demagogue" was her epithet for him. She would go to her grave, poor, distracted woman, convinced that Andrew Johnson had had a hand in her husband's murder.

Abraham Lincoln died at 7:22 A.M. on Saturday morning. Later that day Mrs. Martha Johnson Patterson sat down in her rented house in Nashville to write an anxious letter to his successor. "My dear, dear Father," she wrote, "the sad, sad news has just reached us . . . Are you safe and do you feel secure?"

Mrs. Patterson, oldest of the Johnson children, was a handsome woman of thirty-six who, after the feminine fashion of the time, italicized words profusely. The announcement of Lincoln's death had left Nashville *"wild with excitement,"* Martha wrote. The Tennessee capital, in Union hands since early in the war, had been celebrating the peace that very morning and had "presented a *gala* appearance" but the "stars and stripes have been taken down, and now nothing but the booming of cannon is heard and returning soldiers to camp." She continued:

I never felt so sad in all my life, and poor Mother, she is almost deranged fearing that you will be assassinated. Our distracted and torn up country. How I long to be with you this sad day, that we might weep together at a *Nation's calamity,* and be ever mindful of *Him* who watches over and preserves us from all harm.

The city now presents a gloomy aspect, almost everything is draped in *mourning* and the house we *occupy* is also draped.

Overwhelming as the events of that hour were, Martha was too much woman to consider them the whole of life. A few days later she would see to it that her small son Andrew wrote a letter thanking his grandfather for a suit of clothes and expressing the desire to "see you dear Grandpa since you are President and see if it is my Grandpa yet." Martha also had news of a purely family nature to relate on that terrible Saturday morning. The landlady, Mrs. Brown, she informed her father,

walked in here the other day, and inspected things, without observing the common *ceremonies* of *entering* a *house* . . . but then she is a *rebel,* and nothing better could be expected. I presume she thinks we are an ignorant *sort* of *people,* half civilized and *refugees* from upper E. Tennessee, etc. I will enclose her *note* written to Mother, asking "for the *rooms in her own house."* I made no reply to her note.

Next came a report on other members of the family. "Sister" was in Knoxville after a "pleasant trip," sister being Mrs. Mary Stover, widow of a Union Colonel in East Tennessee, whose military organization "the bridge-burners," had inflicted considerable damage on Confederate troops in the early phases of the war. "Bob" was in his *"usual* condition." Robert Johnson, or Robin as his friends called him, the older of the President's living sons, was an alcoholic. Martha wrote that Bob was at home but he was "not sensible of the *awful calamity."* Martha closed with the hope that "we will . . . hear from you by telegram today."

The telegram for which Martha hoped would not leave Washington until late that night, for Andrew Johnson had a busy day. At 10 A.M., under the chandelier of a parlor in the Kirkwood

House, he took the oath that made him President of the United States. Chief Justice Salmon Portland Chase administered it, holding out the Bible, on which Johnson planted his lips at Ezekiel, chapter 11, verse 21.

Most of the twelve or fourteen men, standing in a circle around them, watched the ceremony with tired eyes, having kept the death vigil of the night before. Among them were all of the Cabinet except Secretary of Navy Gideon Welles and the stricken Seward. Also present was Francis P. Blair, Sr., head of a family that had been prominent in American politics since the days of Andrew Jackson. Retired now and growing corn on his Maryland estate, the old man had come into town the night before, had slept at the home of his son, Montgomery, across the street. Devoted to Lincoln, fond of Johnson, he leaned now on Montgomery's arm, a homely, skinny, yellowing old man who had placed the imprint of his quick mind on a good deal of American history. Also present were a few Senators and a general.

Chase was the first to extend his hand to Johnson in what the stately Chief Justice would later describe in his diary as "sad congratulations." After Chase left the room, the new President began a short speech, a sort of inaugural.

"Gentlemen," he said, "I must be permitted to say that I have been almost overwhelmed by the announcement of the sad event which has so recently occurred." There was no other reference to the tragedy; nor did Johnson broach any of the many-faceted problems confronting a nation reunited in fact but still divided in spirit by the memories of four years of internecine conflict. "As to an indication of any policy which may be pursued by me," Johnson said, ". . . that must be left for development as the administration progresses . . . The only assurance I can now give of the future is reference to the past . . . The best energies of my life have been spent in endeavoring to establish and perpetuate the principles of free government . . . Duties have been mine; consequences are God's."

Tradition and courtesy demanded that Lincoln's Cabinet now

tender their resignations, staying on only if the President asked them to do so. In his closing words Johnson made it clear that he wanted all of them to stay: "Gentlemen, . . . I want your encouragement and countenance. I shall ask and rely upon you . . . in carrying the government through its present perils."

There would be a great deal of criticism of Johnson's brief and awkwardly-phrased inaugural. Much would be made of his failure to mention Lincoln by name, of his frequent use of the pronoun "I" and of his statement that the "Duties have been mine; consequences are God's." Senator John P. Hale of New Hampshire, one of those present at the ceremony, quipped that "Johnson seemed willing to share the glory of his achievements with his Creator, but utterly forgot that Mr. Lincoln had any share of credit in the supression of the Rebellion." Congressman James Gillespie Blaine of Maine found in the President's address disturbing evidence of "a boundless egotism."

This was a charge often hurled at Johnson and one that his habits of speech invited. "I want to say . . . ," he once asserted, "that these two eyes of mine never looked upon anything in the shape of mortal man that this heart feared." Again, harking back to his early days as a tailor, "I do not forget that I am a mechanic. I am proud to own it. Neither do I forget that Adam was a tailor and sewed fig-leaves, or that our Saviour was the son of a carpenter."

The President's predilection for such remarks was irksome, especially to men inclined to mistake the manner for the man. They said that Johnson talked too much about himself. He did, but the defect was a factor in the protective coloration he was at pains to invoke. Aside from the still occasionally-circulated stories of Johnson's drunkenness and his illiteracy—false charges, as it will be shown—he is perhaps best remembered for his combativeness and his stubborn determination. Courage he most certainly had, but he was not a hard man. The stern visage which peers at us from the old photographs of him was not the reflection of an inner toughness, but the shield of an inner tenderness. In this he differed from his predecessor, for Lincoln harbored in the depths of his compassionate being a core of toughness, without which he might never have survived the stresses of the Civil War Presidency.

Johnson was not so fortunate. He was a hard-word, soft-deed man. The hard-word habit was one that he had acquired in whirlwind campaigns for office in the wild mountain country of East Tennessee. The frontier farmers of his homeland expected their political leaders to thunder and revile, and Johnson obliged. He cultivated to a fine point the arts of ferocious speech: the stinging tongue-lash, the ready invective, the smashing epithet. On the stump he could duel an opponent into a corner with flashing words, shower him with billingsgate. But when it came to actions, he tended to gentleness, to conciliation, even at times to timidity.

He was aware of all this. "The elements of my nature," he pointed out, "the pursuits of my life have not made me either in my feelings or in my practice aggressive. My nature, on the contrary, is rather defensive in character." Had his life run differently, had he had a chance at systematic education, he might have eschewed the hurly-burly of politics. He might have become a teacher or minister or chemist. So he said to his private secretary, .Colonel William G. Moore, who made a practice of preserving the President's confidences in a shorthand diary, notable for the keys it provides to Johnson's character. Chemistry was especially appealing to him. "It would have satisfied my desire to analyze things," he told Moore, "to examine them in separate periods and then unite them again to view them as a whole." The book-lined study of the scholar was Johnson's proper niche. Kept from it by birth and rearing, and forced to seek fulfillment in a noisier arena, he was a lonely man—with the added loneliness of being a gifted one who, because of his lack of education, or rather because of his exaggerated awareness of it, was usually ill at ease in the company of other gifted men.

Johnson grew up in Raleigh, North Carolina, where he was born on the night of December 29, 1808. His parents were mudsills, a term given to landless poor whites, presumably because they often lived in shacks with dirt floors and mud sills. Of his mother, Mary McDonough Johnson, little is known other than that she was small and swarthy, that she was addressed by the townspeople as "Aunt Polly" and that she was of Scotch-Irish forbears. Jacob, his father, is believed to have been an immigrant from the North of England, an honest and good-natured man who supported his family by a succession of more or less menial jobs.

When Andy was three, his father became the town hero by plunging into the icy waters of a lake to save the lives of two prominent citizens. The experience shattered Jacob Johnson's health, and a year later he was dead.

A certain charm attaches to Andy's efforts at an early age to satisfy his itch for learning. There were no free schools in Raleigh and money for tuition was out of the question for "Aunt Polly," hard put to support Andy and his brother by taking in washing and weaving clothes on her loom. So Andy found his own school— in the shop of master-tailor James J. Selby. It was the custom of the journeymen tailors, while they sat cross-legged about the shop doing their cutting and sewing, to hire a man to read to them from newspapers, magazines, novels, poems, plays and the debates of Congress. For hours on end the reading went on, and for hours on end, once young Andy had discovered this unorthodox institution of learning, he could be found among the tailors, dark-eyed and eager, listening and learning.

One of the paid readers took note of the boy's interest and gave him the volume he was using. From this book, with the aid of a primer and an alphabet provided by one of the tailors, Andy taught himself to read. The book was an 1810 edition of *The American Speaker* which, despite its title, was a collection of orations by famous Members of Parliament.

When Andy was fourteen Selby took him on as an apprentice. Two years later, frightened by a threat to "persecute" him for a boyish prank, he ran away. For a time he lived in South Carolina. Still later he journeyed westward over the mountains, travelling mostly on foot as far as the Mississippi river. The summer of 1826 found him again in Raleigh, brought home by news that his mother, who had remarried, was in financial difficulties. Unable to find employment in North Carolina the young man once more ventured west, this time taking his mother and her second husband with him.

They settled eventually in Greeneville, Tennessee, a farming center of some seven hundred population in the foothills of the Great Smoky Mountains, ten miles west of North Carolina. There, on December 17, 1827, Andrew Johnson and Eliza McCardle were married in the home of the bride's widowed mother. Johnson was nineteen. Eliza was seventeen, an intelligent young woman, plain yet attractive, with knife-fine features and hazel-colored eyes. Five children would be born to this union. Johnson, at the time of his marriage, could shape the letters of his own name. Eliza had enjoyed some education. She taught her husband to write and do sums, and he supplemented her tutelage by paying a man six cents a day to read to him while he tailored and by joining two local debating societies.

Political life began for him in his twentieth year when he was elected to the town council, the first of the many offices he was to hold. After three terms as alderman and two as mayor, he moved on to the lower house of the state legislature and from there to the state senate. In 1843 he was elected to the first of five consecutive terms in the House of Representatives. He was elected Governor of Tennessee in 1853, re-elected two years later; and in 1857 he went to the United States Senate.

He found his political home in the party of the Jacksonian Democrats. His political creed, once shaped, remained substantially unaltered. He championed the cause of the have-not—of the mechanic, the small farmer and the small business man. "The people need friends," he said. "They have a great deal to bear." He fought concentration of power, whether in government or in business. For 14 years, as a member of Congress, he battled for a Homestead bill that would have enabled any qualified citizen to obtain free a section of land in the public domain in return for his promise to settle and cultivate it for a given time.

As for slavery, *the* issue of his times, here Johnson's course was occasionally erratic, but on the whole his attitudes and his votes were those of an orthodox Southerner. More exactly, they were those of a border-state Southerner, inclined to face North on economic issues and South on cultural ones.

"My position," he announced in 1850, "is that Congress has no power to interfere with the subject of slavery, that it is an institution local in its character, and peculiar to the states where it exists, and no other power has the right to control it."

He recognized that slavery was a blight on the economy of the South, a ball-and-chain on the ankles of its white workers. As he put it when Emancipation came, "I think we are freeing more whites than blacks in Tennessee." In private conversation he conceded that "as an institution," human bondage was "opposed to the spirit of Christianity." He knew that to the generality of Southerners, slavery was more than an economic institution, capable of being valued at so many millions of dollars; he thought that great as were the evils of slavery they were less than the consequences of emancipation. In Johnson's time the word "integration" did not bear the special meaning it would take on later, but in its broad sense integration was what he feared. In common with other Southern leaders, Johnson shrank from the burden of social-readjustment that the abolition of slavery would thrust upon the South.

When Johnson entered politics in 1829, the Civil War was already in the making. He was serving his first term as Governor when in 1854 the last attempt to resolve the differences between North and South fell to the ground with the repeal of the Missouri Compromise of 1820. Reaching the Senate in 1857 Johnson watched with alarm the divisive agitation of the Abolitionists of the North. He was equally alarmed by the Fire Eaters of the South, a small but articulate group of secession advocates. In Johnson's opinion the Fire Eaters were "conspirators" bent on deluding the Southern masses into an unjustified war of independence. It was not his belief, and never would be, that the protection of slavery was their prime motive. What was driving the secessionists, he contended, was a fear of popular government; they were distressed by the growing power of the people, a trend against which they hoped to insulate the South by separating it from the North where the popular voice was loudest. Uneasy as the times were, Johnson was slow in detecting in them the signs of impending conflict. As late as 1859 he was confident that "all the factionists of this government" can never "pull it to pieces."

The events of the next few months were such as to make him eat those words. As the critical Presidential election campaign of 1860 took shape, Johnson's party split over the slavery issue. The northern Democrats named Stephen Douglas of Illinois as their candidate, the southern branch named John C. Breckinridge of Kentucky. Into the battle edged a third party, calling itself Constitutional Union, representing anti-secession conservatives throughout the country and advancing as its candidate John Bell of Tennessee. The newly formed Republican party nominated the little-known westerner, Abraham Lincoln, and from South Carolina, home-base of the Fire Eaters, came the threat that, if the railsplitter were elected, secession would follow.

The day of reckoning had arrived and with it a day of personal decision for Andrew Johnson. He was a states-rightist, but he was also convinced that the Federal Constitution was a compact for perpetuity from which no member-state had the right to withdraw. While he dreaded the effects on the South of the destruction of slavery, he was certain that slavery could not survive a civil war. Given these beliefs, the nature of his personal problem was clear. When the break came he must either stand by slavery or by the Union.

During the campaign he did his duty as a Southern Democrat. He toured Tennessee and nearby states, beating the drums for Breckinridge; but no drums were ever beat more feebly. A document published for the use of campaigners castigated Lincoln as a "Black Republican." Johnson made use of the document but avoided the epithet. On Monday November 5, the day before the election, he was in Gallatin, Tennessee. His co-speaker was Col. J. J. Turner. After they had completed their speeches, the two of them and some political associates retired for tea as the Colonel's guests and the talk went to the morrow. Johnson predicted that Lincoln would win, that the South would seize on his election as a pretext for secession, that civil war would follow and that the South would lose and slavery be destroyed. He paused at this point and got to his feet as though aware of the import of his next statement on Tennessee politics.

"When the crisis comes," he said, "I will be found standing by the Union." Later, talking to another group of Southerners, he made clear the basis on which his decision had been reached. Reiterating his conviction that civil war would spell the end of slavery he said, "If you persist in forcing this issue . . . against the government, I say in the face of Heaven, give me my government and let the Negro go."

The Senate to which Johnson returned in December of 1860 was long on words and short on temper. Even a routine motion to print the usual number of President Buchanan's message unleashed a protracted row. The mood of Congress reflected that of the country as a whole. American history had become a ticking time-bomb. Everywhere ears were cocked, waiting for an explosion that everybody realized was coming but that only a sprinkling of men on either side of the Mason-Dixon line wanted to hear.

Throughout the North men were grappling with questions as old as the Union itself. Did a state have a right to secede? If a state did secede, rightfully or otherwise, was there anything the Federal Government could do about it? In the closing weeks of 1860 secession was being talked up everywhere. John C. Burch, representing California in the House, wrote home that since the Union was going to pieces anyhow, his state might as well get on the bandwagon. Rapidly germinating, according to the New York *Times,* was a "strong movement . . . for a great middle confederation to be called the 'Central United States' or the 'Federal Republic of Washington.'" It would include, the *Times* was informed, nine northern and southern states and the Northwest Territory. New York City resounded with talk of converting that booming metropolis into a free city like Venice, a proposal heartily endorsed by its pro-Southern mayor, Fernando Wood.

In the White House a pious and lachrymose old man cowered before the storm. James B. Buchanan of Pennsylvania loved the Union. He also loved the South. The war clouds were in the sky when he took office, and his initial determination was to keep the peace by making every possible concession to Cotton State interests. When he realized, belatedly, that all the concessions in the world could not silence the agitation making for war, he scarce knew what to do. He termed his course a "policy of forbearance," aimed at letting the South fire the first shot if—God forbid!—a first shot there had to be. Since he was not President of the North alone but of all sections of the country, this policy was the only one he could legitimately pursue. Unfortunately he was incapable of implementing it in any constructive way. At a time when the country needed leadership, he simply mirrored its distraction. His message to Congress, a few days before the opening of the South Carolina secession convention, tackled the questions of the hour in a spirit of yes-and-then-again-no. As Senator Wade of Ohio observed, it consisted of three propositions: (1) South Carolina had just cause to secede, (2) she had no right to secede, and (3) if she did secede, the Federal Government had no right to stop her. Seward of New York, soon to leave the Senate for Lincoln's Cabinet, said ironically that the message showed "conclusively that it is the duty of the President to execute the laws—unless somebody opposes him; and that no state has a right to go out of the Union—unless it wants to."

It was against this background of confusion that Andrew Johnson rose in the Senate on Wednesday, December 18, 1860, to announce his personal stand to the country as a whole for the first time. It was a dramatic moment. In Charleston the South Carolina secession convention was well under way. Johnson spoke to a crowded chamber, with its galleries filled. Word had spread that secession would be his topic, but there had been no foreknowledge of the position he was going to take. Afterwards many would declare that the impact of his words derived not so much from the words themselves, as from the circumstances under which they were uttered.

"Mr. President," he said, ". . . if the doctrine of secession is to be carried out upon the mere whim of a state, this government is at an end. It is no stronger than a rope of sand, its own weight will crumble it to pieces, and it cannot exist. If a state may secede why, as Madison asks, may not other states combine and eject a state from the Union?"

He agreed with those who contended that the Federal Government did not have the right to coerce a state, but what was happening in the South, he argued, was not being done by States but by the individuals living in them. Those individuals were subject to the national laws. When they defied those laws, it was not a case of the Federal Government having a right to act. Under the Constitution it had no choice but to act.

Although Johnson's statements shared headlines with the news that South Carolina had seceded, they produced a sizeable reaction and went a long way toward dispelling indecision throughout the North. Typical was the statement of a Tennessee Union man, long one of Johnson's political opponents, that his words were "a powerful light in the darkness and the gloom of the hour . . . the first message of courage to the almost despairing North."

There were later speeches, all of them ringing changes on the theme of Union. In the wake of Lincoln's inauguration and the outbreak of hostilities, Johnson introduced and the Senate passed a conciliatory resolution stating that the North was not fighting a war of subjugation or conquest, that it had no desire to interfere with slavery, where it already existed, that its only aim was to preserve the Union.

In the spring and early summer of 1861 Johnson was once more in Tennessee, fighting to keep his own state loyal. It was a losing battle. During the preceding February the people of Tennessee had voted against secession. Then came Fort Sumter, followed by Lincoln's call for troops. Talk of war was one thing. Actual hostilities and a Presidential proclamation that many Tennesseeans regarded as a threat to liberty and fireside were something else. Within an hour after news arrived that the batteries in Charleston had opened fire, sixty thousand Tennessee Union men deserted to the Confederate cause. Secession sentiment swept the large-plantation counties of Western and Middle Tennessee. Only in Johnson's small-farm homeland, the thirty counties of East Tennessee, did Union sentiment hold firm. In a second plebescite in June, large Confederate majorities in the rest of the state overwhelmed the East Tennessee Union majority and carried the state into secession. But the last-ditch labors of Johnson and other Union leaders did not go to waste. East Tennessee would provide at least 35,000 volunteers to the Northern army. Of these, 13,000 were actuated by personal loyalty to Johnson.

Back in Washington by mid-summer, Johnson kept a close eye on military developments in the West. In East Tennessee, the mountaineers, refusing to acknowledge the Confederacy, were staging what later generations would speak of as the rebellion against rebellion. In August a Confederate army invaded the area, and conscription was enforced. Sinewy farmers, hostile to secession, were dragged from their homes, stuffed into Confederate gray and shipped South. Thousands of men fled, making their way North to cast their lot with the Federal forces. A kind of guerilla warfare, with men sallying forth to harass the Rebels by night, living in caves by day, followed.

In Washington Johnson nagged at the authorities, demanding military aid for his embattled homefolk. He found a receptive ear both in Abraham Lincoln and in George B. McClellan, newly-named General-in-Chief of the Armies. But the pertinent Union commander in the West, Don Carlos Buell, took a dim view of moving into East Tennessee. Even after receiving orders to do so, he temporized and delayed. Before this impasse could be relieved, the course of events was changed by the sudden and decisive action of a grubby little man, who had been persuaded to resign from the regular army because of his fondness for the bottle and whose name was Ulysses S. Grant.

Grant's seizure, in February of 1862, of Forts Henry and Donelson in northern Tennessee had the effect of placing in Union hands large sections of Western and Middle Tennessee, including Nashville, the state capital.

To Andrew Johnson the joy of Grant's victories was the joy of half-a-loaf. East Tennessee was still under Confederate control and would remain so until 1864. To Abraham Lincoln the victories spelled an opportunity to get started on the healing work of reconstruction and restoration. A man would have to be found to do it, and early in March Lincoln asked Johnson to resign his Senate seat to become military governor of Tennessee.

As military governor Johnson's chief task was to restore his state to civil status. It was a task beset with difficulties, not the least of which was a continuously shifting military situation. Tennessee was the scene of more Civil War battles and engagements than any other state except Virginia. Nashville itself was subject to repeated Confederate threats. Twice, during the summer of 1862, the city was isolated, without communications with the North. From September 15 to November 10 it was once again in a state of siege. There were two serious attempts by Confederate raiders to take it, but both were beaten off by the Union garrison and on the evening of November 10, Major General William Starke Rosecrans, commander of the newly-renamed Army of the Cumberland, arrived to make Nashville his headquarters. His presence brought a period of relative calm and security to the Tennessee capital.

There was no respite for the hard-pressed Unionists of East Tennessee, however. Still in Greeneville in early 1862, in Johnson's home on Main Street, were the Governor's wife and the youngest of their children, eight-year-old Andrew, called Frank. Eliza Mc-

Cardle Johnson was only fifty-two, but the trials she was under-going were making her an old woman. In common with the other women of the neighborhood she was in the mountains in all weathers, carrying food to the cave hide-outs of her son-in-law, Dan Stover, and his "bridge-burners."

On April 18 Jefferson Davis imposed martial law on all of East Tennessee. Six days later Mrs. Johnson was ordered to take her son and pass beyond the Confederate lines. She was given 36 hours, a difficult demand under the circumstances. She was a sick woman, ill with consumption, as tuberculosis was then called. Her son was a victim of the same illness and would be for some years. Because of her pleas, the order was softened to the extent of per-mitting them to remain in the area, but the Johnson house and servants were confiscated at once. Eliza and her boy were driven into the street, to make their way as best they could to the home of a relative miles distant. In the fall Mrs. Johnson requested per-mission to join her husband. There was a delay at Murfreesboro while redtape was unravelled in Richmond. October was at hand before she reached Nashville with her small son, a broken woman destined to be the prisoner of a sick room for the remainder of her life.

Nonetheless it was a joyous reunion. The Johnson's elder sons, Charles and Robert, both in Federal blue, were stationed at a near-by camp. Charles was serving in his professional capacity as a surgeon. Robert was a colonel with the First Tennessee Cavalry. A house was rented and the soldier-sons came and went. It was a pleasant interlude, one the Johnsons did well to make the most of. Shortly came the news of the death of son-in-law Dan Stover, exhausted at the age of thirty-five by the strains of guerilla fighting. In January Charles was thrown from his horse and killed. Charles had been a wild young man, fond of alcoholic sprees, but likeable and cheerful. His mother never fully recovered from the shock of his death.

From time to time Governor Johnson sought to scare Tennessee's rich, slave-owning secessionists into the Union fold by threats of seizing their property. How little he meant this is shown by his prompt action when an officer of the Nashville military command did the very thing to which Johnson had been giving lip-service.

The officer was a Colonel Truesdail. Acting with the tacit consent of his immediate commander, Truesdail organized a secret police. When Johnson learned that this cabal was making arbitrary arrests and confiscating property, he lost no time in getting in touch with General Rosecrans, Truesdail's superior. Johnson was "blankety-blanked" if he was going to put up with the interference of Truesdail and his aids in the private lives of the citizens. That, he told Rosecrans, was no way to win supporters for the Union. There was no rest for Johnson, or for Rosecrans, or for the telegraph lines to Washington until Colonel Truesdail's private police were disbanded and the confiscation of property halted, never to be resumed.

There will be reason, at a later point, to recall this incident—and also another incident of Johnson's military governorship, his ill-starred "Moses" speech on the night of October 24, 1864.

A contemporary newspaper has preserved this occasion in flamboyant verbiage. Johnson spoke from the south portico of the Tennessee capitol to a crowd including practically the entire Negro population of Nashville. In front of him, according to the Cincinnati *Gazette,* "the street was filled up by a mass of human beings, so closely compacted together that they seemed to compose one vast body, no part of which could move without moving the whole. . . . Over this vast crowd the torches and transparencies, closely gathered together near the speaker, cast a ruddy glow; and, as far as the light extended, the crowd could be seen stretching either way up and down the street."

Johnson's opening words dealt with Lincoln's Emancipation Proclamation, effective the year before. He pointed out that "for certain reasons . . . the benefits of the Proclamation were not applied to the Negroes of Tennessee." It was generally assumed that Johnson himself had asked Lincoln to exempt Tennessee from the proclamation as a means of holding in line the state's pro-Union Whigs, many of whom were slave-owners. Be that as it may, on this emotion-packed October night Johnson was ready to tell his Negro audience that the hour had come to remove "the last vestiges" of slavery. Without reference to the President or any other person, he announced, "I, Andrew Johnson, do hereby proclaim freedom, full, broad and unconditional to every man in Tennessee."

When reverberating cheers, shrilling fifes and rolling drums had faded into echoes, Johnson went on. He turned now to the aristocrats of Tennessee:

Who has not heard of the great estates of Mack Cockrill, situated near this city—estates whose acres are numbered by the thousands, whose slaves were once counted by the score, and who early espoused the Confederate cause? Who has not heard of the princely estates of General W. D. Harding, who by means of his property alone outweighed in influence any other man in Tennessee? . . . Harding, too, early espoused the cause of treason. . . . It is wrong that Mack Cockrill and W. D. Harding, by means of forced and unpaid labor, should have monopolized so large a share of the lands and wealth of Tennessee; and I say if their immense plantations were divided up and parceled out amongst a number of free, industrious and honest farmers, it would give more good citizens to the commonwealth, increase the wages of our mechanics, enrich the markets of our cities, enliven all the arteries of trade, improve society, and conduce to the greatness and glory of the state.

The representatives of this corrupt and (if you will permit me almost to swear a little) this damnable aristocracy . . . charge us with favoring Negro equality. Of all the living men they should be the last to mouth that phrase; and when uttered in their hearing, it should cause their cheeks to tinge and burn with shame.

Negro equality indeed! Why, pass any day along the sidewalks of High Street where these aristocrats more particularly dwell— pass by their dwellings, I say, and you will see as many mulatto as Negro children, the former bearing unmistakable resemblance to their aristocratic owners!

Colored men of Tennessee! This, too, shall cease! Your wives and daughters shall no longer be dragged into a concubinage . . . to satisfy the brutal lusts of slaveholders and overseers! Henceforth the sanctity of God's holy law of marriage shall be respected in your persons, and the great state of Tennessee shall no more give her sanction to your degradation and your shame!

It would appear from the Cincinnati *Gazette* account that at this point Johnson's audience was quite carried away. " 'Thank God,' " the newspaper story runs, " 'Thank God' 'Thank God' came from the lips of a thousand women." Johnson, veteran of a hundred frontier canvasses, was carried away, too. Looking out upon "this vast throng of colored people," as he put it, he was "almost induced to wish that, as in the days of old, a Moses might arise who should lead them safely to their promised land of freedom and happiness." The Cincinnati *Gazette* concluded: " 'You are our Moses!' shouted several voices, and the exclamation was caught up and cheered until the Capital rung again!"

It was a dramatic scene in Nashville that misty October night, and an unusual speech to issue from the throat of conservative Andrew Johnson. Its words would echo tauntingly on the fretful winds of later years.

By late June, 1863, General Rosecrans was no longer in Nashville. He was leading the Army of the Cumberland eastward to do battle with Braxton Bragg at Chickamauga creek near Chattanooga, Tennessee. September 19 and 20, the dates of the battle, were funereal days for the North. The Army of the Cumberland might have been destroyed had it not been for the eleventh-hour holding action of General George H. Thomas and his men—action that added to "Pap" Thomas' string of nicknames that of "Rock of Chickamauga." Two months later the Army of the Cumberland, now under Thomas' command, made it up, eighteen thousand men streaming up a mountain wall in the face of cascading enemy fire to rout the Confederates from Missionary Ridge.

The Battle of Missionary Ridge put Chattanooga in Union hands and Chattanooga was the gateway to East Tennessee. The result was that in the opening days of 1864 all of Tennessee at long last came under Union sway and Governor Johnson was able to speed up his efforts at reconstruction.

The general terms under which Tennessee could resume civil government had been laid down in Lincoln's only official action on reconstruction, his so-called "Ten Per Cent" Proclamation of December 8, 1863. The proclamation offered to pardon all citizens of the seceded states, with a few exceptions, who were willing to swear allegiance to the Constitution. It provided that a government set up in any Southern state by one-tenth of its pardoned qualified voters would be recognized as a "true" government by the Federal executive. To this was added the proviso that each such government must pledge acceptance of emancipation.

Led by the military governor, the campaign to establish a civil government in Tennessee was getting up steam early in 1864. Harsh experience had taught Johnson the importance of honoring a telegraphed request from Lincoln that precautions be taken to keep the state under loyal control. When Johnson announced an election for the first Saturday of March, he called for an oath far stiffer than the simple oath of allegiance suggested in the Presidential proclamation. No man could vote who was not willing to swear, "so help me God," that he would not only support the Constitution but that he ardently desired "the suppression of the present insurrections and rebellion against the government of the United States, and the success of its armies and the defeat of those who oppose them."

It was a difficult oath for any Tennessean who had ever harbored or still harbored a flicker of hope for a Southern victory. The Nashville *Press* came out openly for perjury. So did a cavalryman called Richardson. "Take any oath that the Federals may prescribe," he urged secessionists, "but . . . control the election at all hazards."

Under these strained conditions the day of the voting came and went—and was a heartbreaking failure. The vote was between 40 and 50 thousand, but in many counties there was no election at all and in general the requirements of the Ten Per Cent Proclamation were not met. Johnson had to start all over again. Not until April of 1865 was he able to report to Lincoln that once more Tennessee was under a civil regime loyal to the Union.

The end of that same month found Johnson en route to the national capital. His nomination for the Vice Presidency in June of the previous year was the outgrowth of a series of political maneuvers. Their precise nature is still open to question but the items which stand forth are these: In the Presidential campaign of 1864 the party in power, casting off its regular name, convened in Baltimore as the National Union Party. Two considerations impelled the Republicans to this strategy. One was their desire to mitigate the stigma of sectionalism clinging to a party recruited almost entirely in the North. The other was their desire to attract the support of War Democrats and other non-Republican Unionists. In public Lincoln gave no indication of whom he wanted on the ticket with him, but behind the scenes his actions were those of a man determined to nationalize his party further by the nomination of a War Democrat as his running mate.

That his final choice was Johnson would be the testimony of Simon Cameron and Alexander K. McClure, the bosses of rival Republican factions in Pennsylvania.* Into the ear of each, separately and privately, the master-politician in the White House dropped Johnson's name with the result that at the Baltimore convention the two antagonists functioned as one in support of the Tennessean, throwing Pennsylvania's 52 votes his way on the first and final ballot.

So it was that Johnson, in the spring of 1865, found himself on his way to Washington. Early that winter he had been ill with what

---

* See Alexander K. McClure, *Abraham Lincoln and Men of War-times*, pp. 106-108, 115, 117, 438, 439; and by the same author, *Old Time Notes of Pennsylvania*, vol. 2, p. 133 *et seq.* See also Carl Sandburg, *The War Years*, vol. 3, p. 69 *et seq.* For a detailed presentation of the contrary view —namely that Lincoln did not select Johnson behind the scenes—see Charles Eugene Hamlin, *The Life and Times of Hannibal Hamlin*, p. 591 *et seq.* and 611.

was apparently a malarial fever. In January, convalescent but shaky, he had written Washington to see if there were any precedents which would permit him to take his oath of office as Vice President in Nashville and remain there until sometime after inauguration day. He was informed that other Vice Presidents-elect had done what he was suggesting, but Lincoln telegraphed that "it is unsafe for you not to be here on the 4th of March. Be sure to reach here by that time."

Johnson was in the national capital by the first. On the evening of the third he attended a stag party in his honor at the Capitol Hill quarters of John W. Forney, secretary of the Senate and editor of newspapers in Philadelphia and Washington. The party lasted well into Saturday morning. Liquor was plentiful and when Johnson awakened on inauguration day, in the words of his friend and secretary, Benjamin F. Truman, he "felt much chagrin at his unsteady condition."

For two days rains had been drenching the city and on Saturday morning it was pouring in torrents. Because of these conditions the schedule for the day was put on a flexible basis. If the rain continued both Johnson and Lincoln were to take their oaths of office and deliver their addresses inside the Capitol. If not, the second half of the program, Lincoln's inauguration, was to be held outdoors on the East portico.

The rain ceased altogether even as Johnson was speaking in a Senate chamber filled to more than its capacity by the members of Congress, the heads of government, the cream of the diplomatic corps and the brilliantly-garbed elite of Washington society. Women predominated in the crowded galleries. As retiring Vice President Hannibal Hamlin opened the ceremonies with a brief speech of farewell, a gentleman representing one of the South American republics entered the diplomatic gallery, lost his footing in the sea of crinoline around him and fell clattering down the aisle. There was another stir, minutes later, when Mrs. Lincoln arrived, wearing "a black velvet dress trimmed with ermine."

After Johnson's part of the program was completed and after

the dignitaries on the Senate floor had left the room in solemn procession, the eighteen hundred gallery occupants piled out of the building in wild confusion. Apparently those in charge of the proceedings had neglected to make arrangements for directing spectators out of the Capitol onto the grounds for Lincoln's speech. Everybody rushed for the same door, the main entrance to the Senate wing. It was a stampede. People moved not where they wanted to go but where the crowd propelled them. A number of ladies were lifted off their feet and hurtled, crinolines in full sail, from man to man down the stairways above "a mass of struggling humanity." Already an enormous throng was gathered on the grounds and now the privileged holders of gallery tickets debouched into the area. The impression of an outraged *Times* reporter was that "not one person in fifty got within hearing distance of Lincoln." Such was the setting in which, in a five-minute address beginning about one o'clock, were heard some of the noblest words ever spoken by an American President: "With malice toward none, with charity for all. . . ."

But before these luminous phrases became a part of history, Andrew Johnson had made a spectacle of himself. His downfall began in the Vice President's room off the Senate chamber. Escorted there late in the morning by Senator James Rood Doolittle of Wisconsin, Johnson awaited the beginning of the ceremonies in the company of the retiring Vice President. A Boston *Commonwealth* newsstory describes the scene:

There was nothing unusual in his [Johnson's] appearance except that he did not seem in robust health . . . Conversation proceeded on ordinary topics for a few minutes, when Mr. Johnson asked Mr. Hamlin if he had any liquor in the room, stating that he was sick and nervous . . . Brandy being indicated, a bottle was brought by one of the pages. It was opened, a tumbler provided, and Mr. Johnson poured it about two-thirds full . . . When [it was near] twelve . . . Mr. Hamlin rose, moved to the door near which the Sergeant-at-Arms stood and suggested to Mr. Johnson to come also. The latter got up . . . said, 'Excuse me a moment,' and walked hastily back to where the bottle was deposited. Mr. Hamlin saw him . . . pour as large a quantity as before into the glass and drink it down like water. They then went into the Senate chamber.

All eyes were trained on the two men as they mounted the dais. Hamlin took the chair and made a brief and gracious address. When he had finished he asked Johnson if he were ready to take the oath. Johnson said he was but before Hamlin could administer it, Johnson had plunged into his speech.

It was apparent at once that his two tumblers of brandy were playing havoc with his wits. The first reaction was an amazed hush. Then a murmur began, principally among the dignitaries on the floor. "What's wrong with him?" was heard, and "He must be sick."

Johnson was to speak for seven minutes, but once wound up he couldn't stop. On and on he went, his voice loud and unclear, his words tumbling over one another and losing themselves in their own echoes. Lincoln entered the chamber as he was speaking, and for this poignant moment we have the recollections of Mr. Forney, among others. Forney wrote later that he would never forget Lincoln's expression as he "took his seat facing the brilliant and surprised audience, and heard all that took place with unutterable sorrow." No anger from Lincoln, according to Forney, no indulgence in shocked indignation, only the quiet comment that what happened was "a severe lesson for Andy, but I do not think he will do it again."

It is relevant at this point to discuss Andrew Johnson's habits. In a hard-drinking age, he was an abstemious man. For this we have the testimony of many reliable individuals who because of their official positions were in daily contact with him for years at a time. Although scores of newspapers promulgated the myth of "Andy the Sot," the fact is that, so far as history knows, Johnson got drunk only twice in his life. The second fall from grace occurred six years after he left the White House, a failure. On January 26, 1875, Johnson sat in a room of the Maxwell House in

Nashville, awaiting the results of a vote in the Tennessee legislature that would send him back to Washington, the first ex-President ever to be elected to the Senate. Waiting with him that winter day was his friend A. G. Goodlett. Johnson, Goodlett would recall years later, "had been awake all the night before, and he was very nervous. A glass of brandy acted upon him as it did the day of his inauguration. . . ."

The similar circumstances surrounding the two events suggest that Johnson's behavior on inauguration day in 1865 was not so much a compound of liquor and illness as it was the reaction of a man momentarily overwhelmed by success and gratitude at his part in a momentous occasion. His speech itself bears witness to such a conclusion.

"Deem me not vain or arrogant," he said, according to a somewhat smoothed-out version of his inaugural address, "yet I should be less than human if under such circumstances I were not proud of being an American citizen, for today one who claims no high descent, one who comes from the ranks of the people, stands by the choice of a free constituency in the second place of the government."

So much attention was bestowed on the manner of his talk that little or none was given to its content. Actually it was unobjectionable. His theme was that in a democracy the power resides in the people and that the higher the governmental office a man holds the more constantly he should remind himself of this fact. At one point he undertook to remind the members of Lincoln's cabinet that they too were subject to the popular will. Addressing each of these eminent personages in turn, he omitted titles. It was *"Mr. Seward," "Mr. Stanton," "Mr.—"* But poor Johnson! his memory was not working. Leaning over to Colonel Forney, "What is the name of the Secretary of the Navy?" he asked; and having received the requested information he went rambling on. He stumbled over the words when he finally took his oath and, having sat down, would have risen and made a second speech had he not been restrained by the men around him.

Lincoln would later characterize this incident as "a bad slip," and Johnson's enemies would make the most of it.

During the 41 days of life remaining to Lincoln after his second inauguration, Andrew Johnson took no conspicuous part in the affairs of the nation. On the Monday following his "bad slip," he presided over the Senate. Then old Preston Blair and his son Montgomery whisked the new Vice President off to Silver Spring, the elder Blair's country estate seven miles from Washington. There for several days Johnson rested and repented.

Returning to the capital he began making preparations for the visit to Tennessee that would never materialize owing to the assassination of his chief. On April 4, 1865, he was in Richmond with the President. Fire had gutted large sections of the Confederate capital preceding its surrender the day before. Through its devastated streets President and Vice President walked for a mile and a half, accompanied by a group of dignitaries and reporters and guarded by only four Union officers and ten sailors.

Exactly how much Lincoln and Johnson saw of each other during the weeks before Lincoln's death is not known. There is evidence that on occasion Lincoln avoided interviews sought by Johnson, but there is no evidence of any strain between them. The New York *Evening Post* quoted Lincoln as speaking "warmly" of his Vice President to a White House caller, saying of Johnson's misstep on inauguration day: "He is too much of a man for the American people to cast him off for a single error."

Sometime, soon after the inauguration, the two men did get together for a conversation that Johnson would recall in detail during a public address not quite a year later. The topic was Lincoln's views on the reconstruction of the South and his eagerness to see the Thirteenth Amendment, recently submitted to the states, incorporated in the Constitution. The atmosphere was cordial, with mutual agreement on all issues discussed.

Lincoln was hardly the man to forget that of the 22 Southerners sitting in the Senate at the onset of the war, Johnson alone had remained loyal to the Union. He was unlikely to forget the dangers and the indignities which Johnson had endured because of his stand. Several times, during the war, the Tennessean had come within a hair's breadth of being lynched by aroused Southerners. On one occasion the attempt of a hothead to pull his nose had forced him to physical combat. "No one," Lincoln once remarked, "has the right to judge Andrew Johnson who has not suffered as much and done as much as he for the Nation's sake."

The two men had known each other since 1847 when, as members of Congress, they frequently messed together on Capitol Hill. Antithetical political outlooks discouraged real intimacy but a mutual respect had long existed. During the conflict the President confided to an associate that while other war governors gave him considerable trouble, "Andrew Johnson . . . never embarrassed him in the slightest degree." As for Johnson, he regarded Lincoln as "the greatest American of them all." Equally devoted to the Union and of the same mind on the problems of reconstruction, the Republican President and his Democratic Vice President were in profound rapport.

They were together on Lincoln's last day when, shortly after noon, Johnson called at the White House at the President's request. Edward D. Neill, chaplain of a Minnesota Regiment, was in the executive office when Johnson arrived. Neill stayed long enough to see the President hurry across the room to grasp his visitor's hand. Then the chaplain left, leaving President and Vice President alone for another discussion of immediate issues.

It was their last conversation, of course. The next morning Lincoln was dead and Andrew Johnson was President.

II

THE RADICALS

No page in American history is more moving than that which tells of the deep and spontaneous mourning which swept the northern half of the country at the death of Abraham Lincoln. As for comment on his successor, it was mixed. Andrew Johnson had been popular in the North prior to his unhappy behavior on the day of his inauguration as Vice President but since then an element of distrust had lodged in the hearts of many citizens.

On the morning of Lincoln's death, at the St. Nicholas Hotel in New York City, a stunned gentleman roared his reactions at a reporter from the New York *World*. "A drunkard for President!" he trumpeted. "Great God, that we should come to this!" The reporter elicited similar outbursts from others. "What will become of the country?" a lady wanted to know.

Petroleum Nasby of the Toledo *Blade* sharpened his nib in anticipation of a messy administration. The famed wit, whose writing had given Lincoln so many chuckles, envisioned the dead executive's successor as torn "between two conflictin' forces: the desire acquired, to be a respectable man, and the disposition natural, to be a Dimocrat." Iowa's scholarly Senator James W. Grimes was "full of borebodings." "Johnson," he wrote his wife, "is loyal enough but a man of low instincts, vindictive, violent and of bad habits."

At the other end of the gamut was the optimism of Horace Greeley, erratic founder-editor of the Republican New York *Tribune*. Johnson, in Greeley's opinion, possessed "rare qualifications" in that as a Southerner himself he knew how far the rebellion had "perverted" the South and would know "how to temper justice with mercy." James Gordon Bennett's independent New York *Herald* compared the new Executive favorably with Oliver Cromwell and Andrew Jackson. "As Joshua was to Moses," quoth the *Herald,* "so we expect Andrew Johnson to be as the successor of Abraham Lincoln." Scathingly critical of Johnson as Vice President the leading Democratic organ, the New York *World,* adopted a wait-and-see attitude on President Johnson. The effects of Lincoln's death, the *World* said, "will be mainly such as his successor's personal character and political opinions, especially on the subject of reconstruction, shall determine."

The news was slow in penetrating the South. As late as April 22, in the Georgia town of Griffin, the hospital worker, Miss Kate Cumming, was shrugging aside gossip that Lincoln had been assassinated and that the Confederacy had been recognized by France, England, Spain and Austria. "None of our people," she wrote in her Journal, "believe any of the rumors, thinking them as mythical as the surrender of General Lee's Army."

As the truth took form, the general reaction was one of shock. During the war informed Southerners had softened their estimates of Abraham Lincoln. Little by little it had dawned on them that there was a largeness about the "miserable and contemptible despot," as the Confederate Congress had labeled him in 1863. As hope for a Confederate victory faded, the conviction grew that under Lincoln a defeated South would be treated with dignity and fairness.

But what was there to look forward to now? In the eyes of most Southerners Andrew Johnson was a turn-coat, a Southerner who had deserted his own people. Repeatedly Johnson had denounced the leaders of the Confederacy as traitors, once citing "halter and noose" as their appropriate reward. "Andy the bloody-minded tailor," people in Richmond were now calling him.

Only one sizeable group of men looked on Johnson's accession with unmitigated delight. This group was composed of the Radicals of the Republican party. Made up originally of a small body of anti-slavery zealots, the Radicals were also known as the "iron-back" element, the "ultras," the "vindictives" and the "Jacobins" in memory of the extremists of the French Revolution. An accurate understanding of what they stood for is most satisfactorily attained by reference to the political situation during Lincoln's administration. Throughout this period the Democrats exerted little influence on Federal affairs. The reason for this was that the booming guns of Fort Sumter had torn still another rent in their already fractured party. The Northern membership subdivided into War Democrats, who supported the Union war effort, and Peace Democrats, who endorsed the right to secede in principle and whose support of the war was lukewarm at best. With the Democrats "busted" and "gone-up," in the words of a contemporary satirist, the only effective "loyal opposition" to Lincoln was that provided by the Radicals of his own party.

Lincoln's long dispute with these men revolved around three questions:

1. What was the North fighting for?
2. What should be done about slavery?
3. What should be done with the South after the war?

Lincoln's answer to the first of these questions was that the North was fighting to preserve the Union and the Constitution. The Radicals' answer was that the North was fighting to create a new and better Union, and to hell with the Constitution.

Lincoln's answer to the second question was that, under the Constitution, neither he nor Congress had the power to abolish the institution of slavery in the states where it existed even though most of those states had seceded. Lincoln's Emancipation Proclamation, let it be noted, did not abolish slavery. Issued as a war measure it theoretically freed the slaves then living in most of the states in rebellion, leaving intact the institution of slavery itself. The Radicals wished to abolish slavery without reference to the Constitution.

Since Lincoln died before reconstruction could be launched on more than a piecemeal basis, his answer to the third question was never fully ennunciated, but we can surmise the general lines of it. "Blood cannot restore blood," he said, "and government should not act for revenge." At his last Cabinet meeting on April 14, 1865, he declared that it was "providential that this great rebellion is crushed out just as Congress has adjourned and there are none of the disturbing elements of that body to embarrass us. If we are wise and discreet, we shall reanimate the Southern states and get their governments in successful operation, with order prevailing, and the Union re-established before Congress comes together in December." To these words the President appended the fervent hope that there would no persecution of Confederate leaders, no bloody work. "No one," he said, "need expect me to take any part in hanging or killing those men, even the worst of them. . . . Enough lives have been sacrificed. We must extinguish our resentments if we expect harmony and Union."* Unquestionably, had Lincoln lived, he would have used the powers of his office in an effort to give the South what his iron-back opponents contemptuously called a "tender peace." The Radicals, of course, wanted a "hard peace."

Later, during the Grant administration, the Radicals would degenerate for the most part into puppets on the strings of North-

---

* In this presentation of Lincoln's last remarks on reconstruction, the author has taken the liberty of converting to first person paraphrases of the President's words by his Secretary of the Navy, Gideon Welles. Welles describes Lincoln's last Cabinet meeting in his article, "Lincoln and Johnson: Their Plan of Reconstruction . . ." in the *Galaxy* magazine, vol. XIII (1872), p. 526 *et passim*. Even more detailed and revealing is Welles' discussion of the same Cabinet meeting in a remarkable letter to Johnson, dated July 27, 1869. This letter is in the Johnson papers at the Library of Congress, vol. 154, number 24795 *et seq*. See also John G. Nicolay and John Hay, *Complete Works of Abraham Lincoln,* vol. X, p. 85.

eastern industrial interests. But during the times of Lincoln and Johnson, their leaders were men of diverse and in some cases even irreconcilable economic views, and generally speaking economic considerations were secondary to their desire to maintain the supremacy of their party in national affairs. They reasoned that since the Republicans had taken the lead in seeing the war through, they should take the lead in shaping the peace.

To this end they wanted to see the South brought to its knees. Its plantation oligarchy must be stripped of influence. Its white Democrats must be largely disfranchised and its slaves freed and given the franchise on the assumption that, grateful to their bene-factors, the Negroes would forever vote the straight Republican ticket. The rationale of the Radicals was a compound of humani-tarianism and vengeance, idealism and power-hunger.

Riding herd on the ultras were some of the shrewdest political strategists America has known. During the last years of the war their leader in the House was Henry Winter Davis of Maryland. Tall and slender, Winter Davis was arresting to look at in a sandy, wavy-haired, curly-mustached way. When it was known that he was about to speak, the House cloakrooms emptied. In a high tenor voice that whipped through the fusty air of the chamber, he orated like an angel—a "fallen angel," according to one critic, who saw in Davis a man who would rather "rule in hell than serve in heaven or on earth."

In 1865 Davis' Baltimore district returned him to private life. For a time he continued to exert considerable influence on Jacobin circles from a distance. Then on the evening of December 29, taken ill only a week before, Winter Davis smiled as his wife spoke of a visit he had been planning to make. "It shows the folly of making plans even for a day," he said. At two o'clock the next afternoon, 49-year-old Winter Davis was dead.

His passing removed one of the most magnetic men ever to hold sway over a political faction. He was succeeded by a man of even greater personal magnetism, Congressman Thaddeus Stevens of Lancaster, Pennsylvania, who dominates much of our story.

In the Senate the Radical forces were more or less conjointly field-marshalled by two men of widely different character and personality. One of them was Massachusetts' Charles Sumner, dedicated, ponderous, cosmopolitan and elegant, a product of Beacon Hill aristocracy. The other was also a descendant of New England aristocrats, but during a life spent on the frontier, the elegance had rubbed off—at least from the outer man. Inwardly he had a certain sensibility; but all in all he was a man of violent spirit and coarse body. His name was Benjamin Franklin Wade and he hailed like a maverick wind from Ohio.

These men and their associates carried much weight in party councils. It was the Radicals who urged Lincoln to issue the Emancipation Proclamation long before he came to do so, and who would have preferred a far more sweeping and less "Constitutional" document than the one Lincoln eventually unveiled. It was the Radicals who struggled in vain to deny the President a second term by replacing him with a nominee of their own persuasion in 1864. It was the Radicals who after Lincoln's re-election were saying, in the words of one of them, that the President "must accept our views . . . or we will find means to ruin him. We want to subjugate the South completely and reduce it to a territory governed by the North." And as Lincoln made it increasingly clear that he had no wish to see the South subjugated, the Radicals began muttering among themselves the dread word "impeachment."

One of the men whom the Radicals had viewed in 1864 as a Presidential possibility was that colorful political adventurer from Massachusetts, Major-General Benjamin F. Butler. During the week preceding the assassination he was in Washington. Restlessness had brought the enterprising Butler to the capital. Recently relieved of his duties after holding active command longer than any other political general on the Union side, he was a military leader with no one to lead and a politician without portfolio. In short, he was looking for a job, preferably a Cabinet post, but if no such post were available something else would do so long as it suited the 47-year-old General's energies and talents.

In his mind was a plan for building an Isthmian canal with the labor of Negro soldiers. He mentioned the scheme to Lincoln who referred him to Seward who was inaccessible because of his recent carriage accident. Realizing that for the moment there was nothing he could do for himself in Washington, Butler on the morning of Friday, April 14, 1865, entrained for his home in Lowell, Massachusetts. He was in Jersey City when news of the assassination reached him.

Years later—after Ben Butler's death—the New York *Tribune* would sum up his career in six words: "He was seldom out of sight." Butler did have high visibility. He was a huge man with a powerful body and the head of Jove, a slightly cockeyed Jove owing to the congenital droop of one of his eyelids. He had a broad forehead, a fringe of thin hair around a bald crown, squinting eyes obscured by pointed lids, a sharp nose and a nervous sniff. He was a man of swiftly changing moods, now speaking with the purr of a gentleman, now with the snarl of a bully. The Booths of Maryland were the recognized leaders of the acting profession of that day, but no more gifted ham than Ben Butler ever strutted his hour on the national stage.

Butler was frequently outraged by the allegation that his father was a pirate. It is known that John Butler was a sea-going man, although present in the bosom of his family long enough to sire three children by his first wife and three by his second. The last of them was Benjamin Franklin Butler, born in Deerfield, Massachusetts on November 5, 1818. Ben was four months old when his father died, prosaically, of yellow fever in the British West Indies. Money was scarce, and when Ben was ten his mother moved to Lowell and set up a boarding house. Ben read endlessly, and his memory was such that he rarely forgot a fact once he had absorbed it from the printed page.

During his boyhood Ben absorbed certain political convictions. His father had been an ardent Andrew Jackson Democrat, and though Ben never knew him, the elder Butler's views permeated the household. At an early age Ben was staunchly opposed to the Whigs, and to aristocrats in general. Most of the residents of his mother's boardinghouse were factory girls working in the woolen mills of Lowell. Ben liked these pleasant and high-minded young women, and from them acquired an intimate knowledge of the hard lot of the working class. This gave him for the rest of his days a genuine sympathy for the oppressed. In his late teens his ambition was to attend West Point. When he failed to get an appointment, owing to a lack of proper connections, his dislike of the privileged hardened into a lifelong principle.

His college was a small Calvinist institution in Waterville, Maine, later known as Colby, where attendance at chapel was compulsory. Bored with the long-winded sermons, Ben petitioned the college president to excuse him. His grounds were that Calvin had decreed that the number of the elect was small, that he (Ben Butler) was obviously not one of them and that, therefore, further attendance at chapel could only increase the torments of hell by making him familiar with the blessings of grace without enabling him to take advantage of them. The petition was denied.

Admitted to the bar in early manhood, Butler rose rapidly. He was a hard worker, a thorough researcher, an imaginative and spectacular trial lawyer. Along the way he branched out into sundry businesses. By the time he was 35 he could point to a bank account of $140,000.57 as the fruit of his own efforts. When he saw the Civil War in the offing, he hastened to the office of Governor Andrew of Massachusetts. He pointed out that the soldiers of the state militia would soon be enduring wintertime service under conditions different from the drilling in armories to which they were accustomed. Butler's point was that the soldiers needed overcoats. They got them—from the Middlesex Mills of Lowell, in which Butler was one of the largest stockholders. If Papa was a pirate, son was a chip off the old block.

Naturally when he entered politics along about 1840 he did so as a Democrat. In 1859 he was an unsuccessful candidate for

Governor in Whig-dominated Massachusetts. For a time he was a leading spirit in a coalition movement involving Massachusetts Democrats and Free Soilers. Then in 1853 General Caleb Cushing, the state Democratic boss, handed down an edict. Democrats interested in patronage must hew to a party line that had become, in effect, pro-slavery.

Weakest link in the chain comprising the Compromise of 1850 was the fugitive slave law which required Federal marshals and their deputies to return captured runaway slaves to their masters forthwith. The slave was given no legal protection; on the simple say-so of his master, he was to be returned without trial or investigation. It was one of those laws which breeds disrespect for law itself. On the popular level this disrespect took the form of the Underground Railroad. On the legislative it took the form, in several states, of so-called Liberty Laws. Privately Butler disapproved of the fugitive slave law. Publicly he supported it to keep his standing in the Massachusetts Democratic machine.

No other aspects of his party's program on the eve of the war gave him any apparent trouble. When Stephen Douglas's ill-fated popular sovereignty law of 1854 initiated a battle between pro-slavery and free-state settlers in Kansas, Butler put the blame on the Emigrant Aid Societies, northern groups set up to promote organized anti-slavery immigration to "bleeding Kansas." He supported the indefensible Lecompton constitution, an attempt to fasten slavery on the state of Kansas. He applauded the 1857 Dred Scott decision by which the Supreme Court handed down the dictum that a Negro had no rights a white man need respect. During his gubernatorial campaign he asserted that if by insurrection the Republicans did succeed in effecting emancipation, it wouldn't do the Negroes any good because they were the members of an "inferior race." Finally, as a delegate to the fateful Democratic National Convention of 1860, he cast his vote fifty-odd times for Jefferson Davis. And when the party split, Butler campaigned for Breckinridge, the candidate of the Southern Democrats.

The result of these actions was that when Lincoln was elected and war came, Butler found himself beyond the pale, politically speaking. Now it was that he demonstrated his capacity for self-rehabilitation. Overnight, in a remarkable political somersault, Butler cast off his past like a shedding snake to become a War Democrat. He threw himself into raising troops for the Union. He not only raised the troops and helped the State procure funds for equipping them, he at the same time catapulted himself into a permanent brigadier-generalship over the heads of dozens of more experienced officers. Later he was promoted to Major-General and in 1862, in a letter to Lincoln, he was describing himself as the senior officer of this rank, a statement which was incorrect.

Following the first exchange of gunfire at Sumter, the city of Washington was practically defenseless and wide open to invasion. Hastening southward with his troops, Butler was instrumental in bringing reinforcements to the frightened capital. His next maneuver was a surprise invasion of Baltimore where he brought a pro-secessionist movement to an end and thus helped save border-state Maryland for the Union. Still later, for eight months, he was Military Governor of Union-held New Orleans where he issued his unforgettable "woman's order" asserting that if the ladies of that city continued to insult occupying Yankee soldiers they would be treated as women of the street, an announcement that sent a gasp of horror throughout the South.

The rest of Butler's career as a general added no lustre to military annals. But as the war proceeded Butler's political influence waxed—and Butler's politics altered. The change began at Fortress Monroe in southeastern Virginia whence Butler was sent in May of 1861 to take command. He had been on hand only two days when he found himself face to face with a problem that sooner or later was bound to pester Union forces. Three runaway slaves took refuge in the eighty-acre fortress at Hampton Roads. What was to be done with them? Should they be returned to their owner, or should they be kept? If kept, how should they be regarded, as slaves or as freed men? The problem was a knotty one because the North had announced that it was fighting only to preserve the Union, that it had every intention of respecting the Constitutional status of slaves as property.

It was a dilemma for a states-rights and strict-constructionist Democrat who only a short time earlier had called the Negroes an inferior race. But Butler was equal to the occasion. He discovered that the slaves' owner had been using them to help build Confederate fortifications. Ergo, as property, the three Negroes were "contraband" of war and would not be returned.

The whoops of joy that the word "contraband" produced in the North were loudest among the Radicals. Like all actors Butler could resist anything but applause and the applause that now arose in ultra circles was music to his ears. It became even more beguiling when in November of 1862, after a series of rows with foreign consuls in New Orleans, he was relieved as military governor. As one man the Radicals protested his dismissal. A short time later, in a rousing oration at the Academy of Music in New York City, he was giving voice to ideas that would have been unthinkable to him a few years earlier.

He told a cheering audience that the time had come to face the fact that after the war the Union should not be restored as it had been before. The seceded states, he said, should be treated as conquered areas and the Federal government should confiscate the property of the slave-aristocracy and distribute it among those Southerners who had remained loyal to the Union. Benjamin F. Butler had joined hands with the Radicals.

Hearing of Lincoln's assassination in Jersey City, on his way home, Butler at once decided to return to Washington. Before doing so, he made a quick visit to New York. At about the same hour as Butler reached New York on the Jersey City ferry, an eminent attorney and distinguished Columbia College alumnus emerged from his house on East Twenty-first Street. His name was George Templeton Strong, and he was treasurer of the "Red Cross" of the Civil War, the great privately-financed organization called the Sanitary Commission. Strong recorded his impressions of this day, during the course of which he heard Ben Butler speak. In his diary under the entry date "April 15, Saturday," he concluded his first paragraph with the words, *"Eheu* A. Lincoln!" *"Up with the Black Flag now!"* he continued, and went on:

What a day it has been! . . . Tone of feeling very like that of four years ago when the news came of Sumter. This atrocity has invigorated national feeling in the same way . . . People who pitied our misguided brethern yesterday, and thought they had been punished enough already, and hoped there would be a general amnesty including J. Davis himself, talk approvingly today of vindictive justice and favor the introduction of judges, juries, gaolers, and hangmen among the dramatis personae . . .

Thence to Wall Street. Immense crowd. Bulletins and extras following each other in quick contradictory succession . . . The temper of the great meeting I found assembled in front of the Custom House (the old Exchange) was grim. A Southerner would compare it with that of the first session of the Jacobins after Marat's death. I thought it healthy and virile. It was the first great patriotic meeting since the war began at which there was no talk of concession and conciliation. Its sentiment seemed like this: "Now it is plain at last to everybody that there can be no terms with the woman-flogging aristocracy. Grant's generous dealing with Lee was a blunder . . . Let us henceforth deal with rebels as they deserve. The rose-water treatment does not fit their case."

That sensitive, learned George Templeton Strong, a charitable and gentle soul, should write in these terms is a measure of the impact of Lincoln's murder on public feeling. A forest fire of vindictiveness was sweeping the North. Ben Butler, speaking in Wall Street at noon at the meeting which Strong describes, asked his audience to tell him what fate should be meted out to the assassins whom he implied included all five million Southern rebels. He was gratified by the chorus of "Hang them! Hang them!" In grim preview of the content of hundreds of sermons preached the next day, on the feast celebrating the Resurrection of the Prince of Peace, Butler concluded with this lofty thought: "Perhaps I may say reverently that this dispensation of God's good providence is sent to teach us that the spirit of the Rebellion has not been broken by the surrender of its armies." In other words, let the war go on. Ben Butler's pious reaction to Lincoln's death was that of the Radicals generally; they were united in the conviction that politically the turn of events was heaven-sent.

Having informed his Wall Street audience that he was returning at once to the capital "in order to be present to give any assistance in this crisis of the country," Butler made the journey back to Washington, taking ten hours by ferry and rail. Presumably he got there late Saturday night, although this is not certain. On Easter Sunday he was emphatically on hand.

Since 1861 the Radicals' main instrument for promoting their policies had been the Committee on the Conduct of the War, composed of four senators and four members of the lower House. In no previous war had propaganda played so large a role. The Committee had contributed heavily to this development in the form of news releases based on endless investigations of Union generals and Union defeats. There were always one or two moderates on the Committee but its prevailing tone was extremist. Its Senatorial heavyweights were Ben Wade and tall Zachariah Chandler of Michigan. The House representation took its Radical flavor principally from John Covode of Pennsylvania and the gentle and doctrinaire George Washington Julian of Indiana.

Congressman Julian, a strong-featured man of considerable moral courage, had a literary bent. His *Recollections* provide a detailed picture of Radical activities over the tragic weekend. Saturday afternoon the members of the Committee on the Conduct of the War met in caucus for several hours. Andrew Johnson had been a member prior to his resignation from the Senate in 1862. Julian knew him well and personally harbored some doubts about him. But his misgivings were not shared by most of his fellow Radicals. They were in high spirits, convinced that Johnson was their man. The Tennessean had cause to hate the leaders of the Confederacy. Surely, the Radicals reasoned, he would soon repudiate the policy of "unconditional forgiveness" on which his predecessor had so rashly embarked. Discussion during the caucus turned on the necessity of changing the Cabinet to rid it of its "Lincoln influences."

Saturday night the Committee members called on Johnson. Ben Wade gave the new President a verbal slap on the back. "By the gods," he exclaimed, "there'll be no trouble in running the government now." It was mild verbiage for squirrel-gun-toting, "Bluff" Ben Wade, whose profanity once drew a protesting letter from a distressed Brooklyn lady.

Throughout the war Johnson had frequently voiced his belief that "treason must be made odious." In reply to Wade he tossed the old record onto the turntable. "I hold that robbery is a crime," he declaimed, "rape is a crime, *treason* is a *crime* and crime must be punished. Treason must be made infamous and traitors must be impoverished." At these stirring words from probably the best stump speaker ever produced in America, the cup of the Radicals overflowed.

Ben Butler, getting together with the Committee members on Sunday, was delighted to learn that the consensus was that he should replace Seward as Secretary of State. He himself called on President Johnson Sunday night. He mentioned his willingness to take over Seward's duties—just let the President say the word. The President smiled—and said nothing. Instead he brought up the matter of Grant's terms to Lee at Appomattox. Lee and his soldiers had been permitted to return to their homes with the understanding that as prisoners of war on parole they would not be molested during good behavior. The President asked Butler's opinion as to whether those terms still applied. Butler said he thought not since the war was now over. He thought that General Lee should be hanged. Johnson listened attentively, and Butler climaxed the conversation by tendering what he considered a piece of good advice. The President, he lectured the new President, "must not administer the estate of Lincoln."

It was a well-turned phrase, and at the moment no doubt Ben Butler considered it a fair estimate of the shape of things to come.

III

OF HOPES DEFERRED

For the first forty-five days of his administration, Andrew Johnson did not share his thoughts on reconstruction with the public. That is, he did not share them in a clear and categorical manner. The country was left wondering. In the words of Representative George Washington Julian, "What would the new President do?" Would he go the Radical way or the Lincoln way? Congress was in recess and would be until the following December. Ahead of Johnson in April of 1865 were almost nine months, during which he was free to initiate the reorganization of the South according to his own lights.

Most Radicals continued to regard him as their white hope, none more so than Charles Sumner.

Senator Sumner, a Bostonian and Harvardman, was a strange individual. Fifty-four in the summer of 1865, he was a man of magnificent manner and impressive appearance: six feet four, of sturdy physique, clean-shaven, heavy-visaged, almost handsome with his burning blue eyes and chisled features. Brown hair overhung a beveled forehead in a profusion of carefully-arranged negligence. He was fond of distinctive garments, usually effecting spats and rich colors.

He did not merely walk; his movements were those of a man on parade. There was no informality about Sumner, no relaxation. Many of his contemporaries found him a person at once difficult to admire and difficult not to. Henry Adams was fond of him but Sumner's mind, he thought, was "a pathological study"; it had "the calm of water which receives and reflects images without absorbing them." Of similar content was the comment of Confederate General Richard Taylor, son of former President Taylor and himself a man of culture. Sumner, in Taylor's purview, had "studied everything and digested nothing."

The Senator had traveled widely in Europe. There he had developed lasting friendships with some leading intellectuals, and had annoyed others. Thomas Carlyle burred that Sumner was "the most completely nothin' of a man that ever crossed my threshold— naught whatsoever in him or of him but wind and vanity." Vanity there was. General Grant made it the subject of one of his rare flashes of wit. Told that Sumner put no faith in the Bible, Grant quipped, "No, he didn't write it." But wind and vanity did not sum up Charles Sumner. His career exhibits a certain nobility, a stoic determination to see his country honor the high assertion of the Declaration of Independence that "all men are created equal." To the frequent claim that this or that compromise had settled the slavery question, he ringingly retorted, "Nothing can be settled which is not right."

He was not a ham, like Ben Butler. Still there is reason to suspect that the Charles Sumner we meet in the pages of history is precisely the man he meant for us to meet. What we see is a self-edited Charles, an android, a synthetic. He himself made the curious assertion that never, even in the privacy of his bedroom, did he allow himself to assume a position that he could not assume with dignity in the Senate of the United States. He rehearsed for his speeches, standing for hours before a pier glass, trying out gestures and facial expressions. He was given to riffling through dictionaries and books of synonyms, seeking new ways to express what were often not particularly profound thoughts. He could be very fussy about niggling matters. Was the correct expression "prophetic voices *concerning* America" or "*of* America?" This was the question about which he was consulting the Librarian of Congress and his friend, Henry Wadsworth Longfellow, on the last day of his life.

He was not complex. His adult life was strung on a single line, fueled by a single passion, dedicated to a single idea—the freeing and the elevating of the American Negro. When he moved away from this worthy cause he often became uninteresting or unsuccessful, or both. He married rather late in life, too late, perhaps. The lady was pretty and young, too young, perhaps. It didn't work. She left him soon and tragically, as was to be expected. It is not easy for a woman to live with a man who has become a theory.

His background was the cream of Boston society and a long line of Yankee forbears. There was no silver spoon, however. His father, Charles Pinckney Sumner, was an unsuccessful teacher, then an unsuccessful lawyer and finally a satisfactory deputy sheriff, struggling with the help of his seamstress-wife to bring up nine children on less than a thousand dollars a year. It was genteel poverty with all of its proud penny-pinching, and unadmitted despair. The elder Sumner was stern and gloomily Puritanical. Young Charles never got along with his father and never forgave himself for not getting along.

Charles and his twin sister, Mary, were the first-born, coming along in 1811. He loved Mary, and her death in 1845 left him torn with grief. Thereafter he appears to have reserved his affection exclusively for oppressed-people-in-the-mass-and-at-a-distance. Julia Ward Howe, the lively-minded author of *The Battle Hymn of the Republic,* found Sumner a man of "large qualities," but she was amused by his "small defects." "Sumner to tea," she wrote in her diary one evening. "Made a rude speech on being asked to meet Edwin Booth. Said, 'I don't know that I care to meet him. I have outlived my interest in individuals.' " Mrs. Howe's comment: "God Almighty, by the latest accounts, has not got so far as this."

Informed that Mrs. Howe had so written, Sumner was pained. "What a strange sort of book your diary must be!" he declared. "You ought to strike that out immediately." Of his humorlessness and literalness there were other anecdotes. At an official ball he told a young lady that the two of them were fortunate "for, standing here, we shall see the first entrance of the new English and French ministers into Washington society." The young lady replied, "I am glad to hear it. I like to see lions break the ice." Sumner thought that one over. Then, "Miss——, in the country where lions live there is no ice."

Coming to the Senate as a Free-Soiler in 1851, succeeding to the seat of Daniel Webster, Sumner made the chamber ring with his mellifluous orations. His vocabulary was extreme: "Abomination, disgusting ordure, loathsome stench." Such expressions, rolling from his tongue, meant that he didn't approve of the proposition at hand. He always overstated his case, and when he assailed an individual, it was without the slightest awareness of the impact of his words on the person under fire. Early in his political career he denounced a vote cast in Congress by an old friend as one that "cannot be forgotten on earth; it must be remembered in heaven. Blood! blood! is on the hands of the representative from Boston." When the offended Representative terminated their friendship, Sumner expressed himself as unable to see what the Congressman could possibly have against him.

During his famous "Crime Against Kansas" speech in the Senate in 1856, he mounted a violent attack on Senator A. P. Butler of South Carolina. Butler, he charged, "has chosen a mistress . . . who though . . . polluted in the sight of the world, is chaste in his sight. I mean the harlot, slavery!" In the House of Representatives at that time sat tall, dark Preston S. Brooks of South Carolina, shirttail cousin of Senator Butler. Brooks heard this part of Sumner's speech. Enraged by the insults to his kinsman, he informed his friend, H. A. Edmundson, that he was going to give the Massachusetts Senator a thrashing. Brooks' plan was to wait outside the Capitol and challenge the Senator when he came out. Edmundson advised against this. He pointed out that Sumner was a big man, that the slighter Brooks would stand little chance in a fair fight. So, armed with a heavy cane, Brooks slipped into the chamber and waited until the Senate had adjourned and the room was almost empty. Then, while Sumner sat trapped between his chair and a desk that was fastened to the floor, he rained a series of slashing blows on the helpless man's head. For the next three years Sumner was an invalid, unable to attend to his Congressional duties. As for his assailant, Brooks died suddenly and at a young age in 1857. It is a revealing comment on Charles Sumner that throughout the rest of his own long life he never evinced the slightest personal resentment. Years later, when Brooks' name was mentioned, he said: "What have I to do with him? It was slavery, not *he,* that struck the blow."

Lingering in Washington for several weeks after the assassination, Senator Sumner was a regular caller on the new executive, sometimes alone, sometimes with Chief Justice Chase or Senator Wade. From these conferences Sumner came away in a state of euphoria. From his modest bachelor quarters on New York Avenue flew ecstatic letters to friends in this country and abroad. He was confident that President Johnson saw eye to eye with the Radicals on the reorganization of the South. On May 2 he was writing his scholar-friend Francis Lieber that he was "charmed" with Johnson's sympathy, which was entirely different from his predecessor's. "I said during this winter that the rebel States should not come back except on the footing of the Declaration of Independence and the complete recognition of human rights. I feel more than ever confident that all this will be fulfilled. And then what a regenerated land! I had looked for a bitter contest on this question; but with the President on our side, it will be carried by simple avoirdupois."

Since no Radical's hopes were higher, no Radical was more

dashed, more shaken, more distressed than the magnificent Sumner when on May 29 President Johnson broke his silence and made public his own reconstruction plan. Its elements will concern us later. All that need detain us at this juncture is its over-all intent. In spirit, if not in detail, Johnson's program was Lincoln's program.

IV

A CASE OF MISTAKEN IDENTITY

Among the Radicals, President Johnson was now berated as an "apostate," as a man who had "betrayed the men who elected him." All summer long and into the autumn plaintive letters went back and forth.

From Thaddeus Stevens to Sumner: "Is there no way to arrest the insane course of the President in 'Reconstruction'?"

From Sumner to Stevens: "Can anything be done to stop this wretched experiment which the Pres. is making?"

From Butler to Wade: "All is wrong, we are losing the first results of this four years' struggle."

From Sumner to Secretary of War Stanton: "The mischief already done seems to me incalculable."

From Sumner to Wade: "Can you give me any comfort with regard to the policy of the President?"

From Sumner to Wade again: "You are silent. What say you? I feel unhappy."

And from an outraged constituent to Wade: "Don't let Johnson Tilyscare Congress."

It was during the silence of which Sumner complains that Wade penned for Sumner's eyes a letter that apparently was never delivered, at any rate not in the form in which it has been preserved among Wade's papers at the Library of Congress. Portions of this colorful missive were scratched out as too strong, perhaps, to be entrusted to the mails. The Ohio Senator wrote:

The President is pursuing and I believe is resolved to pursue a course in regard to reconstruction that can result in nothing but consigning the great Union, or Republican party, bound, hand and foot, to the tender mercies of the rebels we have so lately conquered in the field and their Copperhead allies in the North.

What had impelled Johnson to his folly? Wade saw behind the President's reconstruction policy the shadow of a dead man. Johnson had taken his stand, he was certain, in response to the outpouring of praise for his predecessor after the assassination.

I can but believe [he wrote] that the extravagant eulogisms of Mr. Lincoln have had the effect of impressing Mr. Johnson with the idea that Mr. Lincoln had made himself exceedingly popular by his negative, non-committal, hesitating, shilly-shally policy, and has induced him [Johnson] to become the feeble copyish [*sic*] of a very feeble original.

Little comfort these words would have been to Sumner had he received them. He was suffering the pangs of personal betrayal. "I do not understand the Presdt.," he protested to Wade on August 3. "He said to me 'I agree with you on this question. There is no difference between us. We are alike.' Whose influence has brought about the change?"

Sumner's last phrase, "the change," is notable. It was the Radicals' belief, never abandoned, that Johnson had come into the Presidency a raging Radical lion. In the course of half a dozen weeks he had been metamorphosed into a Lincolnian lamb. Some beguiling tongue had lured him from the path of righteousness. Nor were the Radicals long in giving a name to the possessor of this beguiling tongue. It was the quaint little man from Auburn, New York, Johnson's Secretary of State and Lincoln's before him. Johnson had been all right on the subject of reconstruction, Thad Stevens said, but then "Seward entered into him and ever since they have been running down deep places into the sea." This Radical surmise must have been gratifying to Seward. Adroit, good-humored, loquacious and ambitious, the little Secretary rather fancied himself as a power-behind-the-throne.

But facts are facts and dates are dates. On April 15, when Johnson took over, Seward was a prisoner of his bedroom, doubly injured by his carriage accident and by the assassination attempt of the night before. It was May 9 before he was able to receive Johnson and the Cabinet in the parlor of his home, and Secretary Welles' first-hand account has it that this was a social visit and little more. It was May 20 before Seward was able to resume his duties. Even then he had to be carried by chair from his home across Lafayette Park to the State Department offices in the north wing of the Treasury building. Four days later Johnson presented his reconstruction plan to his cabinet. Five days after that he announced it to the public. As one of the Secretary's biographers, Frederick Bancroft, has observed, Johnson's program was formulated before Seward, his broken jaw still encased in wires, was "able to talk without great pain."

But what of the Radical contention that the President executed a quick political somersault? Does this also not rest on a tissue of dubious evidence and wishful thinking? It does, and Secretary Welles was writing history when he asserted that "No change of policy took place," that Johnson took over the Presidency determined "to carry out the policy of his predecessor."

The Radicals' assumption in mid-April that Johnson would travel their road was a case of mistaken identity. They simply did not know their man. The major aim of the Radicals at this point was to utilize the reorganization of the South as a means of preserving Republican hegemony over House and Senate. In retrospect their belief that Johnson would be sympathetic to this goal seems naive. Johnson was a Democrat. His nomination for the Vice Presidency at the 1864 Republican Convention in Baltimore was an accident of Civil War politics. In his formal letter of acceptance, he took care to make clear that his political identity remained unaltered. Only four months earlier he had told a crony that "if the country is ever to be saved it will be done through the old Democratic party."

Such leading Radicals as Thad Stevens and Butler wanted to see the Southern states reduced to "conquered provinces." Yet as early as November of 1863, in a letter to his friend, Montgomery Blair, Andrew Johnson was urging the then Postmaster-General to warn Lincoln against "the proposition of states relapsing into territories and held as such." Three days after Lincoln's death he was telling an Indiana delegation that "Upon this idea of destroying states, my position has been heretofore well known, and I see no cause to change it now . . . Some are satisfied with the idea that the States . . . are to lose their character as States. But their life-breath has only been suspended. . . ." The central government's job, he concluded, was to resuscitate them as states.

Thad Stevens was willing for the South to "be laid waste and made a desert." This was not a sentiment likely to appeal to the last Southerner to occupy the White House for generations to come. More in keeping with Johnson's love of homeland was his statement to his Indiana visitors on April 18, 1865, "that I intend to bring back peace to our distracted country."

"We especially insist," Stevens was thundering at his Pennsylvania neighbors in the fall of 1865, "that the property of the chief rebels should be seized . . ." In this connection, Johnson's prompt and violent protest against the confiscation of rebel holdings in Nashville will be recalled.

Stevens, Sumner and some of the other Radical leaders wanted the right to vote to be extended immediately to the newly freed slaves. As a states-righter Johnson could not be expected to go along with a demand that the Federal government reach into the Southern states and dictate their suffrage laws in defiance of the Constitution.

Much of the flimsy evidence that Johnson toyed briefly with a

Radical program rests on those ecstatic letters Sumner was writing in April and May of 1865. There is no reason to question Sumner's reports of what the President said to him and *vice versa,* but the conclusions the Senator reached were not necessarily justified by the facts he himself presented. Reporting on his conferences with Johnson in a letter dated May 2, Sumner wrote that the President wanted to do everything possible to promote reorganization of the South "without distinction of color." To which Sumner added that the President desired that this "movement should appear to proceed from the people." The Senator perhaps would have been less optimistic had he given more weight to Johnson's reservation.

Why then for several weeks were most of the Radical leaders so certain of Johnson? One answer is that there was a single point on which the Radicals and the President saw eye to eye. Both believed that some of the leaders of the Rebellion should be punished. Time, the swift subsidence of the hysteria provoked by Lincoln's murder and, above all, the genius of the American people for forgetting a grudge—these and a number of legal complications were to render the point academic. Jefferson Davis and a score of Confederate leaders would be seized, charged with treason and imprisoned for periods ranging from a few months in most cases to two years in the case of Davis. But in the end none would be tried, none convicted. Not many years hence most of them would once again be full-fledged citizens, some of them sitting in the United States Congress—a state of affairs which, when one considers the executions which usually follow a war of rebellion, makes the Civil War the most atypical revolution in history. It was too much so for Andrew Johnson, who would go to his grave convinced that an example should have been made of a token few of the top Confederates.

Johnson had his reasons, such as they were. One was his belief that the bulk of the Southern people had been dragooned into the war by a few influential men. Those men should be taught a lesson. Another was the offshoot of the legal turn of his mind. Speaking to some White House visitors, among them a Mr. James R. Hubbell,

Johnson said that Jefferson Davis should be permitted to set up his defense and then be tried for treason in a civil court. The President's reasoning, as reported by Hubbell, was that it might be useful to the government in some future crisis to have a clear and precise definition of treason. As to whether Davis should be executed, if found guilty, the President did not say. Hubbell's observation was, "I suppose he [Johnson] knew he had the authority if Davis were . . . convicted . . . to pardon him."

During the first forty-five days of his administration most of Johnson's utterances revolved around this one point on which he and the Radicals agreed. No doubt those who were misled, and there were several doubting Thomases from the start, were misled by this fact.

The President provided his future enemies with another basis for misinterpreting his attitudes. During these early days he was acutely conscious of the awkwardness of his status as a Southern Democrat in an atmosphere dominated by Northern Republicans. Moreover, he harbored a healthy respect for the mischief of which the Radicals were capable. He was bent on keeping them at bay until he had time to ascertain the facts and devise and project his own reconstruction policy.

On the last Saturday in April Chief Justice Chase was urging Johnson to issue "some simple declaration that the colored people are free and are citizens and therefore entitled to vote." A sincere friend of the ex-slaves, a man who often went along with the Radicals but was never of them, Chase said that such a declaration would glorify Johnson's name, as the Emancipation Proclamation had glorified that of his predecessor. Johnson's reply was that he wished to go slow for the time being, because "I am new and untried and cannot venture what I please." Sumner, in his letters, quotes the President as saying frequently that he did not wish to "give a handle to party."

In short, the President was listening to everybody, nodding at everything and staying as far away as possible from controversial issues. In the bosom of his official family he made no bones as to what course he intended to follow. At his first Cabinet meeting he said his policy "in all essentials would be the same as that of the late President." In public he tended to pursue a non-committal course, confining most of his speeches to reiterating in violent tones and in sundry forms his assertion, "Treason must be made odious, and traitors must be punished and impoverished." This was a safe theme. It conformed to the mood of the Northern people, still angry and resentful at Lincoln's assassination, and it set well with the Radicals.

Among the President's callers on the day of Lincoln's death was Governor William M. Stone of Iowa. Stone asked Johnson what he intended to do about the South. The President's reply, as paraphrased by Stone, was that "he would deal kindly and leniently with the mass of people in the South and with the rank and file of the authorities, regarding them merely as the victims and sufferers of the rebellion. Nevertheless he would not pursue any policy which would prevent the Government from visiting punishment on the guilty, as the cause of the rebellion." These expressions, a few hours after Lincoln's death, form a fairly accurate preview of the reconstruction policy on which Johnson would embark a few weeks later.

On the third day of his administration, he terminated a visit by an Illinois delegation with a brief speech. Glancing over a copy of his remarks, taken down by a stenographer, the President noted that he had promised to continue the Lincoln policies. He demurred, saying that he believed that his meaning had been misconstrued. Standing by was his friend, Preston King, a former Senator from New York. King, with his baby-face and mountainous body, was a stalwart Lincoln Republican, a sensitive and intelligent human being, and probably Johnson's closest adviser at this point. When the corpulent New Yorker suggested that the reference to Lincoln be stricken, Johnson nodded. Apprised of this incident, the Radicals glowed, taking it as another indication that the President was in their camp. They could have as reasonably concluded that Johnson, who was an honorable man, had no intention of riding on the çoattails of his predecessor and that in the eyes of the public he meant to assume full responsibility for the success or failure of his policies, from whatever source they came.

It seems clear that he did not alter his course, and to the evidence that has been mentioned may be added a further incident as reported by the Blairs, old Francis Preston, Sr., and his sons, Montgomery and Frank. The old man had been Andrew Jackson's journalistic whip and a member of Old Hickory's "kitchen cabinet." Opposition to the extension of slavery into the territories and a belief in graduated emancipation had carried him out of the Democratic party and his sons had followed. All three had been active in setting up the Republican party and in bringing about the election of Lincoln.

Scarecrows in appearance, the Blair men had no straw in their heads. Frank and Montgomery rose to political prominence in Missouri. Frank remained a westerner but in 1853 Montgomery migrated to Washington. There, as a lawyer practicing in the Supreme Court, he defended Dred Scott in 1856. During the war Frank commuted between active service as a general in the field and a seat in the lower house of Congress. Montgomery served as Postmaster-General until his outspoken opposition to the Radicals compelled Lincoln, to keep peace in the party, to ask for his resignation. As for the old man, he devoted himself to a fruitless attempt to end the bloodshed at an early date and to forestall the harsh peace the Radicals were demanding.

> How do the little busy Blairs
> Improve the shining hours,
> And load their minds with ponderous cares
> To close this war of ours.

So ran a jingle in the unfriendly press when in January of 1865 the old man twice travelled to Richmond in an unofficial effort to negotiate a truce with his long-time friend Jefferson Davis.

Politicians on the grand scale, the Blairs were into everything.

Although Johnson considered them "among the best and most sensible men in the country," he once wryly remarked that they were "a peculiar family" in that an important governmental vacancy never occurred but what the Blairs were certain that one of them was "the very man to fill it." Always loyal to their friends, the Blairs were quick to rally to Johnson's defense when he disgraced himself on the Saturday of Lincoln's second inauguration. Having carried Johnson off to Silver Spring, old Blair and his son Montgomery sounded out the Vice President on the issues of the day. Later they expressed themselves as satisfied that with a few exceptions Johnson's views on reconstruction were identical with their own and with those of Abraham Lincoln.

Before further attention is given to the events of Johnson's administration, it is necessary to look at one of the pivotal figures of those events, a man of unique and puzzling character.

V

IAGO IN THE WAR DEPARTMENT

His name was Edwin McMasters Stanton and Lincoln, fondly enough, called him "Old Mars." As Lincoln's Secretary of War he was to the administrative aspects of the Union Army what Grant was to the military. Had Old Mars rested on his Civil War laurels, history would no doubt have accorded him a secure niche in her hall of fame. As it is, thanks to his conduct afterwards, his fame rests on a shaky foundation.

He was a podgy little man with feminine hands and small feet, unimpressive except for the piercing eyes behind steel-rimmed glasses and the long, perfumed beard—black with a white streak down the middle—that pointed at the world like a cocked index finger.

Born, reared and educated in Ohio and rising to hard-earned eminence as a lawyer there and in Pennsylvania, Stanton was a scold with the temperament of a washerwoman and the mentality of a wayward genius. No man is all of one piece, but "Old Mars" was of so many pieces as to suggest that at times he must have met himself along the way. Brought up by a Quaker father and a Methodist mother, he was a convert to the Episcopal Church, a man who hated immorality with the fury of a fanatic and practiced what he hated. He was a pillar of strength to Lincoln and a traitor to most of his other superiors. He was a tender father, a loving husband, a sycophant to those who could give him help and a bully to those who sought his.

Prompted by diverse stimuli, he exhibited sniveling cowardice and a mad courage. It was his practice in his early manhood to carry in his vest pocket a beautifully sheathed dagger, seven inches in length. Long after all the other top members of Lincoln's government had put the fear of assassination out of their minds, Stanton was keeping soldiers around his house and going nowhere without a bodyguard. As a small boy he witnessed the sudden death of his doctor-father from apoplexy. From then on he himself lived in dread of dying in the same manner. In court, where as a brilliant trial lawyer he often whipped himself into a frenzy of oratory, he would rip off his coat and loosen his collar as the proceedings approached their zenith.

There were also incidents of courage. While a young lawyer in Columbia, Ohio, he slept and took his meals at the home of a Mr. Howard, a "steam doctor." Cholera struck the city in 1833. One afternoon during the plague the steam doctor's daughter, Anna, served Stanton his dinner at two o'clock. When he returned for tea a few hours later he was informed that Anna had been stricken and was already dead and buried. Seized with the horrifying but (as it turned out) groundless suspicion that the young woman had been interred alive, Stanton ran all the way to the cemetery and dug up the newly-made grave with his own hands.

He was a stunningly effective attorney. His civil cases, many of them involving issues of national importance, made new law. His courtroom methods were the admiration and envy of the bar. An opposing counsel named Roderick Moodey once remonstrated with Stanton's hammer-and-tong manner of examining witnesses.

"Make your appeals to the court," Stanton snapped, "and quit whining."

"I don't think a whine is any worse than a bark."

"Oh yes, Mr. Moodey, there's a difference—dogs bark and puppies whine."

If so intricate a man can be summed up, it could be said that his actions rang a thousand and one changes on a dominant theme— his overweening desire to be top-dog in every situation. A humorist of the day composed this couplet:

> He wrought for the *nation* a vast deal of good,
> But woe to the *man* who in his way stood.

In conversation with a public spirited Unitarian minister, the Reverend Henry W. Bellows of New York, Stanton ground out a few words of self-revelation. Dr. Bellows was in Washington in connection with his work as co-founder of the Sanitary Commission. In 1862 the Commission engineered the removal of an incompetent Surgeon-General and his replacement by young and dynamic Dr. William A. Hammond. Stanton had no use for the Commission. In his talk with Bellows he said that he "detested" the organization.

"But why, Mr. Stanton," he was asked, "when it is notoriously doing so much good service?"

"Well," Stanton replied, "the fact is the Commission wanted Hammond to be Surgeon-General and I did not. I did my best . . . but the Commission beat me and got Hammond appointed. I am not used to being beaten and don't like it, and therefore I am hostile to the Commission."

Never a professional politician, Stanton was a confirmed anti-slavery man with a Democratic background. During the war he veered over to the Radicals. This he had a right to do. What is seemingly unanswerable is that a man of his great abilities should have chosen during Andrew Johnson's administration to play the role of spy within the President's household. Why at meeting after meeting of the Cabinet did he pretend to go along with Johnson while all the time working hand in hand with his enemies? Was he mentally unbalanced, as was not infrequently rumored? Is the clue to his behavior to be found in George Templeton Strong's observation that Stanton was " 'incorruptible' in the ordinary sense" but easily corrupted by his own "prejudice and passion"? Was there in him perhaps a taste for melodrama; did it please him, in some unfathomable way, to assume the character of Iago in the Tragedy of Reconstruction? If so, it was a curious last act for a man to write for his own life.

In the course of a sensational criminal trial, shortly before the war, Stanton introduced into American judicial procedure a device destined to be a stumbling-block to justice in succeeding generations. The incident, a *cause célèbre* of its day, began shortly after noon on a winter Sunday in 1859 when energetic Congressman Daniel E. Sickles of New York happened to glance out of the second-floor window of his white brick mansion on the west side of Lafayette Square in the national capital. Hot words escaped the Congressman as he saw, striding along the street, the blond, six-foot figure of Phillip Barton Key, son of the author of the *Star Spangled Banner* and "the handsomest man in all Washington Society." A few minutes later Key was turning off the avenue into Madison Place, east of the square. Simultaneously Sickles, having hastened around the square via H Street, was approaching him from the opposite direction. There was a gun in Sickles' hand. His first shot missed and Key dodged behind a tree. Two more shots— three, according to some witnesses—pitched Key into the gutter, fatally wounded.

Sickles' motive? Key had been sleeping with his pretty dark-haired, much younger wife. Stanton defended him in a twenty-day trial. Conscience-stricken Mrs. Sickles admitted all in a signed confession, containing the pathetic words "I did what is usual for a wicked woman to do." Notwithstanding Sickles' own reputation for philandering, it was a foregone conclusion that he would escape punishment on the grounds of the "unwritten law," not to mention the double-standard. But Stanton took no chances. Prior to the trial he leaked to the press information designed to arouse public sentiment on the side of his client. He won the case and with it the dubious honor of inaugurating the practice of trying such cases in the newspapers.

It was not the last time that "Old Mars" would take to the press in the pursuit of his own ends. He did it again during the early days of Johnson's administration, this time in connection with an incident which began in a ramshackle farmhouse near Hillsboro, North Carolina. Here, at two on the afternoon of the Tuesday after Lincoln's death, two military leaders met for the purpose of closing the books on the war. One of them was General Joseph E. Johnston, commander of the largest Confederate force remaining in the field following the surrender of Lee. The other was Major-General William Tecumseh Sherman, U.S.A.

Sherman was a tall man given to quick and impatient movements as though galvanized by inner shocks. A muscular frame, a raw neck, a thin mouth, a ragged beard, flashing black eyes and red hair completed the picture. If in the light of history this pungent Ohioan casts an exceptionally long shadow, it is because the outer man hid rather than revealed a certain quality. There was something in him that put him in tune with the sufferings and longings of other people. It was a capacity that can play havoc with a man's internals. Now and then it made "Cump" Sherman act in a strange manner. Oftentimes seeing him hesitant and scattered in a crisis, people said he was "crazy."

In the Vicksburg campaign he was Grant's right-hand man, and there the two officers acquired a lasting respect for one another. They fought in the same way, hard; and for the same reason, to get the horrid mess over with. War wasn't Sherman's only hate. There wasn't a Rebel he despised with anything like the intensity he reserved for Northern newspapermen with their peeping-Tom ways and loose tongues. He picked a good many bones with the correspondents, and at the end of things he picked one with Secretary Stanton.

In the last week of March, 1865, Lincoln was paying a visit to the headquarters of General Grant aboard the Steamer *River Queen,* tied to the wharf at City Point on the James River in

Virginia. Sherman had joined them and on the afternoon and morning of March 27–28, the red-haired General and the President had a long talk in the presence of Grant and Admiral David D. Porter. Sherman asked Lincoln what his plans were on reconstruction. The President's reply, according to Sherman's *Memoirs,* was that all he wanted from the South was the surrender of her armies. Given that, the people "would at once be guaranteed all their rights as citizens of a common country." Nor was that all. "To avoid anarchy," the President said, the Southern state governments currently in office would be recognized "as the government *de facto* till Congress could provide others."

Those were the words of Sherman's Commander-in-Chief, and they were the words which guided Sherman when in the farmhouse near Hillsboro on the afternoon of April 18, he wrote out and he and General Johnston signed a set of terms under which all remaining Confederate armies were to be surrendered. The Sherman-Johnston pact provided that, following military submission, the civic and property rights of all Southern citizens would be guaranteed by the Federal government and all present Southern state governments would be recognized.

Signed on Tuesday, the pact reached Washington the following Friday. At eight o'clock that night it was considered by Johnson and his cabinet in an emergency meeting. Disapproval was unanimous. Several reasons were advanced. Making no mention of emancipation, the clause of the pact guaranteeing Southern property rights was believed to be open to misconstruction. It could be cited by Southerners as a basis for demanding compensation for their slaves. The clause recognizing the rebel governments ran counter to the prevailing Northern conviction that such governments could not be trusted—a fact to which Lincoln had bowed, shortly before his death, during his quickly-abandoned attempt to give limited recognition to the rebel legislature of Virginia. Finally, there was the fact that Lincoln had ordered Grant, in negotiating with Lee, to confine himself to "purely military matters."

The upshot of the Cabinet session was that Sherman was ordered to resume hostilities and Grant was sent South to see that he did so. Sherman accepted disapproval of his peace terms like a soldier. "I admit my folly," he wired Stanton, "in embracing in a military convention any civil matter." In accordance with Grant's instructions, he informed General Johnston that their agreement was void and that his powers were now limited to accepting the surrender of Johnston's army, and that alone, on the same terms Grant had given Lee at Appomattox. Johnston acceded to this arrangement and it was consummated a few days later.

At this point the curtain should have come down on the matter. But it didn't. Stanton kept it up by releasing to the press two distorted accounts of what had happened. One release carried the insinuation that Sherman had been bribed to make peace terms that would permit Jefferson Davis, then in flight, to get out of the country with a fortune in Confederate gold—a fortune that existed only in the imaginations of Stanton and other Northern firebrands. Both news releases were full of omissions. No mention was made of the fact that Sherman had acted in good faith, carrying out what he believed to be the wishes of his Commander-in-Chief. No mention was made of the fact that prior to Grant's arrival in North Carolina, Sherman had received no word of Lincoln's instructions with reference to Appomattox. Nothing was said of Sherman's ignorance of the suppression of the rebel legislature in Virginia or of the fact that his pact with General Johnston was labeled tentative subject to approval. The clear implication of both news stories was that Sherman had been insubordinate, and possibly traitorous.

Stanton's leaks to the press were gratuitous smears of a brave and loyal general. Admiral Porter wrote that "Had Mr. Lincoln lived, Secretary Stanton would have issued no false telegraphic dispatches, in the hope of killing off another general in the regular army, one who by his success had placed himself in the way of his own succession." Secretary Welles confided a similar judgment to his diary. "Stanton," he observed, ". . . seems to have a mortal fear of the generals of the armies, although courting and flattering them. He went to Savannah to pay court to Sherman when that officer was the favored general and supposed to have eclipsed Grant, but the latter having gained the ascendant by the fall of Richmond and the capture of Lee, Stanton would now reinstate himself with Grant by prostrating Sherman."

President Johnson had no knowledge of Stanton's garbled news stories until they had appeared and the damage was done. He volunteered as much when a very angry red-haired General called on him in Washington on the eve of the grand review of the armies on May 23 and 24. On the reviewing stand, during the second day of the ceremonies, Sherman shook hands with the President and with all the other dignitaries—except Stanton, whose proffered hand he conspicuously ignored.

It will be recalled that at the time of Lincoln's death the belief was general in the North that his assassination had been plotted by Confederate leaders. No one was more convinced of this than Stanton and no one was less inclined to own up to an error. Having taken the position that Wilkes Booth was merely the long arm of Jefferson Davis, Stanton stuck to it. In the events connected with the Conspirators Trial, a ravening desire to prove himself right dictated his actions and clouded his judgment. As a Radical he also wished to justify a draconian peace for the South by putting the former Confederate government in the worst possible light.

While digging up evidence for the trial, Stanton found a man who claimed to have proof that Booth had been hired by Jefferson Davis to kill Lincoln. The man who brought these tidings to Stanton used many names. He appears to have been born Charles A. Dunham, but the name under which he approached the Secretary of War was Sanford Conover. We have no inkling as to what he looked like other than the interesting remark of a contemporary that his appearance was "extraordinary." On one occasion, in a newspaper notice signed "Watson," Conover offered five hundred dollars reward for the arrest of the "infamous and perjured scoundrel" whom he charged was impersonating him under

the name of Wallace. Watson, Conover and the "infamous and perjured scoundrel" posing as Wallace-Conover were all one and the
same man.

Conover claimed to be a lawyer and perhaps was. His true
profession was that of a suborner of perjury. Not only was he
himself willing to testify to anything for a price, but he surrounded
himself with a group of grog-drenched individuals whom he carefully rehearsed so that they, too, stood ready to testify to anything
in any court on the same terms. An 1866 House Report indicates
that the Bureau of Military Justice paid him and his associates less
than a thousand dollars for their fabricated testimony at the Conspirators Trial.

Conover told Stanton that he could produce "at least three witnesses of unimpeached character," who could testify to negotiations
between Confederate officials and Wilkes Booth. Conover said that
while in Canada, during the last year of the war, he himself had
seen Booth consorting with Clement C. Clay, George N. Sanders
(or Saunders), Jacob Thompson and other Confederate agents.
Conover said that he had it from the lips of some of these reputable
Southerners that the authorities in Richmond had assented to a
plot to assassinate half a dozen Union leaders, including Lincoln
and Johnson.

All this gobbledygook Stanton passed on to the President, and
Johnson, all too willing to believe the worst of Jefferson Davis at
this time, let himself be used. On May 2, 1865, he issued a proclamation offering rewards ranging from $100,000 to $10,000 for
the arrests of Davis and his agents in Canada. The charge was conspiracy aimed at inciting the murder of Lincoln and the attempted
murder of Seward. When Davis learned of this development, at the
time of his capture on May 10, he was startled. "Why Johnson
knows better than that," he exclaimed. "He knows I much prefer
Lincoln as President, to him."

Almost immediately after the assassination the names of all of
Booth's suspected accomplices were known. Only one eluded Stanton's net. This was 21-year-old John H. Surratt of Washington, a

secret dispatch-rider for the Confederacy. Implicated in Booth's original scheme to kidnap the President but apparently unaware of the assassination plan, Surratt fled the country at the time of the tragedy and managed to keep out of sight for almost two years.

The first problem confronting Johnson was whether the suspects should be tried in a civil court or by a military commission. Again Johnson leaned on one of his aids; and again, perhaps all too willingly, he heeded bad advice. Attorney General Speed's argument for a court martial was that the crime took place in the National Capital during wartime and that the victim was the Commander-in-Chief.

On the basis of this dubious reasoning one boy, six men and a woman were placed on trial on May 10 before a military commission consisting of eight generals and two colonels and including such eminent personages as Major-General David Hunter, who presided, and General Lew Wallace, later author of *Ben Hur*. Conspicuous among the prosecutors was Judge Advocate General Joseph Holt. Tall, of imposing presence, and gray-haired, Holt was a Kentuckian and a staunch Unionist. As Buchanan's last Secretary of War and as head of the Bureau of Military Justice under Lincoln, Holt had served his country capably. To this admirable career his conduct as recorder at the Conspirators Trial put a regrettable climax. Consistently he dotted Stanton's "i's" and crossed Stanton's "t's."

Granted that three of the suspects—Herold, Atzerodt and Lewis Payne—were guilty as charged, the military hearings were a miscarriage of justice. The rights of the defendants were not properly protected, and much of the testimony would never have been accepted as evidence in a civil court.

Both in court and in their cells the male defendants were manacled and shackled. Their heads were enveloped in mufflers with holes permitting them to see and breathe, and through which their meals were fed to them. The excuse for this medieval treatment was that before the trial one of the men had sought to kill himself by dashing out his brains.

Conover and his "unimpeached" witnesses performed magnifi-
cently in an effort to convert the hearings into a trial of Jefferson
Davis and other Confederate leaders *in absentia*. One of Conover's
yarn-spinners testified that during the war Wilkes Booth attended a
secret meeting within the Confederate lines. And what happened
at this meeting? The witness was "told" that plans were laid to
kill Lincoln. Two other witnesses testified to seeing Booth share a
drink with a Confederate agent in Canada. A blind citizen of
Richmond related street gossip of rewards offered by the Confederate government for the assassination.

The most celebrated of the defendants was the woman—Mrs.
Mary Eugenia Surratt, 45-year-old mother of the fleeing Confederate dispatch-rider. Brown-haired, with dark gray eyes and
pleasing features, Mrs. Surratt was a simple and unassuming person.
The widow of a Maryland farmer and railroad contractor, she was
the mother of two sons, John and an older brother, and a daughter,
Anna. The testimony shows that Mrs. Surratt was "guilty" on two
counts. She kept the Washington boarding-house where one or
more of the suspects had lived and to which Wilkes Booth had paid
an occasional visit. The other was that at the time of her arrest she
denied knowing the suspect, Payne, although it was known he had
visited her home at least once. This circumstance was suspicious
but hardly criminal. Most of the testimony against her was provided
by two frightened little men who were given to understand by
Stanton and Holt that they themselves might be made defendants
if they didn't say the right things.

One aspect of the affair speaks volumes. J. Wilkes Booth's diary,
taken from his person as he lay dying on the Garrett farm in
Virginia, was not introduced in evidence. Throughout the trial and
for some time thereafter this little book rested in Judge Holt's safe.
Why was it suppressed? Those responsible never put their motives
on record, but they can be guessed. As was later brought out, the
contents of the diary tended to clear both Mrs. Surratt and her son
of any complicity in the assassination. Right after Booth's capture,
Lieutenant Byron Baker, who had removed the diary from the

dying actor's clothing, was closely questioned by Holt, but Baker was not called on to testify at the trial.

John A. Bingham, special prosecutor for the government, wound up the proceedings with an emotional five-day harangue, and on July 3, the members of the Military Court retired to consider their verdict. All eight defendants were found guilty. Four were convicted of being accessories and were sentenced to imprisonment. Two received life terms. They were Dr. Mudd, who had set Booth's broken leg and who was believed to have given the actor's pursuers false information; and Samuel B. Arnold, a wagon-maker accused of providing certain vehicles for use in the plot. A six-year term went to Edward Spangler, a stage carpenter at Ford's Theatre, who was accused of boring the hole which permitted Booth to observe Lincoln's position in the Presidential box. A six-year term went also to Michael O'Laughlin, the boy, whose connection to the crime was not clearly brought out. Ill with fright during the trial, the lad never fully recovered. In 1867 he died. Two years later Johnson pardoned Dr. Mudd, Arnold and Spangler in appreciation of their self-sacrificing work among the sick during a yellow fever epidemic at Dry Tortugas, Florida, where they were prisoners.

The others, including Mrs. Surratt, were sentenced to hang. The date of execution was set for July 7. On July 5 and 6 friends of the Surratt family besieged the White House in the hopes of obtaining mercy from the President. They were turned away by Senator Lane and ex-Senator King, to whom fell the unsavory task of guarding the outer door. Anna Surratt, the unfortunate woman's daughter, fell in a faint on the White House steps, a scene those present would not soon forget. A Washington judge was persuaded to issue a writ of *habeas corpus* to hold off execution until inquiry could be made into the legality of a court-martial in times of peace. The general of the court to whom the writ was issued sought the advice of Attorney-General Speed. He was informed that the writ had been suspended by Lincoln "and especially in this case by Johnson." Back went the General to explain matters to the Judge, and to leave the great writ with him, unexecuted.

Johnson had been confined to his bed with what was called bilious fever since June 26. On July 5 Judge Holt entered the White House by a side door, carrying a number of papers for the President's attention. Among them was the death warrant for Herold, Payne, Atzerodt and Mrs. Surratt. The President signed it, thereby playing his part in a mystery that did not come to light until two years later.

The first act of this little drama was played in the fall of 1866 when John H. Surratt, the dead woman's son, was traced to Rome where he had obtained a position in the Pope's guards. Brought back to the United States, Surratt was placed on trial in the summer of 1867 in a Washington Civil Court, charged with conspiracy to murder Lincoln. The hysteria, prevalent at the time of the Conspirators Trial, had subsided. The jury, made up of some of the city's most prominent citizens, was unable to agree on a verdict and the case was dropped for lack of evidence.

But the Surratt hearings were productive of a sensational disclosure. It was brought out that at the conclusion of the Conspirators Trial, a petition was drawn up recommending that the President commute Mrs. Surratt's sentence to life imprisonment. This petition was signed by five of the ten members of the Military Court.

To Johnson this revelation, appearing in the press on August 4, 1867, came as a thunderbolt. On the following day he asked the Bureau of Military Justice to send him the papers of the Conspirators Trial, containing the death warrant which he himself had signed two years before. On re-examining the papers, Johnson found the recommendation for clemency among them. He then announced that this was the first time he had ever laid eyes on it! To his secretary, Colonel Moore, he voiced the conviction that the recommendation "had been designedly withheld from his . . . knowledge" by Judge Holt. All this, Holt subsequently denied, making it a case of charge and counter-charge. Either the President was lying or in error; or Holt was.

After the disclosures in the John H. Surratt trial in the summer of 1867, one Washington correspondent suddenly remembered that he had known about the recommendation all the time. This man was A. Homer Byington, editor of the *Gazette* in Norwalk, Connecticut, and a correspondent for Greeley's *Tribune*. Byington was a red-hot Radical, to whom all supporters of Andrew Johnson were "copperheads," "rebels" and "robbers," and who deserves a little attention from history if only because he was the author of the remarkable comment that Johnson's lenient Reconstruction policy "out-Herods Lincoln."

Shortly after the John H. Surratt trial, Byington published in his newspaper a Washington Letter, a clipping of which found its way into the files of Secretary Stanton. Byington denied that Holt had suppressed the recommendation in favor of Mrs. Surratt. He wrote that while reporting the Conspirators Trial for the *Tribune* and his own paper he attended the sessions daily and heard all the evidence. ". . . On three different occasions, now distinctly remembered," he wrote, "when your correspondent himself was at the executive office, President Johnson . . . in substance, if not in exact phrase, uttered these words: 'The Court recommended Mrs. Surratt to mercy because she was a woman and for no other reason. If anyone was guilty of that horrible crime, she was. Her treason and conspiracy to destroy the Government were unmistakable. . . . I permitted this woman to be hung from a sense of public duty. I alone am responsible.' "

At the period of which Byington writes there were in Washington sixty-five correspondents, representing seventy newspapers and press associations, in addition to the staffs of nine local newspapers. Of all these reporters only A. Homer Byington heard the President mention the clemency plea for Mrs. Surratt.

Immediately after the Conspirators Trial, Benn Pittman, reporter to the military commission, obtained permission from Judge Holt to print the testimony. Two conditions were attached. One was that Pittman "must publish every word, omitting nothing." The other was that the proofs of the book must be inspected by an officer of the Court. The inspection was made and the official certified to the "faithfulness and accuracy" of Pittman's report. Did this report contain any mention of the recommendation for clemency? It did not; nor did any of the several other publications of the trial issued at the time.

In the 1920's two of Johnson's biographers, Robert W. Winston and George Fort Milton, examined all of the trial papers. Both of these careful students found physical evidence that when the papers were handed to Andrew Johnson, they were arranged in such a manner that there was no likelihood that the President would see the petition for Mrs. Surratt.

It doesn't follow that if Johnson had seen the recommendation, he would have honored it. He told Secretary of the Treasury McCulloch that he regretted his decision to permit Mrs. Surratt to be hanged. He regretted also the fact that the writ of *habeas corpus,* issued on the morning of the woman's execution, was disregarded. But these statements were made later. At the time of the Conspirators Trial Johnson was as anxious as anyone to see Lincoln's assassins punished. His thinking was infected as was that of most of the men around him by the distemper of the times. Winston suggests that Judge Holt may have acted out of a sincere desire to keep the peace, since public knowledge of the clemency petition of 1865 would have increased the agitation among Mrs. Surratt's friends and further embarrassed the Executive. Whatever Holt's motives, formidable evidence exists that he deliberately withheld the petition from President Johnson's knowledge.

Soon after the Conspirators Trial the charge against Jefferson Davis of complicity in the assassination was dropped.

VI

PRESIDENTIAL RECONSTRUCTION

At the end of the war four of the eleven seceded states had loyal civil governments of some sort. The only permanent one was that of Tennessee under William Gannaway Brownlow, known as the "Fighting Parson." In Virginia, with headquarters at Alexandria, was a skeleton organization under Governor Pierpont. In Louisiana and Arkansas there were provisional "Ten Per Cent" governments.

At the last Cabinet meeting presided over by Lincoln on the day of his assassination, Secretary Stanton brought up for consideration a plan for reorganizing Virginia and North Carolina. It was a Radical plan. It ignored the Pierpont government and proposed to destroy the individuality of the two states by lumping them under a single military governor directly responsible to the War Department, which is to say to Old Mars. Lincoln's tactful comment was that the plan needed "maturing and perfecting." He asked Stanton to prepare in its place a plan for each of the states. These plans, he specified, should call for civil governments and the Pierpont organization of Virginia should be recognized. When the revised proposals were in shape Stanton was to have copies printed and distributed to the Cabinet members for study.

This order to Stanton on Good Friday was Lincoln's last contribution to reconstruction. At President Johnson's first Cabinet meeting, on Sunday, the matter was mentioned but Stanton said the printed copies of his revised plans were not yet ready.

That evening Gideon Welles enjoyed a preview of them. A business errand took the Secretary of the Navy to the War Department, and after the matter at hand had been disposed of he and Stanton chatted for a while before the fire. Suddenly there were visitors. Senator Sumner arrived, accompanied by two Representatives from his own state. They were followed by seven or eight others, including Congressmen Schuyler Colfax of Indiana and John Covode of Pennsylvania.

Warm as the room was, it took on a chill edge for Welles. The suspicion seized him that he was witnessing an informal Radical caucus. Within seconds his fears were confirmed. Without preliminary explanation, Stanton took from his desk and began reading the new plans he had drafted for Virginia and North Carolina.

Welles was embarrassed. Here was the Secretary of War divulging Cabinet documents-in-process, papers meant only for the eyes of the President's advisers. One can imagine Welles glancing from man to man in the crowded room—from the monumental Sumner to "Smiler" Colfax, a blondly handsome and garrulous man, to big-framed "Honest John" Covode, owner of a coal company who, during a brawl in the House, had made a name for himself by plunging into the fracas armed with a spittoon. When a messenger entered shortly with a word for Welles, he took the opportunity to murmur his good-byes. He carried into the night the chill conviction that Stanton's friends had assembled by pre-concert, and that Stanton had wished Welles to be present, reasoning that, hearing influential men endorse the Radical approach to reconstruction, the Secretary of the Navy might be won over.

He was not, nor could he be. Behind fifty-eight-year-old Welles' benign eyes and his sacerdotal face in its whiskered nest lay a trenchant and conservative mind. Like many Jacksonian Democrats-turned-Republican-over-slavery, he was still a strict-constructionist and a states-rightist. Welles came of a long line of hard-working and quiet-living New Englanders who had helped settle Hartford, Connecticut. Born of reasonably wealthy parents on a country estate, educated at the Protestant Episcopal Academy in Cheshire and at Norwich University, Welles had studied law and had then made a career of journalism. In 1826 he took charge of the Hartford *Times*. He was a crusading editor. When the highest Connecticut tribunal ruled that a person who didn't believe in Heaven and Hell was incompetent as a court witness, Welles captained the campaign which induced the legislature to change the requirement to a simple belief in God. No Abolitionist, he was eventually led into the Republican fold by a desire to see the "peculiar institution" kept out of the territories. Simultaneously, he left the Democratic *Times* to become a contributor to the Republican Hartford *Evening Press*.

Lincoln's choice of him for the naval portfolio was amusing to some people, for at the time Welles knew not bow from stern nor reef from porpoise. Yet he turned in a singularly successful record in a post almost as vital as that of Stanton's to the Northern military effort. Proud of his Zeus-like curls, his great bush of white beard, gregarious and sociable, the Secretary, underneath his high polish, had many temperamental affinities with Andrew Johnson. Like the President, he made few close friends. Johnson gave his full confidence only to the members of his family, notably to his invalid wife and to the official White House hostess, his daughter, Martha Patterson. Welles gave his full confidence only to his diary. To Welles-the-historian we are indebted. His diary and other published accounts give us our single most detailed look behind the scenes of the Johnson administration. Largely thanks to Welles' record of the crucial Cabinet meetings of May, it is possible to follow Johnson step by step as he creates his reconstruction policy.

Monday, May 8: The Cabinet convenes to consider Stanton's revised proposals for reorganizing Virginia and North Carolina. Seward, of course, is not present. With Johnson are six men.

There is Secretary of the Treasury Hugh McCulloch. Named to his post only two months before, McCulloch is a young-looking fifty-seven. He wears his hair plastered close to a square head, has wide open eyes, a corkscrew twist in either mouth-corner, the beginnings of a double chin. He is a decent and intelligent man. Maine-born son of a prominent shipbuilder, McCulloch can look back on a brilliant career in the banking circles of Indiana. Entering government service under Chase, as Comptroller of the currency, he can take credit for midwifing the national banking system set up during the war. At this moment he probably understands the system better than any man in the country—certainly better than Andrew Johnson. McCulloch will be faithful to Johnson, although there will be times when Johnson will suspect otherwise. Honest men both, but of differing economic outlooks, each will begrudge to the other a reluctant admiration.

Not quite so new to the Cabinet is James Speed, Attorney-General, appointed in 1864. A lawyer of ability, poise and spotless reputation, Speed is proud of having done much to keep his state, Kentucky, out of the Confederacy in the early days of the war. He does not think much of Johnson, and Johnson's opinion of him is that Speed's "wife is the better man of the two." Later Speed will find that he cannot go along with the President's reconstruction views, and he will relinquish his post.

William Dennison of Ohio, Montgomery Blair's successor as Postmaster-General, will in time resolve his own Radical inclinations in the same manner.

Secretary of the Interior John Palmer Usher has already resigned, effective May 15. Both he and McCulloch are Hoosiers and tradition requires one of them to step down. Usher's place will be assumed by James Harlan of Iowa. Educator and pillar of the Methodist church, Harlan, on taking office, will be thrown into a dither on discovering that one of his employees is writing poetry of a disturbing nature. Fired by Harlan, the poet will find a financial haven in the office of the Assistant Attorney-General and go on writing; his name is Walt Whitman.

Stanton and Welles complete the group. The discussion goes on for four hours. Old Mars has no intention of showing his colors, nor is he going to give up without a struggle. Obedient to Lincoln's instructions, he has revised his plans so as to provide civil governments for Virginia and North Carolina. But the manner in which these governments are to be set up is by provost marshals, appointed by and responsible to—Old Mars! Welles' whiskers quiver. What Stanton is suggesting, he demurs, would be an unwarranted delegation of executive duties to the War Department. The other members of the Cabinet take the same view. Now is the moment for President Johnson to show *his* colors. If he has any Radical inclinations, he has only to side with Stanton. He sides with Welles and the others.

Seeing that all are against him, Stanton contents himself with a lukewarm defense of his provost marshals. Then, arguing that since the clause authorizing the marshals is not going to be used and might as well be removed, he takes a pair of shears and cuts away the sentences involved from all copies of the plans. His object, obviously, is to erase the proposition from the record. But he reckons without the diary-keeping Connecticut Yankee; quietly Welles pockets a set of the cut-away sections. He will trot them out later when the time comes to set the record straight for posterity.

Section 8 of the Virginia plan deals with the Pierpont government. The Radicals have no use for this organization. Sumner has belittled it as "the common council of Alexandria." Stevens will soon be describing it as so microscopic that "all its archives, property and effects" could be taken to the state capital in an ambulance. Actually it is not the size of the Pierpont government that bothers Sumner, Stevens and their friends, but its lack of Radical coloration. As written by Stanton, Section 8 of the Virginia plan treats the Pierpont government as an embryo waiting to be delivered. As re-written under Johnson's guidance, the section treats it as an already-going concern.

By the end of the session the Virginia plan has been stripped of its Radical elements. North Carolina presents a tougher problem, since no loyal government of any sort exists there. For this reason the President suggests that detailed discussion of Stanton's plan for that state be held over until the next morning.

Tuesday, May 9: The Virginia plan is put into effect by Presidential proclamation and the Cabinet meets to take up Stanton's revised proposals for North Carolina.

Two words in these proposals touch off considerable discussion. Stanton's suggestion is that the North Carolina government be organized by the "loyal people." Whom, he is asked, does he include under that phrase?

Old Mars' reply is that he includes the Negroes. Welles reminds him of an 1863 Cabinet session at which the secretaries and Lincoln decided that the valid voters of the South were those who had voted in the last pre-war election. Stanton counters with the suggestion that, without debate, each Cabinet member air his views on the question. Stanton, Dennison and Speed favor requiring Negro suffrage in North Carolina. Welles, McCulloch and Usher are opposed to it. As for President Johnson, two years hence, testifying before a Congressional Committee, Stanton will say that at this moment Johnson expressed his views "distinctly" and that his objections "to throwing the franchise open to the colored people appeared to be fixed." Welles' recollection, trustworthy and documented, will be that Johnson did not commit himself one way or the other.

Wednesday, May 24: Johnson breaks silence, presenting the whole of his reconstruction policy to his Cabinet. The session is fully attended. Harlan has assumed his duties and Seward is on hand. There is no dissent from the President's plan. Stanton, although far from pleased, goes along. He reasons that he has done all he can for his Radical friends; his best tactic for the time being is to pretend agreement and await developments.

Five days later Andrew Johnson made his plan public. On May 29 the President issued two proclamations.

One of them, a Proclamation of Pardon and Amnesty, was in effect a variation of Lincoln's Ten Per Cent plan. It will be remembered that Lincoln's proclamation of 1863 provided that with certain exceptions all Rebels upon taking a simple oath were to be pardoned and restored to "all rights of property except as to slaves." While Lincoln did not offer to entertain special pleas for pardon from those excepted from the benefits of his proclamation, he several times indicated his intention of doing so "in due season." A feature of Johnson's 1865 Amnesty proclamation was an offer to entertain pleas for pardon from all excepted individuals. There was also the promise that such petitions would be handled in a lenient manner.

Lincoln barred from immediate forgiveness six classes of Rebels, principally those who had served the Confederacy in high civil or military posts, or who had resigned from such posts in the Federal government or army to aid the Southern cause. Johnson kept Lincoln's exceptions and added to them, bringing the total of excluded classes to fourteen. Of Johnson's additions, only one was of consequence. That was his clause excluding from the general pardon any rebel worth $20,000. Lincoln's exceptions did not affect many individuals, two or three thousand at the most. Contemporary estimates of the number affected by Johnson's exceptions ranged from a hundred thousand to a hundred and fifty thousand, at least half of whom were believed to come under the $20,000 clause.

The other proclamation of May 29 listed the terms under which North Carolina was to be reorganized. During the summer almost identical proclamations would be issued covering all the other Southern states except those four in which reorganization was already under way or completed. For each state except Tennessee (where permanent civil government was in full swing) the President appointed a provisional governor, or recognized the one already in office. Each governor was instructed to take the steps necessary for assembling an organizing convention. The convention was to set up machinery for establishing a permanent government, which in turn would set up the machinery for naming Representatives-elect and Senators-elect to Congress.

The President let it be understood that in his eyes each state would be elegible for readmission to the Union as soon as it completed this process, provided that at the same time it ended slavery within its borders, repudiated its Rebel war debt and voided its ordinance of secession. The eventual fate of the program rested with Congress, since Congress had the power under the Constitution to accept or reject the Representatives and Senators named by the reorganized states.

The emphasis of the President's plan was not on reconstruction as such. It was on restoration. His hope was that the Southern people would rapidly comply with his terms, set up loyal governments and send loyal delegates to Congress. His final hope, on which all else pivoted, was that Congress would accept the Southern delegates and so re-unite the Nation. To put it another way, the President's over-all aim was to complete restoration with all possible speed, thus permitting the Southern states, once more represented in Congress, to have a voice in their own reconstruction.

Restoration first, then reconstruction. Such was Andrew Johnson's policy. Some details would cause trouble, notably the $20,000 clause in the Amnesty proclamation. But viewed as a whole the program was magnanimous and wise. Could it have been carried through, the harsher aspects of reconstruction would have been avoided. The policy was predicated on Johnson's assumption that if reasonable terms were presented, the Southern people would carry them out in good faith.

Was his assumption justified? In some respects yes. The conditions Johnson set forth as the price the Southern states must pay for readmission to the Union were that each state must accept emancipation, preferably by ratifying the Thirteenth Amendment to the Constitution but at the very least by abolishing human bondage within its own jurisdiction. The other conditions were that it repudiate its Confederate war debt and void its secession ordinance. All of these terms, including ratification of the amendment, were eventually met by all of the states except Mississippi, which refused to ratify the Thirteenth, and South Carolina, which failed to repudiate its war debt and worded its resolutions repealing secession and abolishing slavery "by act of the United States Authorities."

However, in another respect the Southern people let Johnson down. Two oaths were involved in the reorganization process. To participate in the election of convention delegates and state and national officers, a qualified Southern voter had only to take the simple oath of allegiance. But to hold Federal office, he was required to take the so-called "iron-clad" or "test" oath prescribed in a law passed by Congress during the war. This was a stiffer oath, calling on the would-be officeholder to swear that he had "neither sought, nor accepted, nor attempted to exercise the functions of any office whatever, under any authority, or pretended authority in hostility or inimical to the United States." Several states elected to Congress men who could not take the iron-clad oath. Georgia, for example, sought to send to the Senate Alexander H. Stephens, former Vice President of the Confederacy.

Johnson was gravely embarrassed. In conferences in Washington and in a stream of letters and telegrams he begged the Southern leaders not to put ammunition in the hands of their enemies by trying to send to Congress men Congress could not possibly seat. He was well aware that any intransigency below the Potomac would be seized upon by the Radicals as justifying their clamor for a harsh peace. For the most part, his pleas fell on deaf ears. The animus of the defiance in the South is not difficult to understand. In the chaos and misery of defeat the people stood in desperate need of intelligent and trustworthy leadership. Instinctively they turned to men they regarded as their natural leaders, the very men who had led them during the war. It was all very human, very natural, and very imprudent.

Notwithstanding these hitches reorganization moved steadily ahead. Throughout the summer and fall conventions were held, permanent governments set up, delegates named to Washington. By the time Congress convened on December 4, 1865, the process had been completed in nine states and was well under way in the remaining two. If Congress accepted the Southern Representatives-elect and Senators-elect, even if some had to be sent home as ineligible and replacements made, the President's Reconstruction program would be a *fait accompli*.

If Congress did not, what then?

VII

THE DICTATOR

Congressman Thaddeus Stevens, the Radical leader, passed most of the summer and fall of 1865 at his home in Lancaster, Pennsylvania. Home was a three-and-a-half story red brick structure set flush with the sidewalk of narrow and tree-shaded Queen Street. There were two front doors, one to his office and the other to the house proper. On one set of steps or the other he was often seen of a summer evening, taking his rest and nodding to passersby. They returned the greeting, addressing him as "Thad" or "Old Thad."

The old man was 73, gaunt of frame and craggy of brow with a thin and hard-set mouth and a shielded look in his dark blue eyes. Lame from birth, he had been an athlete in his youth, riding well and once boasting that he could easily swim the Hellespont after the manner of that other club-footed genius, Lord Byron. He had also once been handsome, but the face that now looked out upon Lancaster in the summer gloaming was grim. Illness had removed his hair and he wore an untidy brown wig. It was for comfort, not vanity. When an admiring lady asked for a lock of his hair, he said "Please, Madame, take it all," and handed her the wig.

His wit was keen, although he himself never laughed. The most quoted of his quips was one made to Lincoln concerning Simon Cameron. Old Thad's long dislike for the Pennsylvania political czar took on intensity when Cameron traded his way into Lincoln's Cabinet and thus frustrated Stevens' desire to be named Attorney-General. Stevens soon had Washington laughing over his verbal slaps at Lincoln's first Secretary of War. Distressed by this, desiring the friendship of both men, Lincoln asked Stevens to curb his tongue, a request Old Thad ignored.

Finally the President said to him, "Surely, you don't think Mr. Cameron would steal."

"Well," was Stevens' hollow-voiced reply, "I don't think he'd steal a red-hot stove."

Lincoln could keep anything to himself except a good story. Soon Stevens' jibe found its way to the ears of Cameron, who hastened to the White House in protest. Summoning Stevens again, Lincoln begged him to retract his remark.

"Glad to oblige you, Mr. President," said Stevens. "I said that I didn't think Cameron would steal a red-hot stove. I now take that back!"

Old Thad's Lancaster neighborhood was not an elegant one. There was a cheap hotel in the block and a beer saloon on one corner. Stevens spent little or no time in the saloon. His much talked-about appetites required other outlets. He had a passion for gambling and his adventures at the faro table were much talked of. There was the all-night game, in the course of which Thad's luck slid from bad to worse. The windows were letting in the first light of dawn when the door of the room was opened by an old teamster who, on Thad's request, had brought him a load of hay.

"What shall I do with this?" the teamster shouted.

"Put it all on the ace of spades!" was the melancholy retort.

On another occasion he emerged from one of Washington's gambling hells, with his winnings (a one hundred dollar bill) in one pocket, and a dollar in the other. As Thad and a friend stepped into the street, a Negro preacher approached them soliciting charity. Handing him what he thought was the dollar, Stevens later discovered that he had parted with the hundred. "Ah," he sighed, "God works in mysterious ways his wonders to perform!"

Another of his passions was women. A lifelong bachelor, his interest in them was exclusively physical, except possibly where his housekeeper, Mrs. Lydia Hamilton Smith, was concerned. Those who knew her called her "comely, exceedingly intelligent and entertaining." Born in Gettysburg in 1813 and reared as a Roman Catholic, Lydia Hamilton at an early age married a Negro carpenter of Lancaster named Jacob Smith. Jacob died in 1844 and Stevens, who had settled in Lancaster the year before, took Lydia into his home. She was first his housekeeper and later his hostess, travelling with him and tending not only to his Lancaster establishment but also to his plain red-brick Washington house on one of the little-frequented back streets of Capitol Hill. Gossip soon spread that she was his mistress, and periodically the Lancaster *Intelligencer,* the local Democratic organ, dilated on this and other alleged aspects of Old Thad's private life. An 1866 issue carried a story describing a visit of Mrs. Smith to the *Intelligencer* office for the purpose of protesting the newspaper's attack on her good name:

Yesterday afternoon we were favored with a visit from a lady . . . of the fashionable hue—about the color of a new saddle. She has long presided over the household affairs of that grim old Mephistophelean septuagenarian who . . . so completely misrepresents the voters of this Congressional district by ignoring everything that seems to have any relations to the interest of the white race.

Mrs. Smith was quoted as threatening to "cowhide the editor" the next time the paper said anything mean about her. In another issue the newspaper declared "There are few men who have given the world such open and notorious evidence of a belief in Negro equality as Thaddeus Stevens."

These crudities were not confined to the Lancaster press but appeared from time to time in newspapers in all sections of the country. Stevens ignored them until the fall of 1867 when charges of adultery and seduction leveled at him by a Southern newspaper prompted him to enter a categorical denial in a letter to his friend and political associate, W. B. Mellius:

I received your letter of the 8th. inst., containing a printed libel from the "Union Spring [Miss.] Times."

In the course of my life I have received a very large number of such attacks . . . I have seldom noticed them—never contradicted them . . . You tell me that this charge may influence your next election. Hence I noticed it. . . . The rude doctrines ascribed to me by the fellow who wrote them, I pass over . . . As to the domestic history, I have only to say, that the whole is totally without foundation, except so far as follows:

From the time I began business (forty odd years ago) I have kept house, through the agency of hired servants, having no female relations. Those servants were of various colors, some white, some black, others of all intermediate colors. My inquiry was only into their honesty and capacity. They have resided with me for various periods, from one month to fifteen years, generally more than one at a time, indeed I believe always so. I believe I can say that no child was ever raised, or, so far as I know, begotten under my roof. Sometimes husband and wife have worked. The one for me, and the other for another, generally at the same time cohabiting together on Saturday night. But I believe none of these ever became pregnant at that time.

This is a longer disclosure than, I believe, I have ever made before of my private affairs. These calumnies and worse, have been frequently published all around me by fellows living within sight of my door. I know of no one who has believed one of them, or scarcely pretended to believe them. Having no ambition for office, no aspirations for fame, I have not found it pleasant to turn aside to encounter the offensive odor of diseased dog secretions.

In the summer of 1865, the old man was only barely started on the career that in after years would make him the subject of more biographical attention than any other American politician of less than Presidential rank. During the war he had become the auto-cratic leader of the Congressional majority. It was said that "Whoever cracked Thaddeus Stevens' skull would let out the brains of the Republican party." He was no demagogue. His primary appeal was to men's intellects, not to their emotions. He whipped them into line with the informed logic of his argument and the sting of his humor. Probably no figure in American history has ever exerted so much power by the sheer force of his personality.

To reporters covering the House of Representatives, the spectacle of the Pennsylvania warhorse in action was one never to be forgotten. Noah Brooks, brilliant California correspondent and friend of Lincoln, found him the "ablest man in congressional life . . . argumentative, sardonic, grim." According to Brooks the old man "spoke with great calmness and deliberation, dropping his sentences as though each one weighed a ton; his voice was low but distinct and he launched his anathemas at his opponents as coolly as if he were bandying compliments."

In invective Stevens was memorable. "The gentleman who has just spoken," he said in the course of a debate, "need not fear that I will make any insinuations or sneer or thrust at him. There are some reptiles so flat that the common foot of man cannot crush them." Irritated by the repeated attempts of a member to interrupt a speech he was making, "I yield," he growled, "to the gentleman from Virginia for a few feeble remarks." Entering the House during an election for speaker, he was met at the door by an agitated member who said he did not know which way to vote because both candidates were rascals. As he reached for his own ballot, Stevens asked: "Yes, but which is *our* rascal?" On another occasion he rebuked Representative Henry Raymond, founder of the New York *Times,* who had a habit of being on all sides of an issue. "The gentleman from New York," Stevens drawled, "has more privileges here than belong to him. He has the advantage of being able to pair off with himself on every question." On still another occasion, finding himself temporarily in the seat of the Copperhead, Vallandigham of Ohio, and hearing some Republican member make an appeal to the Constitution, he lumbered to his feet with an air of indignation. "How dare you, sir," he demanded, "mention the Constitution of the United States in this House!"

We have a vivid pen picture of his speaking habits by the correspondent, J. W. Binckley. Old Thad would rise slowly, and slowly begin. For a time his voice would be so low that only those very close could catch his words. His opening remarks were usually on the ludicrous side, often having nothing to do with his subject. He would look around vaguely, fumbling with his hands. Newcomers would get the impression that here was a man in his dotage who thought he ought to say something but didn't know just what. During this period there would be titters throughout the House. The members would swap jokes at the speakers' expense, and even the page boys would take off the old man's mannerisms. On Thad's part, of course, all this was play-acting. Shortly the real speech would begin. The old man, wrote Binckley, "lifts his long right arm with a wide sweep, the elbow in advance of the hand; contracts his beetling brows, throws up and back his towering head and with a sudden, straight thrust of his long, yellow finger, followed by the whole outstretch of his arm, he sends forth in a thundering tone the iron bolt of his argument." Stevens once remarked that "nothing is so prolix as ignorance." His own speeches were devoid of the purple patches common to the political oratory of the day. Swiftly he got to his point, pounded it home and shut up.

Born April 4, 1792, in the backwoods settlement of Danville, Vermont, he began life under circumstances almost as unpromising as those surrounding Andrew Johnson. His shoemaker-father, Joshua Stevens, was improvident and dissipated. Enlisting at the outbreak of the War of 1812, Joshua was wounded at the defense of Oswego. Whether he died of this wound or simply deserted his family is not clear. In any event the upbringing of the four children was left to Mrs. Sara Morrill Stevens. By dint of working "day and night," as Thaddeus later related, she saw to it that all of them were properly educated. Thad was everlastingly grateful to his mother. He accounted it a red-letter day when, in his moderately affluent maturity, he was able to give her a two-hundred-fifty-acre farm, a dairy of fourteen cows and "an occasional bright gold piece which she loved to deposit in the contributors' box of the Baptist Church." Not that Thad looked on these gifts as discharging his obligation, since "the debt of a child to his mother, you know, is one of the debts we can never repay."

Completing his education at Dartmouth and at the University of Vermont, Thad taught school for a period, read law, passed the bar, and in 1816 hung out his shingle in Gettysburg.

His legal career ran a familiar gamut. There were years of struggle. Then came success as the result of a sensational murder trial in which Stevens, as defense attorney, entered the then seldom-heard-of plea of insanity. Later he went into the iron business, eventually becoming part owner of a forge and furnace to which he gave the name of Caledonia after the county of his birth in Vermont. The Caledonia works were never profitable, but Stevens kept them going rather than deprive the community of its principal source of livelihood. During the Civil War campaign which culminated at Gettysburg, the works were destroyed by Confederate cavalry. Stevens' loss, according to his own evaluation, was "about $75,000." In after years this incident was often cited as explaining his reconstruction views, but there is considerable evidence that on this subject Old Thad's mind was made up long before the destruction of his property.

He achieved his first political prominence in the 1830's as a leader of the short-lived Anti-Masonic party. For some time after the other chief exponents of Anti-Masonry had abandoned the movement, Stevens continued to give it his all. This inclination to fritter his energies on hopeless and sometimes ridiculous causes created the impression in political circles that he was "able but unsafe." It is the surmise of his biographer, Alphonse B. Miller, that it was this reputation that prevented his coming into his own as a political strategist until the last seven years of his life.

Anti-slavery caught his fancy early. Characteristically he plunged into it whole hog. In 1837, three decades before hardly anyone else was dreaming of such a thing, he was advocating suffrage for the

Negroes of Pennsylvania. By 1842 he had put Anti-Masonry behind him and had joined hands with Whiggery, unenthusiastically to be sure and only because the Whigs were opposed to the Democrats, whose economic policies, notably their affection for a low tariff, were at odds with his own. By 1849 he was representing his district in the House, where his maiden speech created a sensation.

I am opposed to the diffusion of slavery [he said], because confining it within its present limits will bring the states themselves to its gradual abolition . . . I am opposed to the extension of slavery into territories now free, for still graver reasons—because I am opposed to despotism. In my judgment, not only the slave states, but the general government, recognizing and aiding slavery as it does, is a despotism.

Retiring from Congress as a lukewarm Whig in 1853, he returned as an ardent Republican in 1859. Three years later he had become the acknowledged dictator of the Republican-dominated House of Representatives.

Such was Old Thad's status in the summer of 1865. When Andrew Johnson took over, Stevens was not sure what to expect. As a delegate to the 1864 National-Union convention, he had bowed to party pressure and cast his vote for Johnson, but with the comment that it was a pity the Republicans had to go down "into one of those damned Rebel states" for a vice-presidential candidate. He took note of the new President's remarks on the necessity of punishing treason, permitted himself a few mild hopes and kept his fingers crossed. When on May 9 Johnson recognized the skeleton Pierpont government in Virginia, Thad concluded that the President was going to follow Lincoln's tender policy on reconstruction and began preparing for the fight ahead.

Twice, during the summer, he wrote to Johnson. On May 16 he called the President's attention to the fact that "Reconstruction is a very delicate question. The last Congress (and I expect the present) looked upon it as a question for the Legislative power exclusively. While I think we shall agree with you almost unanimously as to the main objects you have in view, I fear we may differ as to the manner of effecting them. How the Executive can remoddle [sic] *the States in the Union* is past my comprehension. I see how he can govern them through military governors until they are reorganized." Stevens closed with the suggestion that Johnson hold everything in abeyance until Congress met. "Better call an extra session," he wrote, "than to allow many to think the Executive was approaching usurpation."

Less than a month later, with Johnson's full program under way, Stevens was writing the President to "pardon me for speaking to you with a candor to which men in high places are seldom accustomed. Among all the leading Union men of the North, with whom I had intercourse I do not find one who approves of your policy. They believe that 'Restoration' as announced by you will destroy our party (which is of little consequence) and will greatly injure the country. Can you not hold your hand and wait the action of Congress, and in the meantime govern them (the Southern states) by military rulers? Profuse pardoning also will greatly embarrass Congress if they should wish to make the enemy pay the expense of the war or part of it."

Apparently Johnson did not acknowledge either of these letters. This was a political error. Both letters show a desire by Stevens to avoid an open breach with the Executive. Obviously Johnson should have given them immediate attention. In the tense and suspicion-laden atmosphere of the post-war months, Stevens must have wondered why the President, who was carrying on an extensive correspondence with Southern Union leaders and even some former Rebels, could not find time to acknowledge two letters from the majority leader of the House. That Stevens' thoughts were running in these channels is clearly indicated by his letters to Senator Sumner during this period. On June 3 he wrote:

"When will you be in Washington? Could we collect bold men enough to lay the foundation of a party to take the helm of this government and keep it off the rocks?" On June 14 he put his fears into words: "If something is not done, the President will be crowned king before the Congress meets." On August 26, again to Sumner: "I am glad you are laboring to arrest the President's fatal policy. I wish the prospects of success were better. I have twice written him urging him to stay his hand until Congress meets. Of course he pays no attention to it . . . Get the rebel States into a territorial condition, and it can easily be dealt with. That I think should be our great aim. Then Congress can manage it. We need a good committee on elections. . . ."

Old Thad had held out the olive branch and Johnson had spurned it. Very well, since the President was asking for a fight, let him have it! "Get the rebel States into a territorial condition. . . ." In other words, declare them territories and keep them in that status until such time as Congress decided what conditions they must fulfill as their price for readmission to the Union. "We need a good committee on elections." In other words, set up a body empowered to pass on all Senators and Representatives elected to Congress by the South—for the purpose of excluding most if not all of them.

In Stevens' last letter to Sumner he also wrote that "I would make a speech as you suggest if a fair occasion offered." The occasion arose on September 6 when, in an address to the people of Lancaster, Old Thad set forth his own reconstruction views:

Four years of bloody and expensive war waged against the United States by eleven states . . . have overthrown all governments within those states, which could be acknowledged as legitimate by the Union . . .

Stevens scouted the notion that the excluded states were still in the Union. He cited President Johnson's own actions as showing beyond question that they were not. Under the Constitution the Federal government had no right to meddle in the internal affairs of a state. But even now the President was doing just that. He was compelling the Southern states, as a condition precedent to their return to the Union, to make changes in their governmental structures. If what the President was doing was legal, then obviously the Southern states were no longer states at all. What were they then? Stevens' answer was that they were "conquered provinces" and should be so treated.

As to what this treatment should consist of, that would be for Congress to determine. He himself believed that in fairness to the "starved, murdered, slaughtered martyrs" of the North, the Government should "inflict condign punishment on the rebel belligerents." A mild conjecture presents itself with regard to these vindictive words. Would Stevens have been so drastic if he had thought for one moment that public opinion in the North would sustain him? The question arises in view of one of his subsequent actions. A few months later, discovering that the South was suffering from a dire shortage of lawyers, he proposed and put through the House a resolution designed to permit Southern attorneys to practice without taking the iron-clad oath previously demanded of them. It is not suggested that in asking punishment of the South Stevens did not mean what he said; the point is that his technique was to ask for more than he knew he could get.

Developing the theme of "condign punishment," in this September address, Stevens "especially" insisted that the Federal Government confiscate the holdings of every "rebel belligerent whose estate was worth $10,000 or whose land exceeded two hundred acres." Under this provision the property subject to confiscation would amount to about three hundred ninety-four million acres. Stevens proposed that forty acres of this be given to each adult, male freedman and that the remainder be divided into small farms and sold. Such a procedure, he estimated, would produce about three and a half billion dollars. Let this money, he suggested, be applied to veterans' pensions, to the relief of damages suffered by loyal men in both the North and the South during the war, and to the national debt.

Old Thad was not usually a dissembler. "I am no sycophant," he once remarked. "What I think I say." Yet in the September speech he did not hesitate to engage in verbal hocus-pocus. Castigating Johnson in terms that were milk and honey contrasted to those he would be using three months later, he said that "our late sainted President" was for a time in the hands of the Blairs, Old Frank and his sons Montgomery and Frank Jr. Now, alas, Johnson was in their hands. Thad described the Blairs as "a family of some merit, of admirable audacity and execrable selfishness." It was his impression that the Blairs had a bad habit of seizing the White House, or trying to, during every administration. He said that they had almost lost the re-election for Lincoln, an ironic statement in view of the strenuous efforts Old Thad himself had exerted to that same end. It was a mild speech, coming from the possessor of the most sarcastic tongue in America.

Toward the end of November the Senators and Representatives were converging on Washington for the December 4 opening of Congress. Stevens arrived on the twenty-third, taking quarters for the time being at the National Hotel. Six days later he called on the President.

According to the New York *Herald,* Johnson did the talking and Stevens listened. Stevens' biographer, Miller, has it that the conversation was more evenly divided. Stevens voiced disapproval of the generosity with which the President was granting pardons to Rebels belonging to the classes excepted from his Amnesty Proclamation. He said that the rank and file of the Union-Republican Party in Pennsylvania was opposed to the President's policy and declared that if Johnson refused to alter his course he would not receive any support from the majority of the Republicans in Congress. Johnson gave no indications of yielding but pleaded for harmony, "which appeal Stevens did not heed."

It can be assumed that the two men parted company fully aware that a fight was coming. Having devoted the summer and fall to correspondence with his fellow Radicals, Stevens had his tactics pretty well in mind. In the offing was one of the most thoroughgoing campaigns ever launched against an American President. It would end as an assault on the powers of the Executive office itself.

PART TWO

The Dispute

VIII

THE GRIM PRESENCE

During the same period that Thaddeus Stevens was sitting on the steps of his Lancaster home, brooding on the sad direction that the affairs of the nation were taking, the prime mover in those affairs, Andrew Johnson, was busy with the heavy and multitudinous tasks of a post-war President.

For the first six weeks of his administration he did not live at the White House for the reason that it was still occupied by his predecessor's widow. To Mary Todd Lincoln the death of her husband was only the worst of a series of personal tragedies. There was the loss of her second-born, "Little Eddie," before she and her husband came to Washington. There was the loss in the White House of eleven-year-old Willie, her favorite. Demonstrative, high-spirited and insecure, Mrs. Lincoln returned to the White House on the morning of her husband's death a broken woman, fated to spend the remainder of her days in the shadow world of mental illness.

The doctor's orders were for her to rest but this she would not do in any room her husband had occupied or had been associated with. "Not there! Oh, not there!" she cried of first one chamber and then another. Finally one was found, on the upper floor of the White House.

To Johnson came a black-margined note from Robert, oldest of the Lincoln sons, saying his mother could not "possibly be ready to leave . . . for two and a half weeks." Johnson sent back word that the Lincolns were to remain in the White House as long as they saw fit. They remained five weeks, during which interval the lower floor was without responsible supervision. Into it poured a rabble of souvenir-hunters. The rooms were plundered of ornaments, plate and silverware were carried off, sofas and chairs were hacked to pieces. By the time Johnson moved in on June 9, much of the White House was a shambles.

By way of lodgings the President accepted Representative Samuel Hooper's offer of his house at H and Fifteenth Streets. There he set up bachelor quarters with his friend and adviser, former Senator Preston King. An amusing incident in connection with the President's stay at the Hooper home found its way into the shorthand diary of his secretary, Colonel Moore. On moving in Johnson discovered that "before he could eat a meal, he had to send to market. Enquiring of the servants if there was any wine, he was told 'Yes, a few bottles,' to which he replied, 'Well, you had better take good care of them.' "

A temporary office for the President was provided in the Treasury building in a room adjoining that of Secretary McCulloch. Draped over the door were the two flags that had decorated Lincoln's box at Ford's Theatre on the tragic night. George Templeton Strong, paying a courtesy call, noted what others may have missed. Still visible in one of the flags was the long tear made by the spur of the assassin's boot as he leaped to the stage after the shooting.

Strong was "favorably impressed" by the new President. "Dignified, urbane, self-possessed; a most presentable person," the cultured New Yorker wrote in his delightful diary. The words he applied to rough-spoken Andrew Johnson may seem strange, but similar comments appear in the diaries of Secretary Welles and former Senator Orville H. Browning of Illinois.

Henry Adams, following his one call on the President, was unable
to forget the President's personal dignity and proud bearing. Having
received from Johnson's lips a "little lecture on constitutional law,"
Adams departed with the impression that the tailor-politician was a
"true President . . . perhaps the strongest he [Adams] was ever to
see."

During his weeks at the Treasury Johnson was usually at his desk
before nine, rarely leaving it until five, sometimes, although not
always, taking a few minutes at noon to share a cup of tea and a
cracker with McCulloch. Lincoln, to a greater degree than any
predecessor, had made himself accessible to the public. Johnson
continued the practice, entertaining a stream of well-wishers,
advice-givers, complaint-makers, project-promoters, office-seekers
and patronage-demanders.

After Johnson moved into the White House his schedule intensi-
fied. A work-day that ended at midnight began at seven in winter,
at six in summer. There were long reports to be read and digested,
and orders to be dispatched to subordinates in all parts of the
country. Cabinet meetings were frequent, and correspondence
voluminous.

The President's working quarters were at the eastern end of the
second floor of the White House. A visitor, mounting the stairs
from the ground-floor vestibule, found himself first in a small office
manned by a clerk. Behind this, at the far east, was a long, narrow
chamber known as the reception room. There were two doors in the
north wall of this room, one to the office of the President's private
secretary, the other to a larger room used by the other members of
his secretarial staff. Of the two doors in the south wall of the reception room, one led to a small private telegraph room and the other
to the President's office. The office was fairly large, 25 by 40 feet.
A door in the west wall gave access to the Cabinet room. Between
two tall windows at the south was a writing table, backed by a large
arm chair, but Johnson appears to have done much of his work on
his feet at a tall, many-pigeonholed desk against the south wall.

Until ten in the morning on an average day he wrote, read and studied, usually in this room. From ten to eleven his door was thrown open to the public. After lunch he received distinguished callers, following which the general public was again admitted. If time were available, he took a walk in the grounds at three; but time was rarely available. Dinner was at seven. At eight, taking with him a pet cat and a pot of coffee, he retired to the library—a large oval apartment next to the Cabinet room—for further reading and writing. After his family joined him in early August, it was his practice to emerge along about nine for a brief chat.

Devoid of outside interests, an indefatigable worker, Johnson demanded a heavy schedule of the members of his clerical staff. His attitude toward them was fair, aloof and formidable. One of his secretaries, Frank Cowan, nicknamed him the "Grim Presence," and Cowan's brief memoirs provide an interesting insight into the daily grind of the Executive mill.

"He wanted to do all the work of the executive himself," Cowan observed. "Easy of approach and constantly made personally interested in the details of many cases," Johnson often had his hands full at one and the same time with "the most mighty and the most trivial matters."

As the secretary charged with the signing of land patents, Cowan worked with several other men in the larger of the two chambers north of the Reception room. On taking over his job, Cowan found that he had only a high walnut stand to work at. "Having," as he puts it, "no more backbone than the average government employee," he soon tired of being on his feet and arranged for the stand-up desk to be removed and a table put in its place. Porters were summoned and the stand-up desk was in the process of being taken away when the reception-room door opened and the Grim Presence made his appearance.

For seconds, as Cowan later recalled the scene, the President said nothing. He simply stood there, one hand on the doorknob, scowling so deeply that all work stopped in the room and the porters put down their burden. Then came the following colloquy:

Johnson: "That desk was General Jackson's. I love the memory of General Jackson. Whatever was Old Hickory's I revere. It is about the only thing in the White House that is a memento of bygone years, when the Constitution of the United States was worth more than the paper on which it was printed. I desire that the desk of Andrew Jackson remain in the corner so long as the mantle of its one-time grand possessor is on my shoulders."

Cowan: "But, Mr. President, if the desk is not removed, where will I place my table?"

Johnson: "Where you please; but Andrew Jackson's desk will remain in that corner."

Exit the Grim Presence, closing the door behind him. Cowan had to put his table in the center of the room. For the next two years, he "had the satisfaction of seeing His Excellency . . . walk around it several times a day and stumble against it repeatedly in attestation of his devotion to the memory of the great Andrew Jackson."

One day Johnson, desiring to send a letter to one of his callers, put his head into the secretaries' room, asking "What is the Christian name of Mr. So-and-So?"

"He has none, Mr. President," Cowan replied with mock gravity. "He is a Jew."

The young secretary was "mortified" when Johnson, finding nothing funny in his retort, slammed the door and could be heard calling around in the room beyond, "What is the first or given name of Mr. So-and-So, the Jew?"

There is nothing to indicate that Johnson shared to any degree the racial prejudices of his day. On the eve of the war, hearing Johnson speak with special harshness of Senator Benjamin of Mississippi, Charles Francis Adams got the impression that Johnson harbored "a strong aversion" toward Jews, yet Adams' impression does not appear to be borne out by any other examples. Johnson's friendship for Roman Catholics was demonstrated on numerous occasions. In overwhelmingly Protestant Tennessee, during his stump-speech days, he openly and often denounced the anti-Catholicism of the Know-Nothings, sometimes under circumstances requiring marked courage. In a speech in the House he rebuked those who called the Catholic Church a foe of freedom, pointing out that religious liberty was first brought to American soil by the Catholic settlers of Maryland.

Johnson's wife and his older daughter, Mrs. Patterson, were actively affiliated with the Methodist Church but Johnson himself adhered to no organized religion. It was his practice, during his Presidency, to summon his carriage on Sunday morning and attend church—but the church varied. Sometimes it was the New York Avenue Presbyterian Church, presided over by the eloquent Dr. Phineas D. Gurley. Sometimes it was St. Patrick's Roman Catholic cathedral. Father Maguire, the pastor there, was a clergyman after the President's heart. Johnson liked the fact that Father Maguire preached no politics, hate or malice, and devoted his sermons to the fundamental virtues. Although Johnson inclined doctrinally to the Baptists, he found much to admire in Catholicism. What appealed to him at St. Patrick's, he told Colonel Moore, was the fact that there were no high-priced pews and no reserved seats and that rich and poor were treated alike.

Returning to the White House after church, he often spent the next hour or so discussing the sermon with Colonel Moore, frequently reading aloud from the Bible to illustrate points that had caught his attention. There was a strong religious bent in the man and he remained to the end of his days a spiritual searcher. He dabbled for a brief period in spiritualism and he was also a student of Confucius.

In his earlier days he exhibited a tendency, amusing to the orthodox, to equate religion with what he conceived to be the underlying principles of democracy. A notable instance of this occurred when he took office for his first term as governor of Tennessee. In his inaugural address he declared that when "democracy and religion shall meet and unite, the Millennial morning shall dawn" and that "democracy and the divinity of man are the same."

One of Johnson's problems was his health—the kidney ailment. Acute at intervals, forcing him to bed because of the intense pain, it was always with him. Cowan noted that he did a great deal of his work standing up, finding that position less painful than sitting. He worked ceaselessly, often making of himself for days and sometimes for weeks a prisoner of the White House. Secretary Welles worried about him, and found it a major project to lure the Executive away from his desk for an infrequent boat trip down the Potomac.

Johnson's family had better luck. The Grim Presence found it more difficult to resist the pleas of his grandchildren to join them at play on the White House lawn or on picnics in Rock Creek park or in the meadows surrounding Pierce's Mill. The President loved children, and it was in their presence that he most often displayed his warm but seldom-seen smile. He gave his grandchildren and their companions the run of the White House. It was not uncommon, even when distinguished visitors were on hand, for four or five youngsters to barge into the Executive office, always sure of a welcome from "Grandpa."

Johnson also had a soft spot in his heart for animals. Picking up a basket of grain in his bedroom one August afternoon, he called the attention of Colonel Moore to the fact that the grain had been nibbled. The explanation was that, while making ready for bed, he had spied some mice playing around and had put the basket down so they could have a meal. Subsequently, having gained "the confidence of the little creatures," as the President put it, he made it a practice to sprinkle the hearth with water so his new pets could wash down their food.

With the arrival of the President's family—ten persons in all—the White House took on a sparkle and a bustle. Eliza McCardle Johnson was now 58, but illness and the hardships of the war had so depleted her strength that she was unable to act as her husband's official hostess. Given the choice of bed chambers, she chose a small guest room with a view of the front lawn. There she sewed and read, played with her five grandchildren and chatted with her sons Robert and 12-year-old Frank, who shortly became a student of the Jesuit Fathers at Georgetown University.

Throughout her almost four years in the White House, Mrs. Johnson made only two public appearances. One of these, on the

President's birthday in 1868, was a party for the children. A newspaper woman attending the affair found the President's wife "a lady of benign countenance and sweet and winning manners." Seated in one of the satin and ebony chairs, Mrs. Johnson did not rise as her small guests were presented. "My dears," she said simply, "I am an invalid." According to the reporter, "her sad, pale face and sunken eyes proved the expression."

Frank Cowan, for all his annoyance at the brusque ways of the Grim Presence, was touched by Johnson's devotion to his wife. The young secretary noted that after her arrival, Johnson did more and more of his work in the library, because it was across the hall from his wife's room. Johnson kept the door open, ready to hurry to the invalid's side at the slightest sound of distress.

Mrs. Johnson's illness did not prevent her, as in the past, from being her husband's most trusted counsellor. She exerted a strong influence on him, one that, according to Colonel W. H. Crook, a special officer of the White House, was invariably on the side "of tolerance and gentleness." "Johnson's response to the slightest movement of her hands or her 'Now, Andrew!' " in Crook's words, "evidenced his respect."

To Mrs. Martha Patterson, the older daughter, fell the task of presiding over the White House social life and the supervision of the household. Like her father, Martha regarded her job as a public trust. When Congress appropriated $30,000 for the badly needed refurbishing of the White House, Martha personally supervised the buying and labor and only she could have managed with this inadequate sum.

It was her daily custom to rise at an early hour and, descending to the basement, to skim the milk and attend to the White House dairy before breakfast. Newspaper accounts, notably those of the three women in the Congressional press galleries, testify to Martha's popularity and to her acceptance by society. Even sophisticated Washington could not resist a woman who in a day when exposed shoulders were the vogue continued to wear the high-necked gowns of her native state, and who said: "We are plain people from the mountains of Tennessee, called here for a short time by a national calamity. I trust too much will not be expected of us."

For his first two years much of Johnson's time was devoted to the details involved in processing the individual applications for pardon sent in by Southerners who fell into one or more of the fourteen exceptions to the general pardon extended by his Amnesty Proclamation. For many months, according to the New York *Herald,* these applications flowed into Washington at the rate of four hundred to five hundred daily. In all some 15,000 petitions were received and some 13,500 granted.

Fully ninety per cent of the applications came from Southerners who were barred from immediate pardon because they were worth $20,000 or more. Johnson's decision to make wealthy Southerners sweat for their pardons reflected a complex of motivations. One was his belief that Southerners had contributed to the Rebellion in accordance with their financial standing. Another was his conviction that the curse of the South lay in the fact that its political and economic power was monopolized by a small group, coupled with his lifelong desire to encourage the growth of a Southern yeoman or middle-class. Hence the reason voiced by Johnson in July, 1865 for turning down the applications of some Richmond manufacturers, who needed pardons to obtain funds for resuming operations. Johnson said he was going to leave these Richmond industrialists "for the present, where the law and rebellion [had] placed them" and allow "new men" to do the manufacturing in Richmond.

Whatever the President's motives, the $20,000 exception was a mistake. The handling of the pardons was a severe drain on his time and energies. By mid-summer complaints were appearing in the press, especially in *The Nation,* a new magazine but already an influential one, thanks to the learning and charm of its 34-year-old founder, Edwin Lawrence Godkin. In his maiden issue Godkin was pleading for some way of protecting the President from "pardon-seekers, delegations, and busybodies of both sexes . . . lest they make an end of him." The editor added significantly that the President's time "belongs to the whole nation."

The Southern historian, Ellis Merton Coulter, has suggested that Johnson got a secret satisfaction out of playing Lord Bountiful to "former proud Southerners who had made him in his younger days feel keenly their high position." If Johnson did relish having the hated aristocrats coming to him for favors, he paid dearly for the pleasure. A vivid notion of his burden is provided by John T. Trowbridge, a Northern writer of books for boys, in his account of a tour of the Southern states after the war. Stopping off at Washington in August of 1865, Trowbridge visited the White House on "one of the President's reception days" when pardon-seekers were permitted to call. Trowbridge found the halls crowded. It was a motley group. "Faces of old men and young men were there," he wrote, "some weary and anxious, a few persistently jocose, and nearly all betraying the unmistakable Southern type. It was, on the whole, a well-dressed crowd, for one so abominably filthy." Making inquiries, Trowbridge discovered that nineteen out of twenty were "pardon-seeking Rebels . . . most of them . . . twenty-thousand-dollar men, anxious to save their estates from confiscation." When the President's office was thrown open, a "strong tide instantly set towards it, resulting in a violent jam at the door." Trowbridge, carried in by the crowd, managed to place himself in a corner where he could watch.

He would "scarcely have recognized" the President from any of his published pictures. He got the impression of "a man rather below medium height, sufficiently stout, with a massy, well-developed head, strong features, dark, iron-gray hair, a thick, dark complexion, deep-sunk eyes with a peculiarly wrinkled, careworn look about them, and a weary expression generally." The President's voice struck him as "mild and subdued, and his manner kindly. He shook hands with none."

To each applicant Johnson "put a question or two, sometimes only one, and dispatched him with a word of promise or advice. No one was permitted to occupy more than a minute or two of his time, while some were disposed of in as many seconds." An "interesting but sad scene," was Trowbridge's summation.

The pardoning-process was circuitous and involved. First, an applicant had to be recommended by a prominent individual, usually the governor of his state. Next the application went to the Attorney General who made a recommendation to the President. If the recommendation was favorable and Johnson confirmed it, the Secretary of State was directed to issue the pardon. This process gave birth to a new professional man, the pardon-broker; and all along the line corruption was inevitable.

Of far more essence was the effect of the $20,000 clause on Southern economy. At war's end one of the greatest needs in the South was money. In the beginning there was a strong impulse by the Northern commercial community to take advantage of this by investments aimed at bringing about a quick resumption of trade between the two sections. The impulse petered out as it became obvious that rehabilitation of the Southern economy was going to be long and difficult. Pending receipt of a pardon a businessman's financial standing and property remained in jeopardy, making it impossible for him to function effectively. The $20,000 clause, in other words, was at variance with Johnson's overall intent, which was to bring about the reconstitution of the South as rapidly as possible. It was a small obstacle compared with those the Radicals were even now devising, but it must be listed among the factors responsible for the long economic agony to which the South was about to be subjected.

Quite likely both the South and the North—and certainly Johnson—breathed a sigh of relief when on September 7, 1867, the President issued a second Amnesty Proclamation, eliminating the $20,000 clause and reducing the number of groups excepted from general pardon to three. On Independence Day, 1868, Johnson issued a third Amnesty, reducing the excepted classes to one, and later that year he proclaimed a universal amnesty. By this time—December 25, 1868—what Johnson did about pardons was of less consequence, for the reason that the states had ratified the Four-

teenth Amendment, the third section of which kept some Southerners under disabilities that only Congress could remove. Final, universal, complete amnesty did not come until June of 1898 when
Congress passed and President McKinley signed a bill that extended
forgiveness to all.

Obviously any evaluation of Johnson's reconstruction program,
as revealed in May of 1865, must take into consideration the fact
that he did not want it to remain in effect long. His hope, of course,
was that Congress would accept the Southern delegates-elect, after
which his first Amnesty Proclamation and all its exceptions would
become a dead letter.

Throughout 1865 the public kept a watchful eye on the President's program, and the reaction on the whole was one of approval.
The New York *Herald* found a "unanimous sentiment of the
country in favor of the President's policy." *The Nation* conceded
that it had "the miraculous property of appearing to satisfy all parts
and parties." It was especially gratifying to the industrial interests
of the Northeast who were eager to see the country stabilized. In
late November, with Congress about to convene, Andrew Johnson
was enjoying the confidence of the public to a degree probably
greater than anything Lincoln had known until the closing months
of his life. No one was more aware of the President's strength than
the Radicals.

IX

THE ATTACK BEGINS

By late November Washington was filling up as Senators and Representatives arrived for the first session of the 39th Congress. Among the early arrivals was Schuyler Colfax, Indiana Radical and Speaker of the House. Light-haired and blue-eyed, somewhat under medium height, with a youthful face and manner, "Smiler" Colfax was a back-slapper and a favorite with the newspaper correspondents. Lincoln had viewed him with more amusement than admiration, once telling Secretary Welles that "Colfax is for Colfax under any and all circumstances." Johnson's estimate was that Colfax would have served his country better as the keeper of "a grocery store at some cross roads where he could dilate upon the excellent quality of his wares and chat with a rapid tongue with the garrulous old men of the neighborhood." No sooner had Colfax arrived than his friends gathered at his lodgings to serenade him and demand a speech. Mr. Colfax obliged. It was recognized by one and all that Colfax was to Thad Stevens as a ventriloquist's dummy to its master.

As previously noted the common objective which enabled Stevens and followers to present a solid front was their determination to preserve Republican hegemony in Congress. Obviously Johnson's

reconstruction program was a threat to this. It was a foregone conclusion that all of the Senators and Representatives, named or about
to be named by the eleven unrepresented states, would be Democrats. Their admission to Congress would reduce the nominal
Republican majority in the House from 98 to about 40 and in the
Senate from 28 to about 6. The Radicals' devotion to party domination was the feature that most clearly distinguished their thinking
from that of the Republican Conservatives who, while not averse
to such domination, gave priority to other and more statesmanlike
purposes.

Another aim shared by the Radicals was the desire, pretended in
some cases but sincere in others, to protect the newly freed Negroes
from conditions "bordering on slavery." Common to all Radicals
was a simple but powerful emotion, a hatred of the white South.

Thaddeus Stevens was under no illusions as to the difficulties
ahead. Nominally the House consisted of 141 Republicans and 43
Democrats and the Senate of 39 Republicans and 11 Democrats.
Actually the division was more complex. In both branches there
was a sprinkling of Administration Republicans, men committed to
Johnson's policy. The outstanding Administration Republican in
the House was Henry J. Raymond, founder of the New York
Times. The delightful Raymond, with his pert eye-glasses and his
small gold-headed cane, simply could not hate anyone, and this was
a handicap in an era of extremism. In the Senate there were five
Administration Republicans: James Dixon of Connecticut, Edgar
Cowan of Pennsylvania, James R. Doolittle of Wisconsin, Daniel S.
Norton of Minnesota and James H. Lane of Kansas.

The presence of half a dozen Administration Republicans and a
few other Conservatives in the House was of little consequence
since there the Radicals held the whiphand. The Senate presented
a different picture. In the upper chamber the balance of power lay
with a dozen Republican Conservatives who, while disinclined to
break with the President, were as yet uncommitted. If these men
supported Johnson's policy, they plus the five Administration Republicans and the eleven Democrats could throw the Senate to the

President. Thad Stevens' task was to entice the Republican Conservatives of the Senate into the Radical fold.

His immediate problems in December of 1865 were that the President *had* a reconstruction policy and that it had found favor with the public. Not only did the Radicals have no policy as yet, such proposals as they had aired to date were too extreme to be pushed until the public could be "educated" to accept them. Obviously the Radicals were going to have to use delaying tactics aimed at preventing Johnson from going ahead with his program until they could devise their own and obtain enough support to put it through.

Old Thad was working with this objective in mind, and he was working fast. The country was waiting for Johnson's first message to Congress. If the message caught the popular fancy, the Radicals might find that they had waited too long. Courtesy and tradition demanded that, after preliminary organization, Congress receive the President's message. But courtesy and tradition be damned, Old Thad was thinking. In the days preceding the opening of Congress he was busily creating the steamroller that would put Congress on record against the President before his message could be read. It was to be a *coup d'etat,* a lightning stroke; and there is something fascinating about the way the old fox pulled it off.

On the Friday night before the Monday on which Congress was to convene, Old Thad and some 25 to 30 Radicals, his yes-men, gathered in secret caucus. Referring to his recent talk with Johnson, Stevens predicted that the President would not yield an inch and called for an open break with him. As for the Southern representatives now waiting to be admitted to Congress—let them wait; let them wait indefinitely. Let none be admitted until all of the Southern states had revised their governments and societies in accordance with the outcome of the war and until these revisions had been written into the organic law of the land. Never mind that the delegation from the President's own state, Tennessee, was made up of men of proven loyalty and that Tennessee's new governor, "Fighting Parson" Brownlow, had become a Radical of the purest dye! Let all the Southern states be placed, for the time being, on a territorial status.

Stevens set forth what he considered to be some of the essentials of a proper reconstruction policy: disfranchisement of Southern whites, confiscation of Rebel property, full protection for the civil rights of Negroes and eventually Negro suffrage. When all of the House Republicans convened in caucus the following night, the Radicals were primed to take over—which is to say that Old Thad took over.

At Saturday night's general caucus Old Thad was no longer talking only to the members of his political family. His listeners included Administration Republican Henry Raymond and a respectable number of other Conservatives and lukewarm Radicals. He trimmed his sails accordingly, making no mention of the shape that he thought reconstruction should take. He confined himself to proposals of a tactical nature.

His first, that all Southern representatives be denied admittance for the time being, met with no opposition. None of the Republicans relished the prospect of an influx of Democrats from the South, and even the most conservative believed that guarantees, over and above those prescribed by the President, should be asked of the Southern states before they were received back into the Union. Another of Stevens' proposals was accepted without argument, namely that Smiler Colfax once again be elected Speaker of the House.

With these and other preliminaries out of the way, Stevens delivered his master stroke. He proposed the setting up of what would become the famous Joint Committee on Reconstruction. The Committee was to consist of nine Representatives and six Senators, and all matters relative to "the so-called Confederate States of America" were to be submitted to it for discussion and recommendation before being considered on the floor of the House or Senate. Old Thad knew what he was doing. Instead of squabbling over the details of reconstruction on the floor, with the Democrats looking on and making the most of every feud, matters could be thrashed out in the secrecy of the committee room, thus enabling the Republican party to preserve at all times the appearance of dignified unity.

The proposal was accepted unanimously. The Radicals endorsed it because they knew what it meant. Henry Raymond and his fellow Conservatives endorsed it because they did not. A week or so would pass before Raymond would awaken to the fact that Old Thad had pulled the wool over his eyes. What Stevens was proposing was that the whole business of reconstruction be placed in the hands of a small body—"an irresponsible central directory," as Andrew Johnson would call it—over which Old Thad could exercise control. The House members of the committee would be appointed by Colfax, Stevens' errand boy. The majority of them—five or six— would be Republicans and, of course, Radicals. With such alert Radicals as Sumner and Wade in the Senate, chances were strong that at least two of the Senate members would be Jacobins, in which case Old Thad's control would be complete. Under these circumstances defection from Stevens' program on the floor would still be possible—but difficult. Moreover extreme measures, not yet acceptable to the public, could be held up in committee until the public mind could be "softened" up. Thus the stage was set when Congress convened on Monday morning, December 4, in a buzz of excitement.

One tactic of the Radicals in their assault on Andrew Johnson was to spread the impression that, in inaugurating reconstruction, the Executive was seeking to usurp the powers of the Legislature. The charge was absurd. No American President was more sensitive than Andrew Johnson of the point at which his own powers ended and those of the co-ordinate branches of the Federal Government began. As the 39th Congress was about to convene, the President advised all but one of the Southern representatives-elect in Washington to absent themselves from the opening session. The one man he wanted present was Horace Maynard, representative-elect from the President's own state.

Tall and spare, with a fiery eye, Maynard was an awe-inspiring figure. Although devoid of Indian blood, he was nicknamed the

"Narragansett Indian." With his long black hair, his high brow and his straight, prominent nose, he looked like an Indian chief; and in his harsh voice he spoke with the force and passion of one. As the President's choice for a test case, Maynard was ideal. His reputation for loyalty to the Union was as great and as well known as that of Johnson himself. Secretary Welles had reservations; he was of the opinion that Thad Stevens had "got" to the Tennessean and that Maynard, in return for a promise of future support, had agreed not to protest too vigorously the failure of the House to seat him. As usual the Connecticut Yankee's suspicions appear to have been well grounded, since Maynard was soon to become a Radical.

Deal or no deal, Maynard was on hand when the House of Representatives was called to order at noon. Clerk of the House was Edward McPherson of Pennsylvania. His first job, and the first order of business, was the calling of the roll. At Saturday night's caucus, in accordance with one of Stevens' proposals, a committee had been appointed for the purpose of instructing the clerk to leave off the roll the names of all Southern representatives. In this simple manner were the states of the South to be denied re-admission to the Union.

That this procedure was contrary to House rules was of no moment to Edward McPherson. He regarded Old Thad with an admiration bordering on reverence and was collecting material for a biography of the "Great Commoner."

When the Clerk had reached the "N's" (calling out the name of Niblack of Indiana), Maynard leaped up, waving aloft his certificate of election signed by Governor Brownlow of Tennessee. Old Thad took care of him without bothering to rise. "I call the gentleman to order," he said. McPherson completed his thought for him. "The Clerk," he announced, "rules, as a matter of order, that he cannot recognize any gentleman whose name is not upon this roll."

James Brooks of New York, the Democratic leader, protested. Why, he asked, was the Clerk leaving the Southerners off the roll when the House rule was that the Clerk must read the names of all holders of certificates of election, leaving it up to the members to decide which to accept. Stevens answered that no explanation was needed. "We know all," said the old man, speaking from deep down in his chest. McPherson completed the reading of the roll, and a motion was made that it be accepted. Stevens silenced Democratic protests by moving the previous question, the motion was voted and the door clanged shut on the Southern states.

Then the House was organized with Elihu B. Washburne of Illinois, as the member having seniority, administering the oath to Colfax who made a nice little speech, something to the effect that the stars in our banner were now shining "with a more brilliant light of loyalty than ever before."

At this point the proper order of business was to call for the President's message. But no such call came. Instead Stevens rammed through his resolution setting up the Joint Committee (subject to action by the Senate) and at 2:50 P.M. the House adjourned, without having taken any action by way of indicating that it so much as recognized the existence of an official of some importance in the White House.

It was a great day for the Radicals. When the House reconvened the following noon, its leading spirits were in a mood for horseplay. One of the first things on the agenda was the election of a chaplain, in the course of which Old Thad tickled his colleagues with a pointed reference to Henry Ward Beecher, famed New York Congregational minister. Beecher had made some kind remarks about Andrew Johnson's policy, and Old Thad's comment was that one of the nominees for chaplain—the Rev. Mr. Stockton—was "the most eloquent man in the United States since the fall of Henry Ward Beecher."

Meanwhile a drama of similar content and authorship was being enacted in the more august atmosphere of the Senate. Called to order at noon by LaFayette S. Foster of Connecticut, President *pro tempore,* the Senate met for an hour and a half on its first day. Wade introduced a bill to extend the suffrage to the Negroes of the District of Columbia—a bill that would not become law until two years later; and Sumner introduced bills to protect and enfranchise the Negroes in the South.

The following day leisureliness gave way to speed and excitement. No sooner had McPherson appeared to announce that the House had passed the Joint Committee resolution than Wade was on his feet, moving that the Senate concur. Grimes of Iowa rebuked him by suggesting that he withdraw his motion until a committee could be appointed to go with one already formed in the House to inform the President that both houses were ready to receive "any communications he may be pleased to make." Wade fussed and fumed until these arrangements were made, then once more leaped up to demand that the Senate concur at once in the House resolution setting up the Joint Committee. A rule of the Senate had it that if an objection was made to a motion, it must lie over to the next day. Reverdy Johnson, most able of the Senate Democrats, offered an objection and Wade's motion was put aside.

At two P.M. Robert Johnson, the President's son, appeared below the bar of the Senate with the President's message. Forney, as secretary of the body, read it, and the Senate adjourned.

As would be brought out years later by Professor William A. Dunning, one of the great students of the Reconstruction, Johnson's first message appears to have been written by George Bancroft, the historian. Johnson, of course, was not the first, nor would he be the last President, to seek professional help in the composition of his state papers. He did not fancy himself as a writer and, throughout his Presidency, he suffered acutely from writer's cramp. Whoever was responsible for the felicitous style of his first communication to Congress, its contents were pure Andrew Johnson.

Echoing through the message were ideas that Johnson had developed in earlier speeches, going back as far as the 1840's. Conciliatory in tone, the message was primarily a defense of his reconstruction policy. Johnson conceded that there were risks involved in restoring the Southern states at this point, but asserted that they were trifling compared with those inherent in any program that would keep the Southern states out for a protracted period.

Public response to the message was overwhelming. An avalanche of approval poured in on the White House. Charles Francis Adams, speaking from his post as our Minister to England, said the message "raised the character of the nation immensely in Europe." He wrote his brother-in-law Sidney Brooks that "I know of nothing better in the annals even when Washington was chief and Hamilton his financier." Raymond's New York *Times* found the message "full of wisdom." Greeley's *Tribune* doubted "whether any former message . . . has contained so much that will be generally approved, and so little that will or should provoke dissent." James Russell Lowell in the *North American Review* declared that "Mr. Johnson shows himself not only a disciple of Mr. Lincoln, but proves that he himself possesses the instinct of statesmanship." Godkin's *Nation* said the message had "the style of an honest man who knows what he means and means what he says."

The Radicals were only mildly worried, and their worries became increasingly less as their own campaign gained ground. In the Senate the resolution setting up the Joint Committee of fifteen was not put through with the hot haste that had characterized its passage in the House. The Senators wanted certain changes. As passed by the House the form of the resolution was joint, a type of action that requires the signature of the Executive. This was all right by Stevens. He was dying for a quick show-down with the Executive and presumably confident that if Johnson refused to sign the resolution, the Radicals could muster sufficient strength to pass it over his veto.

Stevens' thinking was deficient at this juncture. Johnson was at the zenith of his popularity. In an open show-down many members of both houses would have hesitated to buck him lest they anger their constituents. Fortunately for Stevens the cooler heads of the Senate changed the form of the resolution to concurrent, a type that does not require the signature of the Executive.

As originally passed, the resolution bound the Senate, as well as the House, to receive no members from the South until the Committee of Fifteen had reported on them, and to surrender to the Committee the privilege of judging the election returns and qualifications of its own members. The Senate refused to abandon these constitutional privileges, and accordingly altered the wording of the resolution insofar as it applied to the upper branch.

The resulting situation was a challenge to Old Thad's skill as a political strategist. He met it boldly. He ordered the House to accept the Senate amendments. By making this small concession, he won his larger end. On December 13 the Joint Committee of Fifteen was voted into existence, an action that halted Andrew Johnson's reconstruction program and served notice on the country that Congress intended to substitute its own.

X

"WAVING THE BLOODY SHIRT"

Even before the Southern representatives were rejected and the business of reconstruction turned over to the Joint Committee, the Radicals had put under way one of their most devastating maneuvers. The present-day term for this maneuver is "propaganda." The word itself was not much used in the 1860's, but during the war propaganda as such had been widely employed on both sides. That the Radicals should continue to employ it after the war was dictated by what they were trying to accomplish. For the better part of a year, right up to the Congressional elections of 1866, they devoted an enormous amount of energy to the task of capturing the Northern mind. To gain support for a harsh peace they sought to convince the people that most Southern whites were still rebels at heart, that Southern Loyalists or Northerners moving into the South lived in daily fear for their property and their lives and that the Southern acceptance of emancipation was mere lip service. Little by little, as the propaganda barrage took hold, it began to sound an even more sinister note—that the President (a Southerner) was conspiring with Northern Copperheads and Southern Rebels to seize control of the government.

What would later be the Grand Old Party was at this time neither grand nor old. Nor was it, strictly speaking, a party; it was a loosely knit aggregation of former Anti-slavery Democrats, Conscience Whigs, Know-Nothings and Abolitionists. Economically its adherents ranged from men like Ben Wade, who advocated soft money and a low tariff, to men like Thaddeus Stevens, who preferred a high tariff and regarded the rights of private property with profound awe. Politically it ranged from men like Secretary Welles, a strict-constructionist and states-rightist, to abolitionists like Charles Sumner. Since the formation of the party in 1854, these diverse elements had been held together by a common hatred of slavery and a common love of Union. With the war over, these issues were settled —unless, of course, the Radicals could show proof that they were still at stake. This the Radicals were bent on doing.

In due time their propaganda campaign would receive an appropriate name, thanks to Ben Butler. Re-entering politics as a member of the House in 1866 Butler delivered a harangue on the sins of the South, in the course of which he held up a blood-stained shirt said to have been taken from a victim of the Ku Klux Klan. The phrase "Waving the Bloody Shirt," was subsequently applied to the Radical drive.

One of the best "wavers" was Charles Sumner. Having spent the better part of a lifetime in the Abolition movement, he had long since learned the importance and cumulative effect of ceaseless agitation. He himself wrote articles for the *Atlantic* and for Theodore Tilton's *Independent*. In letter after letter he urged his Radical associates "to lead public opinion in the right direction" by broadcasting their arguments far and wide. On the Saturday night before the opening of Congress, he lost no time in calling on Johnson.

A two-and-a-half-hour conversation left him with "the painful conviction that the President's whole soul was set as flint against the good cause, and that by the assassination of Abraham Lincoln the rebellion had vaulted into the Presidential chair." The interview closed on a tart note. Sumner pictured for the President some of the "outrages" which, according to him, were being perpetrated by the Rebels in the South on defenseless Negroes and loyal Union men.

Were there no "outrages" in Boston, the President wanted to know. Were no crimes ever committed there? The two proud and stubborn men parted, enemies, never to meet again.

Sumner displayed unwillingness to question the source or accuracy of any atrocity story, no matter how far-fetched. When a correspondent wrote that the slave trade was being revived along the Southern coast, Sumner offered a resolution empowering the Judiciary Committee to look into it. He read into the record letters saying that there was an organized movement in the South to make General Lee the next President of the United States and another to involve the country in a foreign war, in the course of which the South would once more strike for independence. Solemnly and with relish he read aloud the letter of a Northern observer who declared that in those parts of the South "where there are no Union soldiers, I saw colored women treated in the most outrageous manner. . . . They are killed, and their bodies thrown into ponds and mudholes, they are mutilated by having ears and noses cut off." When skeptical Senators asked for the name of this or that letter-writer, Sumner waved their requests aside with the statement that his correspondent was "a trustworthy traveler" or somebody for whom somebody else, also unnamed, had vouched.

The Joint Committee functioned tellingly as a propaganda mill. The House had no sooner acted to set up the Committee than the New York *World* was declaring that "there is a state of peace . . . that is more disastrous than war itself, and such is the peace which the radical majority in Congress have now proclaimed." It was plain to the *World* that, in establishing the Joint Committee, the Radicals were forcing the nation "to enter upon its new career with all its wounds torn open afresh."

To the House contingent Speaker Colfax named seven Republicans and two Democrats. Stevens was chairman, and of the other Republicans all were to prove dependable Radicals, even John A. Bingham of Ohio who, after exhibiting a degree of independence, would buckle under Stevens' taunts and wheel into line. One of the Democrats was A. J. Rogers of New Jersey. Rogers was a Copperhead, and the deft hand of Thad Stevens is visible in his appointment. As one of Johnson's staunch supporters, Rogers could be counted on to damage the President's cause every time he opened his mouth. He was given to regaling the House with harangues dealing with the "natural inferiority" of the Negro. To most members his speeches were a bore; to Stevens they were a joy. Once, while Rogers was singing away, Colfax sought to shut him up by pointing out that the "gentleman's second hour has now expired." Stevens got to his feet, speaking in that languid drawl with which he obliterated his enemies. "I move," he said, "that he [Rogers] be allowed to go on for the rest of the season."

The Senate contingent of the Committee consisted of five Republicans and one Democrat. Heading the Senatorial body and, therefore, nominal chairman of the entire Joint Committee was William Pitt Fessenden of Maine. Tall, spare and pale from ill health and overwork, Fessenden was a man of impeccable character and one of the ablest of the Republican Conservatives. He was uncommitted as yet and conciliatory by nature, and it was taken for granted that as Fessenden went so would go all of the Republican Conservatives. Since these gentlemen held the balance of power in the Senate, the eventual outcome of the battle between the Radicals and the President hinged on their decision.

For Thad Stevens the path was made smoother by the fact that the 39th Congress had more than its share of dunderheads. To the general low level of competence, Senator Fessenden was one of several exceptions. He was that rarity in an emotional age, a man devoted to reason and balanced thought. His speeches were devoid of rhetoric or vituperation, but those who listened carefully were rewarded with flashes of humor. Urged to support a bill to establish a branch mint in Nevada Territory, Fessenden argued that Nevada was still too young and too small. The framer of the bill then asserted that all the Territory needed to make it a good state was "a little more water and a little better society," to which Fessenden replied, "That's all hell wants."

A visitor to Washington in the spring of 1866 was Mrs. Varina

Davis, wife of the former Confederate President. Her mission was to get better treatment for her incarcerated husband. President Johnson received her courteously, listened to her complaints, sent Secretary McCulloch down to Fortress Monroe to see what was going on and, on the recommendation of the Secretary, saw to it that Davis was treated humanely. While she was in town, Varina called on Fessenden, who after listening to her for an hour and a half, wrote his family in Maine that she was "a terrible talker . . . presents everything in the worst light" and that the country might be better off if her husband were let out of Fortress Monroe and his wife shut up in his place.

Just where Fessenden stood as the year 1866 got under way was not clear. "I am ready and disposed," he announced soon after Congress opened, "to support the Executive to the best of my ability." At the same time he implied that this was no out-and-out endorsement of Johnson's policy by asserting that now that the war was over Congress must assume its original supremacy in the affairs of the nation.

On January 15 the Joint Committee set up a sub-committee empowered to hold hearings for the purpose of measuring the degree of rebellion still smouldering in the South. One objective in gathering this testimony was to keep the propaganda machine fueled. To this end most of the witnesses called were men known for their Radical sympathies. Forty-five witnesses were asked to describe what they believed to be the effect of Johnson's lenient pardoning policy. Forty-three replied that at the close of the war the Southern leaders were "humbled and meek" but that, thanks to Johnson's generosity, these same leaders were now as insolent as ever in their attitude toward the North. Sixty-four witnesses were asked if the Southern leaders were still in favor of secession. Fifty of them replied that they were. Twenty-eight witnesses said there was a general reluctance in the South to pay taxes, twelve said that the Southern planters expected compensation for their slaves and destroyed property, twenty testified that the Southern politicians were plotting "to regain the balance of power in the Union" by splitting the Republican party and co-operating with the Northern Democrats.

Among the witnesses summoned were a few men of real standing. When General Lee testified that the generality of Southerners were kindly disposed toward the Negro people and wanted to see them educated, his questioners sought to take the edge off this unwelcome opinion by compelling the honest General to state that in his opinion the capacity of most Negroes to assimilate knowledge was not as great as that of most whites.

Several substantial Southerners made the mistake of using the witness chair as a platform from which to air political theories— Alexander Stephens, for example. The former Confederate Vice President was doing everything in his power to persuade his fellow-Georgians to accept the outcome of the war in good faith. Had he confined his testimony to his deeds, all would have been well. Instead he permitted his questioners to trap him into a political speech, in the course of which he set forth his come-and-go theory of secession. He contended that not only did a state have a right to leave the Union but that whenever it wearied of living in Secessia it had a right to step back in.

Copious extracts of all this testimony was released to the press, with the result that by the time the Committee closed its hearings in late April, the public was pretty well convinced that the South was a "chamber of horrors" and caldron of suppressed rebellion.

Johnson sought to get a line on Southern thinking by sending several men South with instructions to observe conditions and talk to the people. His first choice of a reporter was Carl Schurz, then a resident of Wisconsin. Tall, spindly-legged, with a full beard and a scholar's face, Schurz was at this time a Radical. In his own *Reminiscences* Schurz gives the impression that Johnson was fully aware of this but another contemporary account has it that before invading the South, Schurz "clearly intimated" that he approved of the President's reconstruction policy.

Two versions exist as to how Schurz came to go South as Johnson's emissary. Schurz's own account is that the President asked him to go, but a Union officer, testifying before a Congressional committee in 1867, quoted Johnson as saying that such was not the case, that he had no desire to send Schurz into the South and only did so because of the reporter's "importunity." According to Schurz, there was considerable correspondence between the two men in the spring of 1865. Schurz was displeased with Johnson's reconstruction program and wrote as much to the President whose reply was a telegram, asking Schurz to call on him. The President did not specify what he wanted.

En route east, Schurz spent an evening in Philadelphia with friends who had become interested in spiritualism. A seance was held with the daughter of the house, a 15-year-old girl, as the medium. Schurz called for the spirit of Lincoln, and the pretty young medium obliged. Disclaiming any opinion about spiritualism, Schurz was startled by two of "Lincoln's" prophecies—and even more startled later when both came true. One was that he was to become a Senator from Missouri, to which state he subsequently moved and from which, in 1869, he was sent to the Senate. The other was that Johnson was going to ask him to take a trip. On arriving in Washington the following day, he was requested by the President to tour the South.

Schurz hesitated. The salary offered by the government was low; Schurz was not affluent and he had a family in Wisconsin. He wrote his friend, Charles Sumner, pointing out that, because of the dangers incident to Southern travel, he would have to pay an extra premium on his insurance policy. Sumner replied: "You *must* go. Let me know the *extra* premium on your policy. The friends of cause here will gladly pay it. I write this in earnest and as business. Send me the bill; and do you go at once on your journey."

Schurz went. Leaving Washington July 15, 1865, he spent three months in five Southern states, interviewing scores of individuals and groups. Arrangements were made by Sumner for him to supplement his income by publishing articles concerning his observations in the Boston *Advertiser*. Five such articles appeared over a pseudonym, when the identity of the writer was discovered and the series discontinued. It is conceivable that Johnson, if he knew Schurz's political stand, assumed that the reporter would lay his bias aside and conduct his investigation with an open mind. This Schurz did not do; he saw and heard pretty much what he wanted to see and hear and admitted it in a letter to Johnson, saying that he had found a spirit of loyalty among many of the planters, but that he was painting only the other side of the picture. Nineteen out of every twenty Southerners to whom Schurz talked voiced the opinion that the Negro would never adapt himself to the conditions of free labor. Schurz took this to be the prevailing Southern opinion, which—however erroneous—it was. He then read into it a spirit of rebellion, which it was not.

On Schurz's return Johnson greeted him with more politeness than enthusiasm. He asked for no report, and when Schurz gave him one anyhow, he put it aside. His intention was to forget about it, but Congress forced his hand. On a motion by Sumner, the Senate called for the report and Johnson had no choice but to send it to the Capitol.

Meanwhile, on the President's request, General Grant had made a shorter tour of the South. Johnson, forwarding Schurz's report to the Senate, sent that of Grant along with it. The conclusions of the two investigators were diametrically opposed. Schurz said: "The loyalty of the masses and most leaders of the Southern people, consists in submission to necessity. There is, except in individual instances, an entire absence of that national spirit which forms the basis of true loyalty and patriotism." General Grant was "satisfied that the mass of thinking men of the South accept the present situation of affairs in good faith." The Radicals saw to it that Schurz's report was given wide and laudatory publicity and that Grant's was lost in the shuffle.

Johnson sent other men South. His friend and former secretary, Ben Truman, spent almost eight months travelling through eight of the seceded states. A New England journalist, Truman turned in a report in April of 1866 that showed evidence of an effort to be objective. His observations were thoughtful and shrewd. "Fully

half of the Southern people," he wrote, "never cherished an educated and active attachment to any government that was over them,
and the war has left them very much as it found them." Truman
said the Southern people were "indifferent" to the government but
loyal, adopting toward Washington the same attitude that the North
had adopted toward the administration of James Buchanan. His
conclusion was that "the South—the great, substantial and prevailing element—is more loyal now than it was at the end of the war
. . . and that it will be more loyal tomorrow than today."

What, in truth, was the dominant state of mind in the South with
regard to the Union at this time? The most trustworthy answer is
provided by subsequent history, which proves groundless the major
thesis of the Radicals that there was a significant and organized, or
about-to-be-organized, spirit of rebellion. The generality of people
were not pleased with the outcome of the war. After fighting the
North for four years they could hardly be expected, overnight, to
become red-hot patriots. Neither were they inclined, as Carl Schurz
deplored, to sit around in sackcloth and ashes, shouting *"Mea
culpa! Mea culpa!"* Most of them believed in the cause for which
they had fought and regretted its loss. But heeding the advice of
such able Southern spokesmen as General Lee and Wade Hampton
of South Carolina, they accepted the loss as irretrievable and were
bent on resuming their places as citizens of the United States. Now
and for some years to come, most of them were occupied with the
difficult and sometimes primitive business of keeping alive. Conditions in the South ranged from dire want and even starvation in
some areas to acute privation in most of the others. Naturally, under
these circumstances, there were outrages. For varying lengths of
time many Southern communities were without either military protection or organized government.

Which of the hundreds of incidents reported by the Northern
press were true, partly true or plain fabrication we shall never know.
Their impact on public opinion depended on how they were presented.

Artemus Ward, the humorist, quipped that "Shakspeer rote good prose, but he wouldn't hav succeeded as a Washington correspondent of a New York daily paper. He lackt the rekesit fancy and immaginashun." Actually the level of reportage was higher than Ward's remark might indicate. The newspaper profession had come into its own during the Civil War and many individual reporters were conscientious in their efforts to get the facts and to convey them correctly. Even so, the best of them were handicapped by the journalistic practices of the time. Newsgathering was not yet on an organized basis, aimed at comprehensive coverage. Little attempt was made to achieve objectivity. A reporter assembled his information in a hit-or-miss fashion and usually slanted it in accordance with the policy of his editor.

Some notion of how the South was reported to the North is gained by comparing two of the Washington newspapers. The papers were the *Daily Morning Chronicle,* of which John W. Forney was the editor and proprietor, and the *Daily National Intelligencer,* owned and edited by John Coyle, a friend of the President. During the spring of 1866 both papers were devoting a great deal of space to "Letters from the South." In the Radical *Chronicle* at least half of these dispatches dealt with crimes— murder, house-burning and the like—committed by ex-Rebels against Negroes and white Unionists. In the staid *Intelligencer* fully half of the stories alleged crimes committed by the newly freed Negroes. It is a safe assumption that no Washington citizen who valued his sanity read both newspapers.

Toward the end of 1865 the newly formed Southern legislatures of the so-called "Johnson governments" began passing what were called Black Codes. Their ostensible purpose was to assist the Negro in his transition from slavery to citizenship. But in wording and content, the codes showed that the Southern leaders were making it impossible for him to do so.

The codes differed from state to state but directly or implicitly all of them wrote into law the principle that the Negroes were to be set apart as a distinct group, usually designated as "persons of color." The Mississippi code obliged all Negro orphans to be bound out until they became of age, preferably to their former masters, and the masters were empowered to "inflict moderate chastisement for misbehavior." A section of the law defined as "vagrants" not only individuals who might reasonably be so designated but also all Negroes found assembling unlawfully, "together with all white persons so assembling with them on terms of equality, or living in adultery or fornication with Negro women." Mississippi also forbade Negroes to own land or to rent or lease it "except in incorporated towns and cities." South Carolina decreed that "without a special license" no Negro could pursue any trade or employment except that of husbandry. Alabama permitted freedmen to testify in court only in cases in which other freedmen were directly or indirectly concerned.

The Black Codes generated the conviction throughout the North that it would be unwise to permit the Southern states to re-enter the Union until they had given some sign of a willingness to abide by the rule of law. *The Nation* underscored the point in an editorial. "Freedom of speech and locomotion," Godkin wrote, "of trade, of following all lawful callings, from selling needles to making stump speeches, without let or hindrance, is at the very foundation of free society . . . Without these things, there is no freedom and there can be no progress in civilization, and to talk of the authority of the United States Government being really restored over any state or territory or district in which it cannot guarantee these things to all classes of the population is an abuse of language. All reconstruction, though it gave every black in the South two votes which did not secure these things to both white and blacks, would be a delusion and a snare; and all arrangements for bestowing the suffrage on the Negro, or for coercing his late masters into giving it to him, which do not provide also for protecting him in the exercise of it, and in preparing his mind for the right exercise of it, will prove futile."

The value of Northern reaction to the Black Codes lay in its correctness. The original codes were not enforced for any length of time but their passage cannot be dismissed as a mere tactical blunder. That they represented the line the Southern leaders meant to take is shown by the fact that after reconstruction the codes reappeared in various forms. Those of 1865-66 were speedily suspended by Federal action, but the memory lingered on.

XI

THE PRESIDENT
AND THE NEGRO

The showdown between Congress and the Executive, so eagerly
desired by Thad Stevens, began to shape up soon after the 39th
session convened. It revolved around the Bureau of Refugees,
Freedmen and Abandoned Lands, an agency set up on the day
before Lincoln's second inauguration.

The powers lodged in the Freedmen's Bureau touched on practically all problems produced by the war. As eventually reorganized
the Bureau dispensed relief not only to the former slaves but to all
indigent individuals, colored or white, in the war-stricken sections
of the Southern and border states. The Bureau supported a program
of education for the former slaves and regulated their labor. Pending restoration of the unrepresented states and full resumption of
their judicial systems, the officers and agents of the Bureau were
authorized to adjudicate cases involving infringement of Negro
rights—and to do so without jury trial or privilege of appeal.

Obviously the Freedmen's Bureau began life big with possibilities
for good and for evil, depending on whether its control fell into the
hands of those who wanted to help the Negro or into the hands of
those who wanted to use him. Lincoln sought to get the agency off

to a good start by naming as its head a St. Louis merchant known to be an incorruptible friend of the Negro. When this attempt fell through, Secretary of War Stanton, in whose department the Bureau was placed, persuaded Lincoln to give the post to General Oliver Otis Howard. The appointment had to be held up since in March of 1865 Howard was leading the right wing of General Sherman's forces through the Carolinas. When Lincoln died, Stanton made haste to assure Johnson that the General was Lincoln's choice, and Johnson went along.

Johnson would have done well to have questioned Stanton's motives. A slender and prepossessing New Englander with a full beard and clean-cut features, General Howard neither drank nor smoked, enjoyed a reputation for saintliness and intellectual achievement, was sincerely devoted to bettering the lot of the Negro. Taking over as Commissioner of the Freedmen's Bureau on April 26, 1865, Howard proceeded to direct its affairs according to Stanton's dictates.

The significance of Howard's appointment becomes apparent when one of the most important powers of the Freedmen's Bureau is considered—its control over certain Southern property. During the war some 900,000 acres of Southern land were either abandoned by their owners or seized by the Federal Government. Most of the seizures were carried out under a series of laws put through Congress by the Radicals.

The most drastic of these Confiscation Acts, passed in 1862, obligated the President to inaugurate the "judicial condemnation and sale" of the real or personal property of any Rebel. Lincoln had serious misgivings about this measure as originally drafted. He pointed out that while the Constitution permitted Congress to punish traitors, it specified that "no attainder of treason shall work corruption of blood or forfeiture except during the life of the person attainted." Reluctantly, and only because they saw no way of getting around a possible veto, the Radicals tacked onto their bill a joint resolution stating that no proceedings under the 1862 Confiscation

Act were to "be so construed as to work a forfeiture of the real estate of the offender beyond his natural life."

When the time came to establish the Freedmen's Bureau, the Radicals saw an opportunity to realize the most ambitious of their dreams—their desire to impoverish the Southern planters by stripping them of their property. It could be done by writing two simple provisions into the bill setting up the agency. One provision entrusted the management of all abandoned and confiscated lands to the Bureau. The other authorized the Bureau to divide up the land into 40-acre parcels and then sell or rent these parcels to Negroes and white Unionists.

Unfortunately for the Radicals, into the bill setting up the agency went a little phrase stating that the Freedmen's Bureau could promise purchasers of lands taken from the Rebels only "such title thereto as the United States can convey." And how much title could the Government convey? Not much. Most of the land was simply "abandoned" and had not yet been subjected to judicial action. The United States held title to only some fifty or sixty thousand acres, bid in on tax sales.

The Radicals were checked but not beaten. When Abraham Lincoln died, the Radicals figured that with the aid of a cooperative President they could quickly divide up and distribute all the lands. Once this was done, they reasoned, it would be next to impossible for their owners to re-acquire them through the slow processes of the courts. But when Johnson announced his reconstruction policy, this scheme was threatened. In his first Amnesty Proclamation Johnson decreed that every pardon issued to a Southerner was to carry with it a full restoration of property rights.

For three months after the promulgation of his First Amnesty Johnson issued no specific instructions aimed at returning the lands to their owners. Egged on by Stanton, Commissioner Howard took advantage of the President's silence. Without consulting Johnson, he directed his assistant commissioners in the South to start dividing up the lands. Johnson put a stop to this and the matter came to a head when the Bureau seized the property of a Confederate veteran who had received a special pardon. The President saw to it that the veteran's holdings were returned to him. Then, in a stinging rebuke to Howard, he issued a directive that placed all of the lands, except the trifling few actually owned by the government, beyond the reach of the Freedmen's Bureau—an action which had the effect of ending forever the attempt of the Radicals to punish the planter South by widespread confiscation. But these events were only a skirmish.

The real battle began on the afternoon of Friday January 5, 1866, when a slight, colorless, spectacled little man arose in the Senate to introduce S. No. 60, "A bill to Enlarge the Powers of the Freedmen's Bureau." The man was Lyman Trumbull of Illinois. Born in Connecticut of one of New England's most distinguished families, Trumbull had gone to frontier Illinois as a young man, and there had practiced law and ridden the circuit with his good friend Abraham Lincoln. Physically he was one of those men who attract little attention, but he was as honorable as he was plain, and his speeches were as direct as himself. Like his friend William Pitt Fessenden he was a Republican Conservative. He hated slavery. He also hated the extremism and the vindictiveness of the Radicals. Nothing was closer to his heart than the hope that an open break between Congress and the Executive could be avoided. His bill was designed not only to expand the powers of the Bureau, but also to extend its life indefinitely since as first set up the agency was to exist for only one year after the war.

Democratic opposition was spearheaded by Thomas A. Hendricks of Indiana. The Hoosier Senator found the bill unconstitutional, especially that section which empowered employees of the Bureau to sit as judge-jury-and-court-of-appeal on cases having to do with the civil rights of Southern Negroes. Hendricks dwelt at length on what he considered a proper interpretation of the Thirteenth Amendment ratified into the Constitution the previous December 18. The first section of the Thirteenth abolished slavery and the second enabled Congress to pass "appropriate" enforcement legislation. Hendricks' "judgment" was that under the second section "we may pass such a law as will secure the freedom declared in the first section, but we cannot go beyond that limitation."

Trumbull's reply, delivered on January 19, was that if "the construction put by the Senator from Indiana upon the amendment be a true one, and we have merely taken from the master the power to control the slave and left him at the mercy of the state to be deprived of his civil rights . . . the promised freedom is a delusion." In still another obvious reference to the Black Codes, Trumbull declared that "When slavery was abolished, slave codes in its support were abolished also." If the unrepresented states, he said, would take action to protect the Negro, well and good; if they did not, then the Federal Government must step in and do it for them. Nothing was clearer to Lyman Trumbull than that the government had no right to free the Negro and then wash its hands of him. The North had created the freedman; now the North must see to it that he got a proper start in life. "If the people in the rebellious States," Trumbull asserted, "can be made to understand that it is the fixed and determined policy of the Government that the colored people shall be protected in their civil rights, they themselves will adopt the necessary measures . . . and that will dispense with the Freedmen's Bureau and all other Federal legislation for their protection."

Trumbull was certain that Johnson would go along with his bill. His certainty arose from the President's statement, in his recent message to Congress, that "good faith requires the security of the freedmen in their liberty and their property, their right to labor, and their right to claim the just return of their labor." The Illinoisan's confidence was shared. When his bill went to the President in early February, the impression in both houses of Congress was that Johnson would sign it. He did not. The assumption that he would rested, like the earlier hopes of the Radicals, on a mis-reading of the man in the White House.

Andrew Johnson belonged to that ante-bellum generation of Democrats which produced such men as old F. P. Blair with his wry slogan, "The world is governed too much." Like the senior

Blair, Johnson was a liberal in the old-fashioned sense of the word. He believed that the best government was the least. Lyman Trumbull's Freedmen's Bureau bill was simply too much government. The bill, Johnson said in his veto message, set aside

safeguards which the experience and wisdom of ages taught our fathers to establish . . . for the protection of the innocent, the punishment of the guilty, and the equal administration of justice . . . and for the sake of a more vigorous interposition in behalf of justice we are to take the risks of the many acts of injustice that would necessarily follow from an almost countless number of agents established in every parish or county in nearly a third of the States of the Union, over whose decisions there is to be no supervision or control by the Federal courts. The power that would be thus placed in the hands of the President is such as in time of peace certainly ought never to be intrusted to only one man.

In other words the 39th Congress, as Johnson saw it, was offering to the Executive an enormous power-machine, and the Executive was having none of it. In another section of his message, he deplored what might be called the "Welfare State" elements of the bill. Trumbull's measure authorized the Federal Government, for the first time, to dispense charity on a large scale and to dip into a state and tax the citizens thereof to help support the needy populations of other states. All this was contrary to the intent of the Founding Fathers, according to Johnson, and the fact that eleven of the states had no voice in Congress made the proposed law a case of "taxation without representation."

The Freedmen's Bureau bill was in line with the major outcome of the Civil War. The war had not only preserved the Union, it had also created a nation. The drift of America was away from states rights and states sovereignty toward a greater centralization of power in the Federal Government. In his battle with the Radicals, Johnson's greatest handicap was that he was moving against this tide, whereas his enemies were moving with it.

Of the first 42 measures submitted for his signature, Johnson turned down only two. The Freedmen's Bureau bill received his first veto. During the ensuing months several of the measures disapproved, like the Freedmen's Bureau bill, would have to do with the welfare of the ex-slaves. Are we to conclude from this fact that behind the reasons Johnson gave for his vetoes lurked another and unexpressed reason, namely the prejudices of his class?

When Johnson's attitudes toward the Negro are examined, the first thing that strikes the eye is that his views were not those of the Southern poor whites from which he sprang. Ben Truman, in his report on the South, asserted that opposition to Negro suffrage was far greater among the poor whites than it was among the former slave-holders and the wealthy. Truman's explanation was that "when classes of population are opposed in feeling and unequal in power and influence, the dominating class is oppressive and intolerant toward the inferior in reverse proportion as it is elevated above it. The southern poor whites, conscious as they are of only a slight superiority over the Negro, and knowing that the suffrage and a few minor factitious distinctions are the chief points of their superiority, are jealous over them accordingly. It is they that will resist most stubbornly the Negroes' enfranchisement, as it will remove the most marked of the few slight barriers that separate them from the blacks."

Flagrant hostility to the Negro—the determination to keep him "down" at all costs, which Ben Truman sensed among the poor whites—is not discernible in Johnson's statements or actions. What can be discerned is the paternalism associated with the Southern upper classes. Johnson told a Nashville audience in 1864: "If whites and blacks can't get along together, arrangements must be made to colonize the blacks. . . ." Characterizing emancipation as a triumph of truth and justice, Johnson said:

The only remaining question for us to settle, as prudent and wise men, is in assigning the Negro his new relation. Now what will that be? The Negro will be thrown upon society, governed by the same laws that govern communities and be compelled to fall back upon his resources, as all other human beings are . . . Political freedom means liberty to work, and at the same time enjoy the products of one's labor . . . If he [the Negro] can rise by his own energies, in the name of God, let him rise. In saying this, I do not argue that the Negro race is equal to the Anglo-Saxon . . . If the Negro is better fitted for the inferior condition of society, the laws of nature will assign him there.

In conversation with George Luther Stearns, wealthy Massachusetts Abolitionist and Radical, Johnson set forth views that also found their way into his state papers. To "let the Negro have universal suffrage now," he was convinced, "would breed a war of races." He told Stearns that if he were in Tennessee he would try to persuade his state to "introduce Negro suffrage gradually; first, those who had served in the army, those who could read and write; and perhaps a property qualification for others, say $200 or $250." As President, he conceived his first duty to be to the Constitution, under which the right to say who could vote was a state matter. He pointed out that if he dictated who should and who should not have the franchise in the rebel states, what was to prevent his doing the same "for my own purpose in Pennsylvania?"

Johnson's attitude was not, of course, exclusively a Southern one. Most of the Northerners of his time, including Lincoln, questioned the capacity of Negroes to function on an equal footing with the whites. Lincoln had expressed such doubts in several speeches. "[T]here is a physical difference between the white and black races," he had said at Charleston, Illinois, "which will ever forbid the two races living together on terms of social and political equality. And inasmuch as they cannot so live, there must be the position of superior and inferior, and I, as much as any other man, am in favor of having the superior position assigned to the white race. . . ." Lincoln too favored colonization, a solution to which he clung until 1864 when, following the failure of an attempt to settle 453 Negroes in Haiti, he gave up the idea as impractical.

During the year following the end of the war Northern advocates of universal suffrage for the former slaves were few and far between. Their argument was that to obtain and protect their civil rights the Negroes must first be given the vote. The counter-argument was that their civil rights should be guaranteed some other way, since to put the vote immediately into the hands of former slaves, deprived of education and new to the responsibilities of freedom, would be to place them at the mercy of scheming white politicians.

In the North the belief that ours is "a white man's government," as Johnson put it, was so prevalent that only six of the twenty-five states that had fought for the Union allowed their Negroes to vote; and in one of these, New York, the franchise law was discriminatory. During 1865 the question came up in Connecticut and Ohio and in both states Negro suffrage was turned down by large majorities. During 1867 it came up again when constitutional amendments enfranchising the Negroes were proposed in Ohio, Michigan, Minnesota and Kansas. In all four states the amendments were rejected by popular vote.

Johnson's prejudice was not so much *against* the Southern Negroes as it was *for* the Southern whites. The mudsill from Tennessee never fully grasped the impact of the Black Codes on the Northern mind. He trusted the Southern whites and assumed that left alone they would deal fairly with the Negroes. With this point of view Northerners disturbed by the codes could not go along.

The President was known to be annoyed by the Black Codes but he made no public statement to this effect. His failure to do so was unfortunate. Such a statement would have reassured the Republican Conservatives, whose support he desperately needed. He did urge the Southern states to protect the civil rights of the Negroes. He informed the Governor-elect of Mississippi that all he wanted from the people and legislature of his state was "a loyal compliance with the laws and constitution of the United States, and the adoption of . . . measures, giving protection to all freedmen or freemen, in person and property without regard to color. . . ." When General Thomas, commanding the military district embracing Mississippi, suspended a state law forbidding Negroes to carry arms, the matter was referred to Johnson, who sustained the General.

Mississippi was the first state to hold its organizing convention under the terms of Johnson's reconstruction policy. As the sessions got under way in August of 1865, Johnson sent a telegram to the provisional governor, William M. Sharkey, expressing the hope that his state would "set an example" by writing limited Negro suffrage into its laws. The President suggested giving the vote to all Negroes who could read the Constitution and write their names, or who owned real estate valued at not less than $250. "I hope and trust your convention will do this," Johnson wrote, "and as a consequence the radicals, who are wild upon Negro franchise, will be completely foiled in their attempt to keep the Southern states from their relations to the Union by not accepting their senators and representatives."

Johnson's telegram to Sharkey—and according to James Gillespie Blaine, similar telegrams were sent to other Southern governors —was another example of his desire to pursue the policies of his predecessor. During the establishment of the Louisiana Ten Per Cent government in 1864 Lincoln, in a letter to Governor Michael Hahn, wrote:

I barely suggest for your private consideration whether some of the colored people may not be let in, as, for instance, the very intelligent, and especially those who have fought gallantly in our ranks. They would probably help in some trying time in the future to keep the jewel of Liberty in the family of freedom.

Lincoln's plea was honored in a superficial and ineffectual manner; Johnson's was ignored. Having urged the Southern states to give the Negro the vote on a limited basis, Johnson would go no further. He believed the government had a right to make of the South only those demands dictated by the outcome of the war. The South must accept emancipation and must evidence its loyalty by nullifying its secession ordinances, repudiating the Confederate war debt and electing to office men capable of taking the prescribed oaths. Once the Southern states had done these things, they should be readmitted and allowed to participate in their own reconstruction.

Restoration first, then reconstruction: In appraising Johnson's vetoes, his fundamental premise has to be kept in mind. Much as he disliked the power and welfare-state aspects of the Freedmen's Bureau, he might have signed Lyman Trumbull's bill in February of 1865 if it had been passed by a Congress in which the South were represented. The President indicated as much in an interview with Governor Jacob D. Cox of Ohio, a Republican Conservative. Cox quoted Johnson as saying that he was not against the Bureau but that whether it was extended beyond one year following the technical end of the war should be left up to the Southern states. The President contended that forcing the Bureau on the South would only cause trouble, and that at this point he wanted to do the things that would increase, not decrease, Southern loyalty.

His message, vetoing the bill, reached the Senate on February 19. On the following day the galleries were full as President *pro tem* Foster put the usual motion: "Shall the bill be passed, the objections of the President to the contrary notwithstanding?" By the slim margin of two votes, the motion failed to get the necessary two-thirds and the veto was sustained.

Where reconstruction was concerned, Andrew Johnson had won his first battle with the Radicals—and his last.

XII

PURGING THE SENATE

Already making its way through Congress was another measure important to the Radicals. Introduced by Trumbull was the Civil Rights bill, one clause of which empowered the President to use the United States Army to see to it that the persons and property of Southern Negroes were respected. Taking form were even more far-reaching measures which had no chance if Andrew Johnson could make his vetoes stick.

Thad Stevens was not worried about the House. There the Radicals could muster a two-thirds vote with some to spare. But in the upper chamber, as shown by the vote upholding Johnson's veto, the Conservatives had a slight edge. Two methods for removing it were available. The Radicals could increase their strength in the Senate by reaching out into the West and bringing in one or more of the territories as new states, or by diminishing the strength of their opponents in some other way.

Bringing in a new state was a risky undertaking. The enabling act would have to go to Johnson who might veto it. Even so, fired by desperation, the Radicals tried it.

The territory which they sought to honor was Colorado. At this time Colorado was about as ready for statehood as Secretary

Seward's future "Folly," soon-to-be-purchased Alaska. Neither this nor other technicalities checked the Radicals, but in the end their effort failed due to the honesty of one of their own, Senator Sumner. The Colorado constitution, although framed by Radicals, restricted the suffrage to white citizens. Bringing to bear the full force of his oratory, Sumner argued that the convention setting up Colorado's constitution had been illegal, that to send so much as one Representative to Washington a state needed a population of 127,000, and that the actual population of Colorado was closer to 25,000.

Having failed to gain their ends by addition, the Radicals turned to subtraction.

Sitting in the Senate was one member whose right to be there was perhaps open to a slight technical question. The Senator whom the Radicals decided must be returned to the blessings of private life was John Potter Stockton of New Jersey.

Son of the naval hero, Commodore Robert Field Stockton, and great-grandson of a signer of the Declaration of Independence, the 40-year-old Senator was a man of dignified manner, facile diction and pleasing voice. A successful lawyer, Stockton had been minister resident to the Papal States under Buchanan and was, of course, a Democrat and a supporter of Andrew Johnson. Old Thad had reason to believe that if Stockton were sent home, New Jersey would replace him with an anti-Johnson Republican.

This, of course, was before the election of Senators by popular vote. The system provided by the New Jersey Constitution was for the two branches of the Legislature to convene together in what was designated as "The Legislature in Joint-Meeting" to name Senators and certain other officials. On February 15, 1865, this body assembled to choose a successor to a Republican whose term was about to expire. At this session, in response to a local political situation, a rule was altered. The existing rule had required a majority of the votes cast to elect; the new one required a majority of all members of the Legislature. Having adopted this new regulation the Joint-Meeting, because of a vacancy in its ranks owing to death, adjourned for one month. During the interval it became apparent that under the new rule, nobody could be elected. Consequently, when the Joint-Meeting reconvened its first action was to rescind the rule and to replace it with one stating "that any candidate receiving a plurality of the votes of the members present" was to be considered elected. Stockton received forty votes as against thirty-seven for the leading Republican aspirant. The presiding officer declared him in "with the unanimous acquiescence of the assembly—not a single protest, objection, or even a dissenting murmur being heard." The Joint-Meeting then adjourned *sine die*. The Legislature itself continued in session for another fifteen days, during which period no objections to Stockton's election arose.

Much later a protest signed by all of the Republican members of the New Jersey Legislature was lodged with the United States Senate. Though the protest was dated March 20, 1865, it appears to have been drawn up at a subsequent time; some of the signatures on it were not obtained until one month before the opening of the 39th Congress—that is, October, 1865. By this time it was apparent that in the next New Jersey Legislature the Republicans would have a majority on joint ballot, thus putting them in position, if Stockton were ousted, to replace him with one of their own.

In the Senate the protest was laid on the table from which it found its way to the Judiciary Committee headed by Lyman Trumbull. Most members of the Committee, the majority of whom were Republicans, agreed that the protest was politically inspired. Nor were they impressed with the argument that Stockton was not the true choice of the New Jersey Legislature because he had not been named by a majority, but by a plurality. Trumbull's Committee contended that "in the absence of any law either of Congress or of the State on the subject, a joint meeting of the two houses of the Legislature, duly assembled and vested with authority to elect a United States senator, has the right to prescribe that a plurality may elect."

All but one of the seven Republicans on the Judiciary signed the report, which was brought to the floor January 30, 1866 and which recommended that the Senate vote a resolution declaring Stockton entitled to his seat. The report excited no comment. Busy with other matters the Senate did not even bother to act on it. Stockton stayed put and the matter was forgotten.

That is, it was forgotten until Johnson's veto was sustained and the Radicals decided to take a closer look at the Senate. The man in a position to act for them was Daniel Clark of New Hampshire, the member of the Judiciary who had not signed the resolution confirming Stockton's right to his seat. Acting in the interests of his Radical friends, Clark now persuaded the other members of the Judiciary to bring the resolution to a vote.

On Thursday, March 22, approximately a month after Johnson's victory, debate on the Stockton case got under way. Clark started things with a parliamentary maneuver designed to give the Radicals two shots at their target. He proposed an amendment to the committee resolution, a motion which in essence inserted the word "not." Since after the ballot on this amended motion the question would recur on the original, the Senate would have to vote twice—first on Clark's resolution stating that Stockton was *not* entitled to his seat and then on the committee resolution stating that he was.

Thursday and a part of Friday were devoted to talk. Clark stated the major argument of the Radicals that under parliamentary law and in the absence of statute law to the contrary, the New Jersey Joint-Meeting had no right to change its election rules. Such a change, he argued, could be made only by a bill passed separately in both branches of the Legislature and signed by the Governor.

When on Friday Clark's resolution came up for vote the lineup in the Senate was touch-and-go. There were several absentees. Among them was William Wright, Stockton's New Jersey colleague and fellow-Democrat, who was seriously ill at his home in Newark. Before leaving Washington he had paired on the Stockton case with Lot Myrick Morrill of Maine. One of the first Senators to advocate confiscation of Southern property, Morrill was a Radical of long standing. Earlier in the week he had shown signs of regretting his pair, under the terms of which he was honor-bound to refrain from voting on the Stockton case until Senator Wright returned to Washington.

On Wednesday, after consultation with Sumner and Fessenden, Morrill dropped a note to Stockton. He said that at the time of making his pair with Wright he had not expected the "question to run on . . . so long" and that "to avoid embarrassment" he thought it wise to mention this fact so that Stockton might advise his colleague. Alarmed by this development, Stockton prepared a telegram for Wright, in which he stated that "after allowing you reasonable time to get to Washington" Morrill would "consider himself at liberty to vote in my case." Stockton got Morrill's approval of this message on Thursday and sent it off. Wright, in a telegraphed reply, informed his colleague that he was still confined to his room and would not be able to reach Washington until the middle of next week. He said he had had no direct word from Morrill and trusted that the Maine Senator would abide by his agreement. It was Friday, the day of the vote, when this wire arrived and Stockton brought it immediately to Morrill's attention.

That afternoon the roll was called on Clark's resolution declaring that Stockton was not entitled to his seat. Stockton himself did not participate. Morrill, too, refrained, honoring his pair. The result was a victory for Stockton, the motion failing to carry by two votes. Immediately the roll was called again on the direct question, the Committee resolution affirming Stockton's right to his seat. This time a Radical who had not participated in the previous ballot cast his vote, but again the victory was with Stockton, the resolution carrying 21 to 20.

Now came an unforgettable moment. No sooner was the result of the second ballot announced than every Radical in the chamber began yelling at Morrill, imploring him to save the day. "Vote! Vote! Vote!" came in a chorus dominated by Senator Sumner.

Morrill paled, hesitated, broke. "Call my name," he shouted to the secretary. His name was called, he voted, and the result stood 21 to 21.

Hurt and angered by Morrill's action, Stockton did not stop to

analyze the situation. Had he done so he would have realized that
he was safe. Since the second ballot was a tie the previous one,
confirming his right to his seat by two votes, was decisive. Leaping
to his feet Stockton denounced Morrill for breaking his promise,
pointing out that Senator Wright would not have gone home had he
dreamed that this would happen. Then he directed the secretary to
call his name and the vote shifted again: 22 for Stockton, 21
against him.

Stockton had done himself in. Had he let the tie stand, the
Radicals would have had to give up the battle. As it was they could
now claim that Stockton's vote was illegal and demand another.

There was furious activity on Saturday and Sunday. Among
those receiving the Radicals' attentions was William Morris
Stewart from the recently-created state of Nevada. Simmering with
restless energy, blue-eyed Stewart was no favorite with one of the
women correspondents who objected to his "untidy and slouchy"
appearance and his cowboy manners. He had voted to sustain
Johnson's veto and on Thursday and Friday he had gone along
with the Conservatives supporting Stockton. What happened to him
over the weekend is not a matter of record, but it can be assumed
that the Radical pressures were increased. Monday morning he was
visible in the Senate, but that afternoon as another vote loomed he
decamped, to be seen no more during the remainder of the Stockton
affair.

To Charles Sumner had been confided the task of reopening the
battle for the purpose, as Sumner loftily put it, of redeeming "the
honor of the American Senate." On Monday, Sumner moved that
Stockton's vote of the Friday before be declared null and void
on the grounds that a member should not be permitted to vote
"on anything in the event of which he is immediately interested."
An offer by Stockton to withdraw his vote was brushed aside. The
motion carried and the necessary arrangements were made for
the Senate to vote once again on whether Stockton should retain his
seat. Desperate efforts were made by the Conservatives to stall
off the ballot until the ailing Senator Wright could be on hand. On

Tuesday morning Senator Wright wired that he was acting under Doctor's orders but that he would be in Washington on Thursday. But the Radicals would brook no delay. Sumner pointed out that "There is a Reaper whose name is Death" who might come "among us" at any moment. On Tuesday afternoon, just before the crucial ballot was taken, another telegram came from Wright, stating that he had made arrangements to be on hand and vote the very next day. Nevertheless the test roll-call was had. John P. Stockton was removed from the Senate by one vote.

Climax was followed by anticlimax. Owing to the political setup of the upper house of the New Jersey Legislature, the casting vote there was held by James M. Scovel, the presiding officer. While the Radicals were busily purging the Senate, President Johnson's supporters in New Jersey were not idle. The Johnsonites channeled the federal patronage for the state into Scovel's hands and he returned the favor. He refused to permit the New Jersey Senate to go into joint-meeting with the result that the Radicals, waiting with open arms for a replacement for Stockton, were forced for several months to wait in vain.

But they had not struggled for nothing: Stockton was gone; Stewart had been won over; and at least one other Republican supporter of the President—Senator Edwin Denison Morgan of New York, millionaire patron of the arts—impressed by the Radical strength as demonstrated in the Stockton affair, was reconsidering his position.

In his veto of the Freedmen's Bureau bill, it had been a tactical blunder for the President to include among his objections the fact that the bill had been passed by a Congress in which the South was unrepresented. The Republican Conservatives as well as the Radicals viewed this portion of his veto message as a gratuitous "lecture," an attempt by the Executive to tell Congress what laws it could and could not pass. Senator Fessenden said that were it not for this statement he would have been inclined to vote to sustain the veto.

Fessenden's resentment, the resentment of the Conservatives

generally, emboldened Stevens to undertake one of his cleverest political stratagems. On the same day that the Senate tried unsuccessfully to override the veto, Old Thad urged the Joint Committee on Reconstruction to recommend a concurrent resolution stating that "no senator or representative shall be admitted into either branch of Congress from any of the said [Southern] states until Congress shall have declared such state entitled to such representation."

The resolution was superfluous, since the course it enunciated had already been adopted by Congress. But as usual Old Thad knew what he was doing. His timing was exquisite. Had he proposed such a resolution to the Joint Committee a few days earlier the Republican-Conservative members would have balked at it as a needless slap at the Executive. But now Johnson had had the audacity to tell Congress what laws it could make and the Conservatives were as eager as the Radicals to get back at him. Every Republican on the Committee voted for the Resolution.

Introducing the measure in the House the same day Stevens described the President's "lecture" as a case of attempted "usurpation of the rights of this body" by "another power." His words raised a hullabaloo among Johnson's Democratic supporters. Repeatedly they sought to get the floor from the old man, prompting him to lower his head in feigned terror as he intoned: "There are earthquakes around us, and I tremble; I dare not yield." Repeatedly the Democrats moved to adjourn in an effort to stall off a vote. One of them tried to delay matters by asking to have a memorial read. Although he said it was an "interesting memorial," it remained unread.

Old Thad was at his best. He met parliamentary trick with parliamentary trick and kept the place in an uproar with his quips. In this he had able assistance. Shortly after nightfall a New Jersey member, managing somehow to make himself heard above the tumult, asked if it would be in order for the House to take a recess for one hour while the Doorkeeper had the hall fitted up for a dormitory. A few minutes later Charles A. Eldridge of Wisconsin, the quick-minded Democratic leader, conceded that the Republicans had the power to vote the resolution and called off the resistance. "We have done all we could," he said. "We . . . yield." Old Thad nodded gravely. "The gentlemen accept their condition," he commented, "just as Jeff Davis did his—because they cannot help it."

There was a roar of laughter, and the vote was taken. The resolution passed 109 to 40 with only four Republicans voting with the Democrats. About 30 Republicans tried to duck personal responsibility for an open break with the President by leaving the chamber. But Old Thad was having none of that. When the House reassembled the next day he moved to reconsider the vote to permit the "wavering gentlemen" to go on record. Most of them bowed to the party lash and voted yes. A few days later the Senate endorsed the resolution and Old Thad was in seventh heaven. At long last the Congressional majority, Conservatives as well as Radicals, was committed against the President.

This victory along with the purge of the Senate put the Radicals in a strong position. Whether both houses were now under their control was not immediately apparent—but it would be soon. A test was in the offing. Even as the final roll-call was being taken in the Stockton affair, there was lying on the Senate desk a message from Andrew Johnson vetoing a bill entitled "An act to protect all Persons in the United States in their Civil Rights and to furnish the means of their vindication."

XIII

BAITING THE PRESIDENT

In the degree to which it enlarged the powers of the Federal government the Civil Rights bill of 1866 went farther than the Freedmen's Bureau bill. It not only declared Negroes to be American citizens and listed the rights they were to enjoy in common with other citizens, but it forbade all states to pass discriminatory laws. Any state official who helped to make such laws or to execute them was to be tried in a Federal court and punished if found guilty.

Some of Johnson's closest advisers urged him to sign the bill. Seward, for one; the Secretary of State admitted that the measure was unconstitutional in some respects, but believed that the country needed a law making it clear that Negroes were citizens. Governor Cox of Ohio advanced an equally expedient argument. In actual practice, he told Johnson, the bill's "bark" would prove "infinitely worse than its bite," since Southern legislatures would find it easy to circumvent its provisions. Therefore let the President sign it. By making a concession at this point, Cox reasoned, Johnson could confound his enemies and make himself "fully master of the situation."

From the standpoint of expediency, Johnson would have done well to have followed this advice. But expediency was not his way.

Harmony with Congress, even the possibility of salvaging his own program for the South—these were secondary considerations when it came to approving a measure which in his mind tore to shreds the basic law of the land. As he saw it the bill placed under the aegis of the Federal government rights which had previously been regarded as belonging "exclusively . . . to the states." All the rights listed in the bill, the President contended in his veto message, "relate to the internal police and economy of the respective states. . . .

"I do not mean to say," he added, "that upon all these subjects there are not Federal restraints . . . but where can we find a Federal prohibition against the power of any State to discriminate, as do most of them, between aliens and citizens, between artificial persons, called corporations, and natural persons, in the right to hold real estate?" The President pointed out that several Northern states had laws forbidding whites and Negroes to intermarry. Were the Civil Rights bill to become effective, would those laws have to be abolished as discriminatory?

He found the punitive aspects of the bill especially objectionable. It seemed to him that the bill defined as "crimes" actions which heretofore had been regarded as quite the opposite. The bill made any state official subject to punishment if he tried to enforce any law passed by his state legislature if that law were contrary to the Civil Rights bill. Was it not setting a dangerous precedent for the Federal Government to designate as "criminal" the efforts of a state officer to perform his duties and fulfill his oath? The provision that all cases coming under the bill were to be tried in Federal courts struck the President as a denial of the rights of state courts. Couching his objections in moderate language, he concluded that the bill established "for the security of the colored race safeguards which go infinitely beyond any that the Central Government has ever provided for the white race." It was "another step, or rather stride, toward centralization and the concentration of all legislative powers in the National Government."

In the Senate Lyman Trumbull answered the President's veto

message, point by point. Once again the little man from Illinois averred that warrant for legislation to assist the Negro was to be found in the enforcement section of the Thirteenth amendment. Once again he insisted that the government must protect the ex-slaves. To fail to do so was to leave them to the mercies of the very men who had pushed the Black Codes through the legislatures of the South.

A drenching rain did not prevent the Senate galleries from being full when, after three days of debate, the customary motion to override the President's veto was put by the chair. The day was Friday, April 6. During the preceding week both Radicals and Johnsonites had been active. Senator Wright, Stockton's colleague, had left his sickbed in Newark, travelling to Washington "at the peril of his life." Dixon of Connecticut, an administration Republican, had also been on the sick list during the Stockton affair. He too was still desperately ill but he had a stretcher waiting and ready in case during the roll-call it became apparent that his vote could help sustain the President.

Since the close of the Stockton affair an act of God had intervened on behalf of the Radicals. Solomon Foot of Vermont had died after twenty-three years in the Senate and the Radical governor of his state had replaced him with George F. Edmunds, who had arrived at the Capitol in time for the ballot. The vote of Senator Stewart of Nevada was now certain. Of the other Republicans who had previously supported the President only three were known to be still on the fence. They were Morgan of New York and the West Virginians, Peter C. Van Winkle and Waitman T. Willey.

The ballotting began about seven in the evening. The Senators' names were called alphabetically. When Morgan's was reached and after a slight hesitation the New Yorker voted to override, there was a boisterous outburst in the galleries. There was one more tense moment as Van Winkle voted to sustain the President, but it was all over when on the very next call his colleague Willey voted to override. Dixon's presence would not have changed the outcome. The final vote was 33 to override, 15 to sustain, giving the Radicals

their two-thirds with a vote to spare. Action in the House the following Monday, taken amid exultant cheering which Speaker Colfax
genially overlooked, was automatic.

Andrew Johnson had met his first defeat at the hands of the
Radicals and for the first time in American history an important
measure had become law over a Presidential vote.

From this point on the personal attack on Johnson gathered
strength. It reached its first crescendo just before the Congressional
elections in the fall of 1866, its second on the eve of the Impeachment Trial two years later. Generally speaking, the misrepresenta-
tions concerning Johnson and his motives were either inspired by
the Radicals or broadcast with their help.

Everything Johnson had ever said or done or thought, and hundreds of things he had never said or done or thought, became grist
to the mill. Was not Johnson drunk when he took his oath of office
as Vice President? Did it not follow that he was drunk all the time?

And what about those crowds when the President opened his
doors to pardon applicants? It was common knowledge that many
of the men who went to the White House on those days were not
interested in seeing the President but in female companionship.
There was that "pretty black-eyed" Mrs. Lucy Cobb, for example,
a pardon-broker. It was a "known" fact, known to thousands who
had never so much as set eyes on Mrs. Cobb, that she was frequently closeted alone with the President. And the President's wife,
after all, was a hopeless invalid.

Then there was that irresistible piece of logic: Who stood to
gain most from the assassination of the sainted Abraham Lincoln?
His successor, of course. Could any man be blamed for crediting
the frequent accusation that Andrew Johnson was one of the
conspirators behind J. Wilkes Booth? "I thank Heaven," a Nashville citizen wrote to Thad Stevens, "that you are in Congress now
that the executive branch of the Government has fallen into the
hands of the most graspingly selfish and unscrupulous enemy it has

ever known." The indignant Tennesseean thanked heaven that Stevens had uncovered Johnson's "moral deformity . . . in all its hideousness. He [Johnson] understands *assassination* and what it has done for him and traitors. He has caused the conspirators throughout the Southern states to worship in their hearts the memory of Booth, and no doubt he, Johnson, feels grateful to that assassin."

Then there was the question of education. What schools had Mr. Johnson gone to? None, of course. The American people had put the country's highest office in the hands of an illiterate. And where did he come from? From the backward mountain country of East Tennessee. What more proof was needed that he seldom, if ever, took a bath?

Portions of this piffle-paffle were believed by some of the country's most reputable men. In the spacious third-floor study of his home in Cambridge, James Russell Lowell scanned newspaper accounts of heated words spoken by Johnson under "the influence." In the *North American Review* Lowell described the President's "principles" and his "expression of them" as tainted "with the reek of vulgar associations." He prophesied that Johnson "will be indignantly remembered as the first, and we trust the last, of our chief magistrates who believed in the brutality of the people, and gave to the White House the ill-savor of a corner-grocery. *He* a tribune of the people? A lord of misrule, an abbot of unreason, much rather."

It was reported that Senator Pomeroy of Kansas, calling at the White House one day, had "found the President, his son [Robert], and son-in-law all drunk and unfit for business" and "that the President kept a mistress . . ." Later Pomeroy disavowed seeing the President drunk. But he clung to the story that Robert was drunk, which was probably true. The young man's dissoluteness was a trial to his father who eventually, on the advice of Welles and Seward, sent Robert abroad on a warship in a futile effort to cure him of the alcoholism which was to destroy him at an early age.

A tendency on the part of the public to confuse father and son was responsible for many of the stories of the President's intemperance.

Drunkard, illiterate, faithless husband, vulgarian, traitor, and murderer! Even after a tedious Congressional investigation had proved all these charges as barren as the Sahara, they continued to appear in the public prints and to be hurled in the halls of Congress. A Philadelphian wrote Sumner that "in this man Johnson we see the instincts of 'the mean white' cropping out. He cannot shake off the bootlicking proclivity born & bred in him toward the . . . aristocracy of the south, miserable fool!" A Bostoner proclaimed the President "a vile, sneaking traitor who [had] obtained political goods on false pretenses."

In the House Thad Stevens missed no opportunity to create a laugh at Johnson's expense. In the first month of 1866 the President permitted himself to be quoted in the press as opposed to some of the legislation pending in Congress. Shuffling to his feet Old Thad said it was "kind" of Johnson to "send us his opinion without being asked for it." He devoted the remainder of his speech to one of those displays of mock indignation at which he was a past master. How dare the President tell Congress what bills to pass! Had a king of England ever dictated thus to Parliament in the olden days he would have lost his head. "But, sir," rumbled Stevens, "we pass that by; we are tolerant of usurpation in this tolerant Government of ours."

There was nothing new in all this. Old Thad knew the importance of building *esprit de corps* among his followers by reminding them from time to time that the President was a powerful enemy and that they had better stick together or else. What was new was the slighting manner in which he referred to the Executive. He spoke of Johnson as "one at the other end of the avenue." He called him "an alien enemy, a citizen of a foreign state . . . not . . . legally President." Old Thad's words started a vogue. Increasingly, as the months rolled on, it became a practice on the Republican side of the House to avoid referring to Johnson by his title. He became "the acting President," "the man sitting in the place of the President," "His Accidency," "His Vulgarity."

There was more in this studied insolence than an attempt to discredit an enemy. Old Thad knew that the President had learned his political methods in back-country Tennessee. Ingrained in Johnson was the habit, when called names, of calling back. In short he was a man who if sufficiently goaded could be counted on, sooner or later, to snap back and in so doing say something indiscreet and damaging to his cause.

So Old Thad needled and hoped—and waited.

For a time it looked as if the stratagem were not going to succeed. For weeks Johnson maintained the reserve appropriate to his office. But at long last the day came.

Washington's Birthday, 1866, was set aside by Johnson's friends for rallies around the country in support of his policies. On the morning of the holiday Senator Doolittle called at the White House and asked Johnson not to speak extemporaneously when the crowd arrived. The President assured him that he had no intention of doing so. Secretary McCulloch also called to make the same request. "Don't be troubled, Mr. Secretary," Johnson told him. "If my friends come to see me, I shall thank them and that's all." So matters stood when late in the afternoon the crowd, several thousand strong according to the administration newspaper, poured into the grounds in front of the White House.

Emerging from the mansion, the President hopped nimbly onto a low wall flanking the carriage drive. It was getting dark. A member of his household staff, also mounting the wall, held a lighted candle. The President had some papers in his hand. Apparently he had scratched off a few appropriate words, but in the excitement of the moment he forgot all about his notes and delivered the impromptu speech he had told Doolittle and McCulloch he would not make. There were a few interesting passages. Taking note of current agitation in Congress to amend the Constitution in the interest of the Negroes, Johnson recounted one of his last talks with his predecessor:

> Shortly after I reached Washington for the purpose of being inaugurated as Vice President . . . I had a conversation with Mr. Lincoln . . . We conversed . . . particularly about the subject of amendments to the Constitution. In this connection he said to me, "When the amendment to the Constitution, abolishing slavery, is adopted by three-fourths of the States, I shall be pretty nearly done, or indeed quite done with amending the Constitution, if there were one other adopted." I asked him, "What is that, Mr. President?" He said . . . "It is an amendment which would compel States to send their Senators and Representatives to the Congress of the United States." [There was great applause at this.] The very policy that I am now pursuing was adopted by me under his [Lincoln's] administration, he having appointed me to a particular position [Military Governor of Tennessee] for that very purpose. . . . There is not a principle of his, in reference to the restoration of the Union, from which I have departed—not one.

Had he confined himself to remarks of this sort, all would have been well. But at one point Johnson accused the Radicals of seeking to assassinate him. It was a ridiculous charge that the President would never have made or even thought of under calm conditions. The other was the outgrowth of one of those exchanges with the crowd that Johnson had learned to handle so well in his early campaigns for office. Lambasting the Joint Committee on Reconstruction, he characterized its program as a second rebellion and its leaders as "opposed to the Union." From the crowd came a voice asking him to identify the men he had in mind. When the President replied that it didn't matter "by what name you call them," he was again interrupted by a voice imploring him to list at least three. Johnson obliged, naming Stevens, Sumner and Wendell Phillips. Someone in the crowd asked why he didn't include Forney, secretary of the Senate, who although once friendly to the President had lately placed the columns of his newspapers at the service of the Radicals. Johnson said: "I do not waste my fire on dead ducks."

This retort brought laughter from the President's audience, but the last laugh was reserved for his enemies. They pounced on the assassination charge and the name-calling. Next day's Radical press bristled with accusations that the President couldn't have made such tasteless remarks had he been sober, and contending that he had alienated thousands of his conservative supporters. As time went on and the Radical press continued to assert that the conservatives were offended, more and more of them began to regard Johnson as a not quite responsible man.

It was Thad Stevens who entertained the House with a savage parody. The old man began in his usual way, discursively and with much fumbling about. Quietly he came to his point. He was shocked, he said, at the current rumor that he was an enemy of the President. It was hard for him to see how anyone could credit such a myth when everybody knew how much he admired the President's "integrity, patriotism, courage, and good intentions." At this point there was an interruption, patently pre-arranged. Playing straight man, Hiram Price of Iowa delivered his lines: "I desire to ask the gentleman, with his consent, whether there may not be some mistake here. When I remember most distinctly that the public press of the country for the last few weeks has been repeating the name of a certain 'Thaddeus Stevens' as having been used by the President in a certain speech at the White House, and when I hear a gentleman whom I suppose to be the Thaddeus Stevens referred to speak in such strong terms in favor of the President, I wish to know whether he is the same gentleman or some other."

Stevens let the members have their chuckle before continuing. "Why, Mr. Speaker," he exclaimed, "does the learned gentleman from Iowa suppose for a single moment that that speech, to which he refers as having been made in front of the White House, was a fact?" Stevens hastened to assure his fellow members that no such speech was ever made. The whole thing was a hoax—yes, a hoax. The Copperheads had made up that speech and had attributed it to the President. Nor was this the first time, said Stevens, that such a hoax had been perpetrated on Andrew Johnson. He called the attention of his listeners to the New York *World* of March 7, 1865, when that "leading paper of the Democratic party" had repeated the "vile slander" that Andrew Johnson was intoxicated at the time of his inauguration as Vice President. What is more, the *World* had called Andrew Johnson "this insolent, drunken brute, in comparison with whom even Caligula's horse was respectable!"

Old Thad's spoof had its intended effect, in the House of Representatives and subsequently throughout the whole country.

XIV

THE FOURTEENTH AMENDMENT

The post-bellum impulse to amend the Constitution was a natural outgrowth of the war. Profound changes ·had been wrought in American society. One of them, emancipation, had already been written into the basic law and Northern politicians were eager to do the same with some of the others.

The task of framing the necessary amendments was confided to the Joint Committee on Reconstruction and for months the fifteen members sifted approximately 140 different proposals. Finally, after a previous proposition had bogged down in debate on the floor, Thad Stevens, reporting for the Committee in early May, presented to the House the elements of what eventually would be the Fourteenth Amendment. In its final form the Fourteenth consisted of four sections bound together by a fifth which empowered Congress to enforce the other four.

The opening sentence proclaimed the creation of a new individual—the citizen of the United States. It declared that every person born or naturalized in this country and subject to its jurisdiction was a citizen both of his state and of all the other states. By asserting that America was not a loose aggregation of states but a nation, this portion of the amendment confirmed the decision of Appomattox.

Through the remainder of Section 1 were clauses that would become the life blood of some of America's weightiest judicial decisions. In the Bill of Rights added to the Constitution in 1791 the Federal Government was forbidden to deprive any person "of life, liberty, or property, without due process of law." In the Fourteenth the same prohibition was applied to the state governments. Its framers were thinking of the Negro; it was his life, liberty and property they were striving to protect. Their intentions were good but their language was faulty. As a result, property interests would find shelter under the "due process" clause of the Fourteenth, and so would Big Business. So, interestingly enough, would the right of a state to regulate Big Business when its functions were "affected with a public interest." But of the 600-some cases arising out of the "due process" clause during the next three-quarters of a century, less than 40 would concern the Negro. Another clause of Section 1 of the Fourteenth would serve him better. This clause forbade a state to "deny to any person within its jurisdiction the equal protection of the laws." Generations later a case brought under the aegis of this clause would produce the Supreme Court ban on segregation in the public schools.

The purpose of Section 2 was to resolve the question of how many Representatives the former slave-states should have in the House. There were fifteen such states, including the four border states that had fought on the side of the Union. Prior to emancipation these states were permitted by the Constitution to base their representation in Congress on what was called the "federal ratio"— that is, on their total free populations plus three-fifths of their slaves. Under the 1860 census the federal ratio had given these states 85 representatives, of whom 18 owed their existence to the three-fifths clause. But now there were no slaves. Every Negro counted not as three-fifths but as five-fifths of a person. The change was of little benefit to the border states, but it was of immense benefit to the deep-south states because of the density of their Negro populations. Unless the basis of apportionment was altered, the unrepresented Southern states when they returned to the Union would be sending about twelve more Democrats to the lower House than had been sitting there in 1860.

Here was a situation no Republican could view without misgiving. The basis had to be changed. But how? The simplest way was to give the Negro the vote, but an amendment would apply to the entire nation and the Northern states had indicated unmistakably that they were not yet ready to accept Negro suffrage. So Section 2 of the Fourteenth was a compromise—and a classic example of tortured English. It read in part:

"Representatives shall be apportioned among the several States according to their respective numbers," counting the whole number of persons in each State, excluding Indians not taxed. But when the right to vote at any election for national or state offices "is denied to any of the male inhabitants of such State, being twenty-one years of age, and citizens of the United States . . . the basis of representation therein shall be reduced in the proportion which the number of such male citizens shall bear to the whole number of male citizens twenty-one years of age in such State."

Section 3 barred from state and national office any person who, having once held a state or national office requiring him to swear allegiance to the Constitution, had subsequently supported the rebellion. To this was added the provision of which a later Congress availed itself, namely that the disability could be removed by a vote of two-thirds of each House.

The fourth section was a statement that the Federal Government would not pay the Confederate war debt, pension any Confederate veteran, or honor any claims for compensation resulting from the emancipation of the slaves.

A resolution submitting an amendment to the states for ratification must have a two-thirds vote in each House and therefore does not require the signature of the Executive. The previous Congress had submitted the Thirteenth Amendment to Lincoln, presumably as a courtesy, but the 39th bypassed the President. The resolution was simply registered with Secretary Seward and on June 16, 1866, it was submitted to the state legislatures for ratification. Old Thad had urged that it be sent only to the Northern states and that it be considered ratified when three-fourths of them, nineteen, endorsed it. Steven's presentation of this plea was his last attempt to breathe life into his theory that the Southern states were no longer states at all but merely territories. While this "pernicious abstraction," as Lincoln had dubbed it, served the Radicals well as a propaganda device, it was never taken seriously by anyone except Old Thad himself, Charles Sumner and a few lesser Radicals. Secretary Seward submitted the Fourteenth, as he had the Thirteenth, to all thirty-six states with the understanding that it would not become part of the Constitution until it was ratified by three-fourths of them.

We come now to the South's reception of the amendment, to Johnson's reasons for opposing it, and to its role in the crucial Congressional elections in the fall of 1866.

All of the Southern states either refused to pass on the amendment or turned it down with one exception, the President's home state. As far as the Ultras were concerned, of course, Tennessee occupied a special position. Her Governor, "Fighting Parson" Brownlow, was as Radical as Thad Stevens and the Tennessee legislature had disfranchised all former Confederate civil and military officers and had given the freedmen the same civil although not the same political rights as the whites. When the Fourteenth Amendment was sent to the states, Brownlow immediately called a special session of his General Assembly to endorse it.

His task was not easy. Some members of the Tennessee legislature tried to resign, others ignored the Governor's summons. For a time it looked as if Governor Brownlow would not be able to assemble a quorum. He therefore asked General "Pap" Thomas, commander of the military district which included Tennessee, to

round up a quorum for him. Thomas forwarded the request to the
Secretary of War, and one sweltering July afternoon Stanton
hustled over to the White House to lay it before the President.

Johnson exploded. He said if "General Thomas had nothing else
to do but to intermeddle in local controversies, he had better be
detached and ordered elsewhere." The President's reaction delighted
Stanton. "Pap" Thomas was one of Johnson's supporters and the
Secretary saw in the situation a chance to woo the popular General
away. He said that of course he would inform Thomas of the
President's decision and asked if he should add to it the President's
rebuke. "My wish," was Johnson's reply, "is that the answer should
be emphatic and decisive, not to meddle with local parties and
politics. The military are not superior masters."

Unable to obtain the assistance of the United States army,
Governor Brownlow by July 19 had contrived to have on hand
fifty-four members of the lower house. This was two short of a
quorum. It so happened that two other members were known to be
in Nashville, so Brownlow ordered the sergeant-at-arms to kidnap
them. The reluctant solons were dragged into the chamber and
kept there under guard while the speaker counted them present, the
roll was called and the amendment ratified. When subsequently the
two man-handled legislators got writs of *habeas corpus* from a
judge of the state court, the Brownlow legislature impeached the
judge, tried him and turned him out of office.

Brownlow's official message to Washington contained an in-
sult to the President. "We have fought the battle and won it," he
wired. "We have ratified the constitutional amendment in the
House, forty-three voting for it, eleven against it, two of Andrew
Johnson's tools not voting. Give my respects to the dead dog of the
White House!"

Within minutes after this telegram reached the Capitol, a joint
resolution was before the House declaring Tennessee restored to
the Union. Old Thad thought things were moving a little fast but
he voted yes. The Senate acted with equal speed.

Off to the White House went the resolution, with a significant preamble stating that "said State Government can only be restored to its former political relations in the Union by the consent of the law-making power of the United States." If Johnson signed, he was endorsing the Congressional policy of reconstruction; if he did not, he was keeping his own state out. He signed, and back to the House went the resolution with a message from the President saying he did not approve of the preamble.

On the same day Tennessee's eight representatives presented themselves to the bar of the House and were sworn in. There was no question in the Senate about admitting Joseph S. Fowler, a Radical, but Sumner objected to his colleague, David T. Patterson, husband of the President's daughter. During the conflict Patterson had sworn allegiance to the Confederacy, although with a spoken reservation. The matter was referred to a committee which shortly reported that Patterson had taken his oath under duress, so on the last day of the 1st session of the 39th Andrew Johnson's son-in-law, a staid individual of a rather plodding turn of mind, took his seat in the United States Senate.

Of the remaining ten Southern states, Texas was the first to reject or ignore the amendment. The others followed suit one by one. There was strong feeling about Section 3 which forbade the Southern people from electing to office those men they looked upon as their true leaders. Section 3 barred from office at least 18,000 Southerners, perhaps more. Howard K. Beale, a student of the period, has plumbed the intensity of Southern feeling by asking his readers to imagine the situation in reverse. Had the South won the war, Northerners undoubtedly would have resented a demand that "they repudiate, never to trust again, Lincoln, Grant, Sumner, Stevens, and . . . even all minor state and federal officers . . . except the Copperheads who had in every way blocked the War." The anger of the South at Section 3 was understandable, but so were the emotions that made the Section not only acceptable to most Northerners but in the eyes of many of them a necessity.

Many of them saw in Section 3 only a reasonable device for preventing a recurrence of the tragedy by penalizing the men they held responsible for leading the rebellion. It would be easy for Americans of later eras to look dispassionately at Section 3 and see that it was unwise and unnecessary. But in the summer of 1866 it was a rare American, North or South, who could look dispassionately at any issue connected with the conflict. The Civil War brought to a head the question of whether the Founding Fathers meant this country to be a confederation of states or a nation. The question had been answered, but it had been answered by force. It was impossible for the Southern people to accept it overnight. By the same token it was impossible for the Northern people to change overnight from hate to trust.

Like Andrew Johnson's $20,000 clause, like the iron-clad oath required of Southerners seeking certain political posts, Section 3 was a mistake. To whom could the Southerners turn for competent leadership?

Southerners were not alone in seeing this problem. A few Northern statesmen, seeing it clearly, became voices crying in the wilderness. Several of Johnson's Cabinet complained of great difficulty in administering the national laws in the South because most of the men capable of assuming the necessary offices were not able to take the test oath. From the retiring Governor of Massachusetts, able and slavery-hating John A. Andrew, came this message of good sense: "We cannot reorganize political society with any proper security . . . unless we give those who are, by their intelligence and character, the natural leaders of the people, and who surely will lead them by and by, an opportunity to lead them now." Referring to Johnson's $20,000 clause he called it "impolitic and unphilosophical" of the President to make "one rule for the richer and higher rebels and another for the poorer and more lowly rebels." To which the Governor added that the liberality with which Johnson was handing out pardons indicated that the President had himself come around to this opinion.

The President had. He was as appalled as any other Southerner at the third section of the Amendment. As for the other sections, he had no quarrel with them. His quarrel was with the passage of any amendment pending the restoration of the Southern states. Even more intense was Johnson's opposition to the implication, inherent both in the amendment and in the report of the Joint Committee defending it, that Congress had a right to establish terms under which a Southern state could re-enter the Union. As the President read the Constitution, all Congress could do was accept or reject the individuals elected to it. It did not have the right to say to any state, "You must ratify this amendment—or do this, that or the other thing—before you are *entitled* to representation."

Johnson placed these objections before his Cabinet weeks before the amendment was put in its final form and submitted to the states. For some time thereafter he was silent insofar as the public was concerned. During the pre-election summer and fall he made no direct attack on the amendment. Early in November, after the election, he prepared for delivery to Congress an amazingly conciliatory message implying that he would go along, at least to the extent of not openly opposing the amendment, provided Congress would now fasten its attention on "financial and other measures having for their objects amelioration of the burdens, and a removal of the restraints which the late civil war unavoidably rendered necessary, and the sure and steady development of the resources of the continent." This message was never delivered. The President changed his mind. The message he actually presented bristled with his now-familiar defiance of the Congressional approach to reconstruction, made no mention of the amendment and left no doubt that his disapproval of it remained unshaken.

When in December Alabama showed signs of a willingness to accept the amendment, a leading conservative of the state, after consulting with Johnson in Washington, sent off a wire opposing ratification and the legislature adjourned without taking a vote. A month later the matter came up again in the Alabama legislature and the governor hurried off a telegram to the President, asking his advice. Johnson's reply was on the wires a few hours later. He asked:

What possible good can be attained by reconsidering the Constitutional amendment? I know of none in the present posture of affairs. I do not believe that the people of the whole country will sustain any set of individuals in attempts to change the whole character of our Government by enabling acts or otherwise. I believe, on the contrary, that they will eventually uphold all who have patriotism and courage to stand by the Constitution, and who place their confidence in the people. There should be no faltering on the part of those who are honest in co-ordinate Departments of the Government, in accordance with its original design.

So ran Johnson's course, and a look at the main factors involved suggests that it was not well-considered. The submission of the Fourteenth Amendment to the states presented Johnson with his last opportunity to save the South from the rigors of Radical Reconstruction. Alternatives were open to him. He could have maintained a posture of neutrality from first to last. It cannot be said definitely that his silence would have induced all of the Southern states to ratify, although mild pro-amendment movements in Alabama and South Carolina, both of which were scotched by the President, suggest that it would have.

It is certain that his silence would have found favor with the Republican Moderates in the Senate. These gentlemen were uneasy in their alliance with the Radicals. They were still looking for signs of cooperation at the White House. President Johnson could have attempted a compromise. He might have asked Congress to eliminate the punitive clause, Section 3, with the understanding that he would then urge the Southern states to ratify. Another opportunity for compromise was presented by the failure of Congress to pass an enabling act, recommended by the Joint Committee and specifically stating that any Southern state that ratified the amendment was to be restored to the Union. It would have been statesmanlike of Johnson to request Congress to pass this act in return for his support of the amendment.

It is not suggested that Johnson's error lay in standing by his principles. His chief error was not in what he did, but in how he did it. At no point did the President make an effort to force the Radicals to put their real motives on the line.

He knew what these motives were, as did many contemporaries. In June, 1866, when Congress took its final action on the amendment, the New York *Herald* charged that the Radicals were not sincere. In their eyes the amendment was merely a campaign document. They knew that the Southern states would find it objectionable and hoped they would turn it down, thus justifying Congress in concocting more severe measures for the South. Thad Stevens, ordering his followers in the House to vote for the amendment, conceded that it was not the supreme instrument of reform and vengeance he would like to have seen. But legislation, the old man sighed, was made "by men, not angels." So take "what we can get now, and hope for better things in future legislation!"

The Radicals were not willing to give any guarantees—quite the contrary: in passing the enabling act which let Tennessee back in, they took care to make it clear that the admission of this one state because it had ratified the amendment was not to be taken as a precedent. During the election campaign the leading Radicals refused to make any promises. Was it their intention to restore each Southern state as it ratified or not? They would not commit themselves. Johnson would have caught the ear of the public if he had asked his opponents from a public platform, "What do you have in mind? Do you regard the Fourteenth Amendment as the end of the road or simply as the first of several legislative enactments, each harder on the South than the one before?"

Johnson's adherence to his beliefs, his decision in the end not to conciliate his enemies, cannot be dismissed as mere obstinacy. It was predicated on his realization that the Radicals were not acting in good faith. During the 1866 election campaign, as we will have occasion to note again, the impression was widespread among the voters that Congress intended to ask nothing further of the South than endorsement of the Fourteenth Amendment. Had Johnson forced the Radicals to confess that this was not true, that they had further and more drastic schemes in mind, the election returns might have been different; at the very least Congress, after the election, would have found it more difficult to proceed to extreme measures.

While the debate surrounding submission of the Fourteenth to the states was the most important political development of the pre-election summer, it was not the only one. Some two weeks after passage of the amendment, the country was startled by one of the calamities of Reconstruction—the New Orleans riot.

The New Orleans riot had its roots in the constitutional convention which set up Louisiana's civil government under Lincoln's "Ten Per Cent" proclamation. Assembling in the spring of 1864 the convention—150 delegates from the 48 parishes of the state then more or less under Federal control—met for two months, allowed its members a per diem of $10, piled up a cigar-and-liquor bill of $9,421.55, revised the state constitution to accord with Federal directives and at its final session passed a reconvoking resolution, reading in part "that when this Convention adjourns, it shall be at the call of the President, whose duty it shall be to reconvoke the Convention for any cause." The convention then wound up its business and a few months later the constitution it had framed was approved by the people. At this point the reconvoking resolution ceased to have any validity. The convention could not be reconvened because it no longer existed.

Notwithstanding this fact some of the Radical members petitioned E. H. Durell, the Convention president, to call the body together in the winter of 1866. They said the action was necessitated by the "unsettled conditions of the State government." Their real reason was alarm over the degree to which the state government was falling into the hands of pardoned Confederates sympathetic to the policies of Johnson. Durell refused to cooperate so the Radicals went ahead without him. On June 26 they met at the state capitol in a caucus from which the public was excluded. Only some 40 members were on hand, a number considerably short of the 76 required for a forum under the 1864 rules. Moreover some of the delegates, especially the lawyers, questioned the legality of the proceedings. Undeterred, the caucus leaders issued a "rump proclamation," summoning the convention to meet in New Orleans on Monday, July 30.

Originally a Johnson supporter, Governor James M. Wells had gravitated to the opposition and was secretly supporting the movement. Lieutenant-Governor Voorhees and Mayor Monroe of New Orleans were fighting it. On July 25 Mayor Monroe wrote to General Absalom Baird, acting military commander in New Orleans in the temporary absence of General Philip Sheridan. Monroe informed Baird that he planned "to disperse this unlawful assembly" and to please "inform me whether the projected meeting has your approbation." Baird, replying the next day, said the Convention did not have "the sanction . . . of the military," but that it had a constitutional right to meet and that "no one ought to object" to such "harmless pleasantry." Informed of Baird's reaction, Lieutenant-Governor Voorhees got off a wire to Johnson. "Is the military," he inquired, "to interfere or prevent process of court?" Johnson replied without delay, sending a similar message to Governor Wells. The "military," the President wired, "will be expected to sustain and not to obstruct or interfere with the proceedings of the courts."

On the Friday night before the meeting the city hall across from Lafayette Square was the scene of a torchlit rally. Among the speakers was Dr. A. P. Dostie, whose speech, as reported, was inflammatory. Emigrating from New York several years prior to the war, Dostie had practiced dentistry in New Orleans until secession came. Fleeing North at the start of the conflict he had returned in time to be elected auditor of public accounts in the Louisiana Ten Per Cent government. An impulsive man and a soldier of fortune, Dostie informed his audience that the opponents of Monday's convention were a pack of rebels whose one aim was to keep the Negro from getting the vote. He foresaw an attempt by the

Mayor to break up the meeting and he called on his listeners to be on hand to prevent this. "I want only brave men to come," he shouted. "Judge Abel with his grand jury may indict us . . . and the police with more than a thousand men sworn in may interfere . . ." If so, Dostie predicted, "the streets of New Orleans will run with blood! The rebels . . . want you to do the work and they will do the voting; and will you throw over them 'the mantle of charity and oblivion'?"

Apparently Dostie's worked-up auditors did not catch the import of his question, for the response was a "We will! We will!" The excited speaker rebuked them. "No, by God!" he shouted, "we won't. We are bound to have universal suffrage, though you have the traitor, Andrew Johnson, against you."

Even General Baird was forced to the conclusion that the forthcoming meeting might be something more than a "harmless pleasantry." On Saturday he sent a telegram to Stanton, asking for instructions "at once." He said that he had warned the state and city authorities that he could not countenance their proposed plan to break up the meeting by arresting the delegates "without instructions to that effect from the President." Baird's telegram reached the War Department Saturday night. The next morning it was delivered to Stanton at his Washington home. Old Mars read it— and did nothing.

Monday was meeting day. Warned by General Baird not to interfere, the New Orleans municipal authorities contented themselves with issuing a proclamation asking people to stay away from Mechanics Institute, site of the convention. Beginning at noon, the meeting was attended by only 25 of the original 150 members. Along toward one o'clock a body of Negroes, with estimates varying between sixty and one hundred thirty, marched up Burgundy Street and across Canal in the direction of the Institute, swinging along to the beat of a fife and drum corps and displaying an American flag. By the time they arrived at the Institute, a crowd of whites had gathered in front of the building. A shot was fired, followed by others, the police came running, and the battle began in earnest.

A white flag was protruded through one of the windows. At this point, according to those inside, the police went berserk, crashing into the building and firing indiscriminately at the crowd of whites and Negroes in the meeting hall. When it was all over about 48 were dead, most of them Negroes, and 448 were wounded. Among the fatalities was A. P. Dostie, dentist.

The question of blame was made a burning issue of the Radical campaign preceding the fall congressional elections. Their press attributed the catastrophe to the President's lenient pardon policy. Some accounts went so far as to state that Johnson had been warned of the impending trouble and had done nothing about it. Little credence was given to the President's statement that Stanton, on receiving General Baird's telegram asking for instructions, had failed to forward it to Johnson. As for Stanton, he did not get around to sending the telegram to the White House until almost two weeks after the riot, and only then because the President ordered him to do so.

XV

A THIRD PARTY?

After the passage of the Civil Rights bill over his veto, Andrew Johnson was no longer doing battle with a small group of Radicals; he was locked in combat with practically the whole of the Republican majority in Congress. Johnson might have avoided so complete a break with Congress if he had pursued his own ends with greater decisiveness and vigor.

It is not necessary to turn to his enemies for this judgment. No one was more sympathetic with his aims or fonder of the man than Secretary Welles. Yet it was Welles, in a letter to Orville Browning, who concluded that the chief weakness of the administration was the failure of the President to make the fullest possible use of the powers of his office. A similar verdict was offered by General Sherman. The General applauded Johnson's reconstruction program and chided his brother John, the Senator, for following the rest of the Republican Moderates into the Radical camp. There was no rancor, only astuteness, in the hard-bitten warrior's observation that "Johnson is not a man of action but of theory . . ."

Johnson's enemies repeatedly accused him of using the patronage to further his policies. "The penalty of disobedience," Thaddeus Stevens declared, was "removal from office. He [Johnson] made this rule with the lowest and most trifling ones. A colleague of mine from Pennsylvania informed me that having presented a petition to the neighbors for the appointment of the postmaster to a hundred-dollar post office, he went to the clerk to ascertain why the appointment was delayed and was shown an order on file, signed by Andrew Johnson, directing that no appointment should be made unless it was directed by Ed Cowan." Stevens characterized Johnson's handing over the patronage to Cowan as a case of "Judas Iscariot dispensing patronage through Judas the younger!"

Yet Old Thad was hard put to find instances of Johnson's use of the patronage. The simple truth was that the President did not make sufficient use of this weapon. Civil Service was being talked about at this time, but the Spoils System was still the order of the day. It was taken for granted that a President would utilize it, but Johnson rarely did so. One great source of patronage in the Federal Government was the huge Treasury Department, and the testimony of Secretary McCulloch is that Johnson never interfered with the department even though most of its employees were known to be against his reconstruction policy. Johnson, McCulloch said, "never even suggested that changes should be made for that reason." His verdict was that Johnson was "a man of unblemished personal integrity. He was an honest man and his administration was an honest and clean administration." According to McCulloch the President did not permit himself to become obligated to anyone. He even returned a horse and carriage presented to him shortly after his accession to office.

Johnson's failure to utilize the patronage sufficiently was dictated by his sense of honor. He was a Democrat; the Republicans had put him where he was. With only scattered and unimportant exceptions, he bent over backwards to see to it that the Republicans got the jobs.

Practically all of his sympathetic biographers agree that his besetting weakness as a political leader was procrastination. It was an understandable defect in a man who by nature was a scholar rather than a doer. It was also a ruinous one. While the President considered and temporized, his enemies carried the day by the simple device of getting in their licks before he could decide on a course of action.

He was no sooner in office than his advisers were urging him to renovate his Cabinet with the idea of surrounding himself with men who were popular with the Northern people and in touch with the current thought. The Blairs were forever at the President to make such changes. The Blairs may have had a couple of berths in mind for themselves but, as Johnson admitted toward the end of his life, many of their suggestions had merit.

Among those urged for the Cabinet by the Blairs and others were Horace Greeley, Governor Andrew of Massachusetts and Oliver P. Morton, former Governor of Indiana and later a member of the United States Senate. Johnson refused to consider Greeley for a minute. As he put it to Ben Truman, Greeley was "a whale ashore" and so full of "goodness of heart . . . as to produce infirmity of mind." For Andrew and Morton he had only admiration. At the time Cabinet reorganization was under consideration, Andrew was a Republican Moderate and his presence in the official household would have immeasurably strengthened Johnson's hand with the Republican Moderates in the Senate.

Morton might have served him in another way. It was pointed out by one of the President's advisers that it would be helpful to have one man "in the Cabinet who could be approached by those who were in opposition to the President, and who could thus become a channel of communication between the Executive and Congress." The President had such a man, of course, in Stanton—but Stanton was a dissembler. Morton, on the other hand, would have filled the bill. He was an emotional man but an honest one. Huge and well-proportioned with striking black hair, he was an able political organizer and he had won the confidence of the people by the firmness with which, as Civil War governor of Indiana, he had put down a virulent Copperhead movement in that state. As a member of the Cabinet, he could have provided Johnson with badly needed insight into the thinking of his opponents.

Johnson listened politely to all suggestions, turned them over in his mind—and did nothing. Changes did occur. Postmaster-General Dennison, Attorney-General Speed and Secretary of Interior Harlan resigned. They were replaced by Alex W. Randall, Henry Stanbery and Orville Browning. These changes had the effect of ringing Johnson with men faithful to his views, but they did not strengthen his position with the Republican Conservatives or give him a pipeline to Congress. Johnson's failure to take more drastic action was attributable in part to the fact that as a Southerner he had little or no first-hand knowledge of most of the men whose names were suggested to him.

Still another factor was at work. In the winter of 1867 Colonel Moore noticed that the subject of Cabinet changes had become painful to the President. Any wholesale alteration would call for the dismissal of men with whom he was loathe to part. Out would go Seward whom the President admired and whom he affectionately dubbed the "Old Roman." Out would go Welles, whom he regarded as "a regular old Brick." Johnson confided to Moore that he was appalled at the thought of the "harsh feelings" these men would entertain if he let them go. He confided to Ben Truman that he could not bring himself to dismiss men who had been chosen by "the greatest man of all," Abraham Lincoln.

His handling of the Republican Conservatives in the Senate was marked by tactlessness. Johnson knew Southern politicians, and knew just how to move so as not to step on their toes. But over and over he offended the sensibilities of Northern leaders because he did not understand them. He angered the Conservative Republican Senators by the "lectures" in his veto messages concerning the limitations of Congressional power and by his failure to meet their overtures half way. Worst of all he failed to comprehend that their desire to protect the civil rights of the Negro was sincere and that he must take it into consideration if he wanted their support.

The key figures among the Conservatives of the upper house were Fessenden, Trumbull and Grimes. Fessenden and Trumbull we have met. James Wilson Grimes of Iowa was a man of commanding presence although careless of his appearance, plain-spoken and honest. A Dartmouth graduate, highly cultured, he had been a farmer, a lawyer, a railroad promoter and governor of his state, which he had almost singlehandedly made a stronghold of Republicanism. He and Fessenden were boon companions.

"Grimes," Secretary Welles was writing in his diary in March of 1866, "says he came here at the commencement of the present session kindly disposed to the President and not very hostile to his policy. But he soon found that certain obnoxious Democrats had free access to the White House, and that pardoned Rebels hung around there. He was not satisfied with this state of things, and spoke of it [to Johnson] . . . Soon after he was invited to breakfast with the President, and spent two hours with him discussing all subjects in full and most satisfactorily. Allusion was made to Fessenden, and he expressed a wish that the two should come together and interchange opinions. The President requested him to speak to Fessenden and invite an interview . . . and F. spent several hours [the next day] most satisfactorily at the White House and went over general measures now prominent.

"On the following day appeared the celebrated letter of 'A conversation of the President with a distinguished Senator' [in which Johnson was quoted as critical of pending legislation]. Grimes . . . asked Fessenden if that was his conversation. F . . . said he had had no such conversation, and they soon ascertained that Dixon [of Connecticut, an administration Republican] was the Senator. The two, finding that they were not the only confidants of the President, thereupon left him, and allied themselves to the Radicals."

Trumbull, speaking in the Senate, aired a similar tale of injured pride. He revealed that prior to introducing the Freedmen's Bureau and Civil Rights bills he twice called on the President, leaving copies of the bills and inviting Johnson's cooperation in making them satisfactory. It was a serious oversight for Johnson to ignore these conciliatory gestures. At the very least he could have consulted with

Trumbull before submitting his vetoes, both of which came as surprises to the Illinois Senator.

To mention Johnson's weaknesses as a politician is not to overlook his difficulties. He entered the Presidency without organized backing. The Republicans had put him in office but they did not consider him one of them. Under the circumstances, many leaders of his own party were reluctant to trust him; there was the further fact that he was damned if they supported him and damned if they didn't. His party as a whole was associated in the public mind with Copperheadism. James Russell Lowell called it "That party which had sunk so low during the war that it seemed impossible to sink lower . . ." The New York *Herald,* after analysis of a crucial vote in the House, concluded that the Democratic spokesmen were less interested in Johnson's policies than they were in refurbishing their organization. It followed that whatever support they gave the Administration was undependable since it was merely an accidental byproduct of a partisan bid for power.

There was nothing, of course, to prevent Johnson's using the prerogatives of his office to build a machine for himself. His first step necessarily was to determine on what platform he was going to stand. He had a choice of two. He could either take his stand on the issue of reconstruction, placing his emphasis on the importance of immediate restoration of the Southern states; or he could take his stand on the economic issues confronting the country in the aftermath of war.

There were half a dozen such issues. Government costs had been staggering during the conflict and the post-war Congress aggravated the situation by enlarging the Freedmen's Bureau and by increasing its own salaries sixty per cent. Complaints were loud in the Western states, less so in the East where the cotton-mill owners saw in the Freedmen's Bureau an opportunity to get their hands on Southern property and the raw materials required by New England factories. The high tariff established during the war was still in existence. This combined with a heavy tax program put a disproportionate burden on small farmers and the debtor classes

generally. It was correspondingly favorable to the wealthy indus-
trialists along the upper Atlantic coast. Inflation was another concern. The Government had issued greenbacks during the war. Now
there was a demand, emanating principally from Wall Street, to
have these withdrawn and to put the country back on a hard-money
basis. Another problem was the growth of commercial monopolies,
spearheaded by the clamor in financial circles to give the railroads
a prior claim on the public domain at the expense of potential
homesteaders.

On all these and similar issues the line of cleavage, generally
speaking, was between the industrial East and the agrarian West.
Johnson leaned toward the West. He favored retrenchment in
governmental expenditures, a lower tariff, a tax program more
favorable to the small farmer and the debtor, a brake on monopolies, the reservation of the public domain to homesteaders,
and continued inflation as against contraction of the currency. It
has been suggested by Professor Beale, one of the most penetrating
students of the era, that Johnson's chief mistake was to relegate
these issues to a secondary position and to make immediate reconstruction the heart of his program. On the issue of reconstruction
his enemies were united. Had he presented himself as the champion
of the small farmer and the debtor, he might have driven a wedge
between the Radicals of the industrial East and those of the agrarian
West.

As early as October of 1865 his advisers were urging him to
head up a movement for a third party to be composed of conservatives of all political shadings. Characteristically he dallied.
June of 1866 had come and was half gone before he sanctioned
the idea. What followed was a case of too late and too little. It was
too late because by June many prominent Conservatives, including
Morton of Indiana and Andrew of Massachusetts, had gone over
to the Radicals. It was too little because the fumbling and com-
promising manner in which the movement was carried on defeated
its objective.

Considerable strength might have accrued to Johnson if the

movement had created a new party complete with its own organization, press and candidates. But this was not to be. There were several snags, including the desire of the ringleaders to have the participation of Henry Raymond, spokesman of the Administration Republicans in the House and editor of the influential New York *Times*. Raymond was chairman of the National Committee of the National Union (Republican) Party. He was not inclined to give up the post, although in the end his connection with what was ostensibly a third-party development prompted the Republicans to read him out. Raymond gave his support with the understanding, as Johnson phrased it, that the objective was not to build a new party directly but to "lay the foundation for a *National* party, which would . . . absorb the Democratic party of the North and West, and all of the Union party but the Radicals" and to which the South would also subscribe.

With this ill-defined goal in mind a call was issued for a convention. The scene of this spectacle, officially the National Union Convention, was Philadelphia, August 14-16, 1866. Since no building large enough could be found, a goat pasture was leased and up went a two-story wigwam with seats for 15,000 persons and a 146-foot front along Girard Avenue at 20th Street.

Public interest was intense. After all, this was the first political gathering of a national character since 1860. During the week preceding the convention, delegates poured into Philadelphia from all of the 36 states, the 11 territories and the District of Columbia. From the erstwhile Confederacy came Governor James L. Orr of South Carolina, John Forsythe of Alabama, Stephens of Georgia. From the West came Senator Hendricks of Indiana, George H. Pendleton of Ohio, ex-Senator Charles E. Stuart of Michigan. From the East, Stockton of New Jersey, John Q. Adams Junior of Massachusetts, Major-General John A. Dix and Samuel J. Tilden of New York. Representing the commercial interests were, among others, the inventor and pig-iron magnate, William Kelley of Pittsburgh, and the younger Charles Goodyear of New York.

The Continental Hotel, swathed in bunting, was headquarters.

To this hostelry on August 10 came the executive committee including Postmaster-General Randall, chairman, and Orville Browning, recently named Secretary of Interior. By Monday, August 13, all hotels were jammed, rooming houses were overflowing and vendors of all sorts had established themselves in the vicinity of the not-yet-completed wigwam. The presence of so many Southerners alarmed the natives. The entire police force was put on duty and supplemented by units of the local militia.

Tuesday morning the crowd gathered early at the Wigwam. The weather was threatening and carpenters were struggling to finish the roof. Shortly before noon the members of the executive committee took their places on the platform, the band blared out a tune and the delegates began entering the vast amphitheatre. The big moment came when General Darius Nash Couch of Massachusetts marched in with Governor Orr of South Carolina. The reaction of the North can be savored in the staccato report of the New York *Tribune:* "Had Barnum and his happy family suddenly appeared, they could not have created more astonishment. The convention was on its feet in an instant. . . . Soon the burly form of . . . Orr was seen moving up the left aisle, holding by the arm a frightful looking specimen [General Couch] who appeared more like his captive than his friend." Spectators and delegates cheered, ladies waved their handkerchiefs and the band rendered *Rally Round the Flag* and topped it off with *Dixie.*

General Dix, as temporary chairman, delivered the main address of the Tuesday session. He conceded that "things need to be done" in the administration of the government "and others need to be undone . . . But we shall not have the power to carry out these until we change the political complexion of Congress. This should be our first and our immediate aim." Dix thus sounded the purpose of the meeting which, in the words of Raymond, was "simply to seek the election of members of Congress favorable to the admission of loyal representatives" from the South.

By Wednesday morning the Wigwam was finished and gaily decorated with flags. The crowd, assembling at ten o'clock, was good-humored and noisy. Senator James Rood Doolittle of Wisconsin, one of the masterminds of the event, had been elected permanent chairman. A vigorous man, radiating good health and good will, a masterly lawyer much in demand as a speaker on religious topics, the unswerving Administration Republican delivered Wednesday's major address in a powerful and melodic voice.

At the third and final session on Thursday Raymond read a declaration of principles: ten resolutions, including endorsements of Southern representation in Congress as a constitutional right and the eqvality of states in making amendments. "We call upon you, therefore," he wound up, "by every consideration of your own dignity and safety, and in the name of liberty throughout the world, to complete the work of restoration and peace, which the President of the United States has so well begun."

Then the convention adjourned and on Saturday a committee of seventy, headed by Reverdy Johnson of Maryland, called at the White House to present the Declaration of Principles to the President. Johnson was in good spirits and full of ginger.

"We have seen hanging upon the verge of the government, as it were," he told his visitors, "a body called, or which assumes to be, the Congress of the United States, while, in fact, it is a Congress of only a part of the states. We have seen this Congress pretend to be for the Union, when its every step and act tended to perpetuate disunion . . . We have seen Congress gradually encroach . . . upon constitutional rights . . . We have seen a Congress in a minority assume to exercise power which, allowed to be consummated, would result in despotism or monarchy itself."

Having delivered himself of these tart statements, Johnson thanked the committee. Then with his daughter, Martha, he went across for dinner at the Sewards, where the guest of honor was 28-year-old Queen Emma of the Sandwich Islands, "a very agreeable body," according to Orville Browning, with a "good bust and neck." Apparently a good time was had by all at this gathering, the President little realizing that his uncomplimentary remarks of the afternoon would later be cited by the House as a high crime and a misdemeanor and made the basis of one of the Articles of Impeachment.

The immediate reaction of the public to the Philadelphia convention was favorable. There was a longing throughout the North to see the country once again really united. People were warmed by the spectacle of Northern and Southern politicians sitting down together in harmony. They were impressed by the caliber of the Southern delegates and by the sincerity of their speeches. After months of listening to the Radical tale of a South rotten with violence and disloyalty, it was good to hear responsible Southern spokesmen say that this was not so, that their people were more than ready to abide by the outcome of the war. The enthusiasm of the public wormed its way even into one of the Radical newspapers. The Springfield (Mass.) *Republican* predicted that the stand taken by the Southern delegates would "command respect among the people. It is in vain to assail it with . . . contempt. It will be found to be a reality, and no sham."

But the spirit of good will generated in Philadelphia could not endure for the reason that once the convention was over, it was over. Like a bonfire it was effective only as long as it lasted. No third party emerged, no permanent rallying point for those favorable to what the President was trying to do.

The Radical press loosed a blast of invective and ridicule. The meeting was labeled the "arm-in-arm convention" and much was made of the embarrassment of its sponsors when three Copperheads presented their credentials as delegates and with some difficulty were persuaded to withdraw. The New York *Tribune* observed that a new party "is a vegetable of slow growth and, although Mr. Johnson may plant, and Mr. Seward may water, and other gentlemen may brandy-and-water, with unflagging assiduity, the 'increase' may prove insignificantly small." For once Mr. Greeley's *Tribune,* not always a reliable prophet, was correct. Long before the fall elections the impact of the Philadelphia convention had spent itself.

In September the Radicals countered with two conventions of their own, also in Philadelphia. For five riotous days and nights there were oratory and resolution-passing and much belaboring of the Administration by such Southern anti-Johnsonites as Brownlow of Tennessee. Later the same month the soldiers and sailors of the country favorable to Johnson staged a convention in Cleveland. Still later soldiers and sailors favorable to the Radicals convened in Pittsburgh, with Ben Butler in a starring role.

While the country was being treated to this orgy of conventioneering, an important decision was made at the White House. The President had been invited to Chicago to assist in ceremonies connected with laying the cornerstone of a monument to the late Senator Stephen Douglas. Johnson had never had the slightest use for the "Little Giant" but he accepted the invitation, simultaneously announcing that during his journey he would deliver a series of speeches in defense of his program. Earlier in the year, in a talk to a Southern delegation, he had used the expression "swing around the circle of the Union." His words were remembered and the newspapers appropriated them to designate his journey to Chicago.

Early in the morning of August 28, 1866—at seven-thirty to be exact—Johnson left the White House, accompanied by a party of friends and aides, to begin his famous "swing around the circle," the first large-scale attempt by an American President to carry his cause directly to the people.

XVI

THE SWING AND THE ELECTION

Preparations for the Swing Around the Circle* kept the White House in a bustle throughout the early weeks of August. Except for Welles, who didn't like "pageants," all of the members of the Cabinet were enthusiastic about the project. Stanton was especially so, a fact which gave Welles an idea which he passed on to Johnson.

"Take the War Minister along," was his suggestion. He surmised that the Radicals would do some heckling or worse along the line, and reasoned that if Old Mars were standing beside the President on the speakers' platform, the Radicals would hesitate to throw anything harder than words. It was assumed, in view of Stanton's vociferous approval of the trip, that he could not possibly refuse to go. But he did, alleging his wife's bad health.

In the end the party consisted of about thirty persons, including a number of reporters headed by L. A. Gobright of the Associated

---

* The account of the Swing in this chapter rests to an unusual extent on Everette Swinney's unpublished Master-of-Arts thesis, *Andrew Johnson's Swing around the Circle: the Study of an Appeal to the People* (the Pennsylvania State University, the Graduate School Department of History, August, 1957) and generally speaking Mr. Swinney's analysis of the effect of the Swing on the Election has been followed.

Press. There were three members of the Cabinet. Randall utilized the trip to tend to post-office business and was not always on hand, but Welles was at the President's side from first to last and so was Seward until an illness, toward the end, forced him to cut short his trip. Other members of the tour were General Grant, General Custer, Admiral Farragut, the President's secretary, Colonel Moore, and his reporter-friend, Ben Truman. A social touch was given by several ladies, including Mrs. Welles, Mrs. Farragut and the President's daughter and hostess, Mrs. Patterson.

A sparkling sun warmed Washington on the morning of departure, August 28, 1866. The excursionists laughed and joked among themselves as their carriages rolled out of the White House drive and along breeze-swept streets lined with waving citizens. Among those seeing them off at the station were Secretary McCulloch, kept in Washington by pressing business at the Treasury, and Orville Browning.

The trip began in three special cars, with a fourth set aside for baggage, attached to a regular train. There was a change at Baltimore where the City Fathers and the Marines from Fort McHenry escorted the party from the Camden Street to the President Street depot through cheering onlookers in a scene that the Radical New York *Tribune* admitted was "enthusiastic beyond description." The day's journey ended at Philadelphia where that evening Johnson delivered his first major address. The city council had refused to prepare an official welcome and the Radicals had circulated false rumors as to the time of arrival. Even so the Presidential party was greeted by a crowd that had waited for hours and that blackened Broad Street for blocks beyond the station.

Next morning's journey to Camden, New Jersey, was by water on the steamer *States Rights*. Camden was reached too late to catch the regular train north but William Gatzner, president of the Camden and Amboy Railroad, took care of that. Hastily outfitting a three-car special and splashing it with flags and streamers, he put the happy tourists aboard and joined a noisy band of well-wishers in seeing them off.

The trip northward at an average speed of 30 miles an hour was broken by whistle-stops with demonstrations at every station. At Burlington an admiring crowd came close to pulling the President from the train platform. Cannon roared the expedition in and out of Trenton. At Elizabeth a gathering hailed the President as "Old Gibraltar." At Newark the citizens had set up a speaking stand but the crowd was so heavy the police were unable to cut a path for Johnson, who spoke briefly from the train.

New York's welcome was official and spectacular. At 10:30 Wednesday morning a citizens' committee headed by A. J. Stewart, the merchant prince, ferried to Jersey City to greet the party on its arrival there. On the return trip, two revenue cutters escorted the ferryboat *Colden* and joined the government forts and the vessels in the harbor in frequent salutes. On the New York side Johnson walked arm-in-arm with Mayor John T. Hoffman to an open barouche. Sixty-five vehicles made up the cavalcade which moved slowly through dense and lustily-shouting throngs to City Hall. Buildings along the route were ablaze with decorations. A huge strip of muslin across the front of the Appleton Building bore the words: "Welcome to the President of our whole country. With malice toward none, with charity for all.—Lincoln." An arch erected at Broadway and Fulton displayed the statement, "The Constitution: Washington established it; Lincoln defended it; Johnson will preserve it."

There were speeches in the Governor's room at City Hall. It was old stamping ground for Secretary Seward, once Governor of New York. Mayor Hoffman assured Johnson that the greeting he had received was not merely that due his office but a tribute "to the fidelity, ability and patriotism" of his administration. Deeply moved the President replied haltingly, his words almost inaudible. Then the parade was resumed, up Broadway, Johnson standing in his carriage, hat in hand, bowing from side to side.

At a banquet that evening at Delmonico's, Johnson developed most of the themes that he would sound over and over in the course of his Swing.

On the purpose of his trip: "All that is wanting in the great struggle in which we are engaged is simply to develop the popular heart of the nation. It is like a latent fire. All that is necessary is a sufficient amount of friction to develop" it. The President's objective in coming to the people, he said, was to provide this.

On Reconstruction: Southern extremists, he declared, had tried to dissolve the Union by rebellion. Now Northern extremists were trying to keep the Union dissolved by denying the Southern states "their representation in the Senate and House." The loyal people of the country had put down the Southern rebellion by force of arms. He now called on those same people to put down the Northern rebellion by voting for pro-administration candidates in the forthcoming election.

On his pardon policy: "In imitation of Him of old who died for the preservation of men, I [have] exercised that mercy which I believed to be my duty."

On nationalism: He reiterated his conviction that the war had been fought to preserve the Union, not to assert the power of the Federal government over the states.

The next morning as the procession reached Central Park, General Grant, riding in a magnificent barouche, grabbed the reins from his driver, and challenged any of the other carriages to a race. The President ordered his driver, a Mr. Hewitt, to accept. Two and a half miles farther North, after a lively spurt, he conceded defeat with a wave of his hat.

The speech Johnson had given in New York was a forerunner of all the major addresses of the tour. Here and there he introduced additional themes. At Albany he took public notice for the first time of the Radical smear campaign. He spoke of the "slander and calumny" directed against him and asked, "Fellow citizens of the United States, what is it I have done to thus expose me? . . . If my crime consists of supporting the Constitution of the country, I stand before you tonight confessedly guilty . . . But I have no objection and am willing to place our case before you as a jury. From my early life I have always been willing for the American people to be my triers. It is on them in the past I have relied. It is on them I now rely."

In another address, at another place, Johnson spoke of the Southerners: "This great government cannot get along without the South. . . . Large as it is, it is not large enough to divide . . . I am one of those who believe that a man may sin and do wrong, and after that may do right. If all of us who have sinned were put to death . . . there would not be many of us left."

From Albany the party headed for Auburn, Seward's home. There were stops en route at Schenectady and at Syracuse there was an amazing demonstration staged, according to the Radical Chicago *Tribune,* by 30,000 people. At Salina the President was obviously moved as he stepped onto the train platform to find himself looking out over a dense mass of humanity.

On the first of September, the party reached Niagara Falls. Here Johnson told an uproariously enthusiastic audience that he would prefer to be remembered in history "as the instrument of restoring or participating in the restoration" of the Southern States "and the reconciliation of the people than to be President forty times." Niagara Falls marked the end of the northeastern arc of the Swing. So far the tour had been a series of triumphs and there would be more triumphs before it was over. But the troubles of which Welles and others were apprehensive were in the offing.

They began at Cleveland where the Presidential party arrived shortly after dark on the evening of Monday, September 3. The strain of the journey was beginning to tell on Johnson who was unusually weary, as Welles noted with concern. The crowd waiting at the depot was unprecedented and on the whole friendly, although there were expressions of disappointment when it was learned that Grant, taken ill, had left the others temporarily and was proceeding by boat to Detroit. When the President stepped onto the hotel balcony, Bank and St. Clair Streets below him were jammed with people. Basically the crowd was orderly and respectful, but there was a scattering of drunken rowdies. The President had no sooner begun speaking than the heckling began. Welles was convinced that it was prearranged and a few days later a friend wrote Johnson that forty or fifty men had been planted in the crowd by the local Union League.

"What about Moses?" he was asked. The reference, of course, was to Johnson's offer to the Negroes of Nashville, in the autumn of 1864, to be their champion. The President's reply was in his sharpest manner. He reminded them that their own state, Ohio, allowed only whites to vote. "Let your Negroes vote," he snapped, "before you talk about Negroes voting in Louisiana. Take the beam out of your own eye before you see the mote in your neighbor's."

"What about New Orleans?" he was asked. When the President replied that the riot there was Radical-inspired he reaped a torrent of boos, hisses—and approving cheers. When he started to say that Lincoln, had he lived, would have pursued a lenient reconstruction policy, he was not allowed to finish. The hecklers did not always get the upper hand. When Johnson said "that he that is opposed to the restoration . . . of the states is as great a traitor as Jeff Davis, and I am against both of them," the applause was so great that the catcalls were drowned out. "I love my country," Johnson thundered, "and I defy any man to put his finger upon anything to the contrary. Then what is my offense?" Someone in the audience sent up an answer: "You ain't a Radical!" Almost simultaneously another listener called out "Veto!" The President shot back: "If you do not understand what the Freedmen's Bureau bill is, I can tell you." Someone cried "Tell us!" and the President did so. He saw no point, he said, in freeing the slaves from their onetime masters and then turning them over to a powerful Federal bureau that was costing the taxpayers "a fraction less than twelve million dollars" a year. "Farewell!" said Johnson finally. "The little ill-feelings aroused here tonight—for some men have felt a little ill—let us not cherish them . . . In parting with you . . . let me invoke the blessing of God upon you, expressing my sincere thanks for the cordial manner in which you have received me."

It goes without saying that it would have been more dignified of

Johnson, more in keeping with his high office, if he had ignored the hecklers. But the habits picked up in Tennessee were strong, and reading the various and somewhat contradictory accounts of the scene at Cleveland it is easy to get the impression that the President found the exchange exhilarating. Welles found it depressing. He said as much to Seward, but Seward could see no harm in the President's trading a few words with his audience. The President, Seward thought, "was doing good and was the best stump speaker in the country." Welles' comment was that the President should not be a stump speaker at all.

Toledo was a great success but at Newark the President once again was troubled by hecklers. A man standing near the platform kept bellowing "New Orleans!" "I should like to see that fellow," Johnson said, whereupon according to the New York *World,* the President's friends pushed into view "a billious, cadaverous, brazen, wall-eyed, red-headed object, of the lower stratum of mankind." Johnson stared. "Ah, there you are!" he said. "I thought you would look just about so!"

Ann Arbor turned out to be another trouble spot. A welcoming address, complimentary to the Administration, was delivered by Erastus O. Haven, president of the University of Michigan. In his reply Johnson said that those favorable to disunion must take pause. At this point a group in his audience sent up three cheers for Congress. "What has Congress done to restore the Union?" Johnson wanted to know. This statement produced such confusion that the President was unable to finish his speech.

Chicago was reached on Wednesday, September 5. At next day's ceremonies for the late Senator Douglas, Johnson gave a short, dignified and non-political talk. At Springfield Grant received the longest and loudest ovation but the multitude awaiting the train treated the President with respect. Carriages bore the visitors to Oakwood Cemetery. Arriving there they disembarked in silence and, forming a line of twos, walked arm-in-arm, wordlessly, around the tomb of Lincoln.

At Alton, Illinois, on a clear and sunny Saturday morning, the party left the train and crossed the Mississippi on the steamer *Andy Johnson*. On the opposite shore they transferred to the *Ruth* for the remainder of their journey down-river. As they approached St. Louis, shortly before four in the afternoon, they were met by barges filled with shouting people. Johnson was no sooner in Lindell Hotel than an immense throng, gathering outside, clamored for a speech and the President, appearing on the balcony, gave a short talk. The evening was given over to a banquet at the Southern Hotel. Johnson spoke both at the banquet and later, at the request of a crowd gathered outside, from the hotel balcony. Although this second oration was one of the best-received on the Swing, it contained several of the passages that the Radicals would later turn against Johnson. Not the least of these was one in which he took note of the fact that frequently he had been castigated as a Judas. "There was a Judas once," he recalled, "one of the twelve apostles. Oh! yes, and these twelve apostles had a Christ . . . If I have played the Judas, who has been my Christ . . . ? Was it Thad Stevens? Was it Wendell Phillips? Was it Charles Sumner?"

After Terre Haute came Indianapolis, for Johnson the most distressing experience of the Swing. For two hours, after the President's arrival at the hotel, a mammoth crowd outside kept up a running demand for Grant. The racket was deafening when Johnson and some of the members of his party appeared on the balcony. Johnson started to speak: "Fellow-citizens, it is not my intention to make a long speech. If you will give me your attention for five minutes—." The interruptions became a solid roar, voices in the crowd yelling "No, we want nothing to do with traitors!", an expression that had been thrown at Johnson at other points along the Swing. A chorus of "Grant! Grant!" set in. Johnson tried again: "I would like to say to this crowd here tonight—." Again his words were drowned out, this time by cries of "Shut up! We don't want to hear you!" Johnson hesitated for a few minutes and then left the balcony.

After dinner he came out again, and again his attempt to speak was drowned out by the jeers of the crowd. Again he retired, leaving behind him a tumult. A man carrying a placard welcoming the

President to the city was knocked down and shot at. A friend, hastening to his aid, fired at his attacker. Within seconds the shooting had become general. The police appeared, but before order could be restored one man had been killed, several wounded. The body of the dead man, a Radical by the name of Stuart, was carried away by his friends, who then held a giant meeting at Masonic Hall.

The remaining five days of the tour took the party across Ohio, Pennsylvania and Maryland. There were large crowds at every stop. Most of them were respectful, but at a few points the President was prevented from speaking. When the train halted at New Market, Ohio, some thirty men raised three cheers for Thaddeus Stevens. The President did not attempt to speak, but General Custer made a brief appearance. "I was born two miles and a half from here," the General told the crowd, "but I am ashamed of you." At Steubenville, also in Ohio, there was another mob. The President appeared but expressed doubts that he would be allowed to speak. Many begged him to do so. To them he gave his thanks. To the others he quoted a couplet, based on one of William Cowper's poems, that he had used often in the United States Senate:

"A clever, sensible, well-bred man
Will not insult me, no other can."

Pittsburgh was a second Indianapolis. A throng too large and too unruly for the police to manage greeted the President and his friends as they reached the city. When Johnson appeared on the balcony of the St. Charles for his first talk, Wood Street was choked with people. There were cries of "Tell us about New Orleans" as he started speaking. Some ten minutes later a Radical parade with brass bands marched by. Amidst hoots and cheers, taunts and hurrahs the President said, "I bid you good night," and withdrew. During the evening a banquet audience heard him out attentively and applauded his remarks.

Johnstown, Pa., one of the stops of the next day, was the scene of a catastrophe. A platform, hastily erected for spectators near the railroad station, collapsed as Senator Cowan was introducing the military members of Johnson's party. Breaking in the center, the platform dropped five hundred people twenty feet. Eight died immediately, several others later, and more than a hundred were seriously hurt. Johnson left one of his military aides behind to supervise the rescue work and contributed generously to a fund for those made helpless by the tragedy.

At seven o'clock on the evening of Saturday, September 15, two howitzers on a nearby hill boomed a salute as Engine No. 269, patriotically decorated, pulled the train bearing the Presidential party into the depot of the National Capital.

The tour was over. The President had been away from his desk nineteen days. During this period his opponents had mounted against him a tirade of abuse and distortion beyond anything they had instigated before. The old charge of drunkenness invaded the Radical press. The Muscatine (Iowa) *Journal* called the Swing "nothing more or less than a big drunk . . . a President of the United States reeling to Chicago." The wide credence given the drunken charge becomes fantastic when the simple physical data are put on view. During his less than three-weeks' absence from the White House, 59-year-old Andrew Johnson journeyed 2,000 miles, enduring all the discomforts of nineteenth century travel, and delivered eleven major and twenty-two minor speeches! Not to mention the banquets, the parades, the conferences, and the whistle stops. There were ladies along and highly respectable ones at that.

Ridicule was the Radicals' chief weapon. Thaddeus Stevens set the tone by designating the Swing "a very remarkable circus" which "sometimes cut outside the circle and entered into street brawls with common blackguards."

The manner in which Johnson prepared and conducted his tour made the task of his detractors relatively easy. It was his practice on a speaking tour to make what amounted to only one speech, adding topics and otherwise revising it as he moved from place to place. This system had worked well in Tennessee. Newspapers were few and far between there and usually Johnson's old speech was new to each new audience. Such was not the case in the North where once he had delivered his speech a couple of times, its elements were pretty well known to potential listeners along the line.

Another handicap was that Johnson was not popular with the press. Toward the end of his term in the White House, as we shall see, he developed a keen sense of what would later be called "public relations." But this sense had not made its appearance at the time of the Swing. Johnson's faith in the wisdom of the people was strong to the point of being naive. He was under the impression that if he conducted his office honestly and conscientiously the people would recognize this fact and see through the attempts of his enemies to misrepresent him. He made no effort to ingratiate himself with the newspaper men. As Military Governor of Tennessee, struggling with innumerable and difficult tasks, he had given the reporters short shrift. Some of those covering the Swing had suffered from his brusqueness then and now jumped at the chance to get back at him.

He was a superb speaker. When in his declining years Oliver Perry Temple, one of the President's most critical political foes in Tennessee, put down his recollections of things past, he declared that the difference between reading and hearing a Johnson speech was the "difference between reading a piece of music by note and hearing [it] rendered by a great master." Temple would go to his grave remembering Johnson's "magnetic voice, the action, the earnestness, the fire, the subtle contagion of sympathy and understanding passing from speaker to hearer." Welles, who was worried about the sort of treatment Johnson's speeches were receiving, could see that Johnson's "remarks were effective among his hearers and that within that circle he won supporters."

Unfortunately for his cause, the number of people who got their impression of the Swing from actually hearing Johnson were a drop in the bucket compared with those who got their impression from reading the "partisan press." Everette Swinney, in the perceptive study of the Swing which has been followed in portions of this chapter, has estimated that about a million people heard Johnson talk. But this figure ceases to be impressive when lined up with circulation figures.

The Republicans controlled sixty per cent of the newspapers and magazines in the North, and there were approximately 2,119 Republican journals with a combined circulation of about 4,853,566.

The picture of the Swing obtained by the great majority of Americans was the one purveyed by the Republican press. The burden of its message was that Johnson, sallying forth from the White House in a shameful defiance of tradition, had clowned his way around the country, sullying and besmirching his high office. Johnson was not undignified because he could not be. Spiritually and mentally he was a large man, and everything he did was large, including his mistakes. Welles noticed that the President never indulged in personalities in private conversation. What he had to say about his enemies he said from a public platform, under circumstances which made it easy for them to strike back if they so desired. Toward those men who fought him openly—Stevens and Sumner, for example—he harbored no resentment. He did come to have contempt for Secretary Stanton, not because Old Mars fought him but because he did so two-facedly. But even on Stanton, as his biographer Robert W. Winston puts it, Johnson "wasted no anger."

During the Swing Old Mars indulged in his usual shenanigans. At Cabinet meetings in early August he was loudest of any member in his approval of the forthcoming tour. When Johnson returned to Washington there was Stanton, all smiles and handshakes, at the forefront of the throng gathered at the depot to welcome the President home. But while Johnson was away Old Mars penned a letter to his friend, Congressman James Mitchel Ashley of Ohio, pronouncing the tour scandalous and predicting that "disrespect and demoralization must follow."

"The leading event of the past week," Godkin's magazine the *Nation* summed up, "has been the President's tour . . . It was a gross political mistake, in the present condition of the public mind, for him to take the field as a stump speaker, as it converts the campaign, so far as he is concerned, rather into a context of persons than of principles, brings out his personal defects into unhappy prominence, and causes them to tell terribly against the cause he advocates . . ."

Shortly after Johnson's return to Washington the fall elections for members of the Fortieth Congress began. In the first landslide in American history, the Radicals piled up a smashing victory. Numerically the lineup in Congress remained about the same (185 Republicans and 60 Democrats) but the re-election of leading Radicals, the addition of Ben Butler to the House and Morton to the Senate, and the overwhelming sweep of the Republican vote gave the Radicals, for the first time, unchallenged control of both houses and sufficient strength to override any Presidential vetoes of Radical legislation.

An assumption, prevalent at the time and later endorsed by many historians, was that Johnson's Swing was chiefly responsible for the Radical victory. But this is a view with which it is difficult to agree. The conclusions of Swinney, based on a minute study of the returns, are that generally speaking the people of the North voted as they had been voting for the last eight years. The only significant shift occurred in those parts of the country where Johnson, during the Swing, was actually seen and heard—and that shift was favorable to the President. On this basis Swinney concludes that the Swing was "mildly successful." Unfortunately, like the stillborn third-party movement that culminated in the Philadelphia arm-in-arm Convention, it was a case of too late. The damage had been done before Johnson left the White House to take his cause to the people.

Had there been a third party in the field the voters could have chosen between pro-Johnson and anti-Johnson Republicans. In the absence of such a party no such opportunity was given for the reason that the Radicals controlled the Republican election machine. Moreover the Radicals worked hard at keeping the real issues out of sight by the simple device of relentlessly attacking the

President. Their aim, carried off with tremendous success, was to convince the Northern people that if they supported the President he would promptly turn the country over to Southern rebels and the people would then lose at the ballot-box what they had won on the battlefield.

The election results were no endorsement of the extreme schemes of the Radicals. In fact, those schemes were not yet clearly or widely understood. One of the most popular magazines was *Harper's Weekly,* then under the editorship of George William Curtis. In November, surveying the fall balloting, *Harper's Weekly* interpreted the results to mean that the people wanted a Congress that would see to it that the Fourteenth Amendment was ratified and that the unrepresented states were then brought back into the Union.

The impression thus echoed in *Harper's Weekly* was general among the voters. They had not voted against restoration; they had merely voted for restoration by Congress rather than by the President. They most certainly had not voted for that continuation of the breach between North and South that the Radicals were planning. The people did not want to see the war continued; they wanted to see it ended.

They were not to get what they had voted for. The Radicals interpreted the results to suit themselves. To use a twentieth-century phrase, they took them to be a green light. Now they no longer need confine themselves simply to stalling the President's program. Now they could substitute their own. The South and by extension the entire country was in for trouble.

XVII

RADICAL RECONSTRUCTION

On Saturday, March 2, 1867, a few hours before its final adjournment, the 39th Congress passed over the President's veto a modified version of a bill that Thaddeus Stevens had framed and unsuccessfully sought to put through months before. Entitled "An act to provide for the more efficient Government of the Rebel States," the law destroyed the reconstruction program of Lincoln and Johnson and replaced it with that of the Radicals.

All of the state governments of the South, except that of Tennessee, were declared invalid and merely provisional until such time as new ones were created. In his veto message, which Burton J. Hendrick in his *Bulwark of the Republic* calls "one of the greatest state papers in Presidential literature," Johnson's comment on this provision was that to "pronounce the supreme law-making power of an established state illegal is to say that law itself is unlawful." The President's observation would be echoed later by the verdict of the constitutional authority, Professor John W. Burgess, that "There was hardly a line in the entire bill which would stand the test of the Constitution"; it was "tantamount to the creation of a new sort of Union with another kind of Constitution by an Act of Congress."

Almost a year earlier the President had proclaimed that the

Civil War was over and Congress had concurred in this action. Stevens' reconstruction law proclaimed it on again. For the first time in American peacetime history a large section of the country was placed under military rule. The ten unrepresented states were divided into five districts, each to be commanded by a general officer appointed by the President. In disregard of a recent ruling of the Supreme Court the district commanders were authorized, whenever they saw fit, to suspend the writ of *habeas corpus* and to set up military courts to try civilians for all breaches of law.

All that Johnson had done in the South was to be done over in a different way. This time all male citizens of the proper age, regardless of color, were to vote and hold office except those excluded by Section 3 of the not-yet-ratified Fourteenth Amendment and those "disfranchised by rebellion." Each state was to hold a convention and frame a constitution, enfranchising the Negroes and disfranchising an uncertain number of whites. The new constitution must be ratified by popular vote and approved by Congress. Finally the legislature of the government thus created must ratify the Fourteenth. Once a state had done all these things, it became eligible for readmission to the Union.

Convening on March 4, 1867, immediately after the close of its predecessor, the 40th Congress found loopholes in Stevens' law and an attempt was made to plug these up by supplementary acts. According to Stevens' law the vote could be denied to any white Southerner "disfranchised by rebellion." But what did that phrase mean? Nobody knew, for the reason that there was no law on the Federal statute books forbidding Southerners to vote because they had given aid and comfort to the Confederacy. Consequently there was no legal definition of the phrase, "disfranchised by rebellion." So one of the supplementary acts "clarified" the ambiguous words in a curious way. For all practical purposes the determination of which white Southerners could vote was left up to the military commander in each district. He, of course, delegated this authority to the registration boards. In actual practice then whether a white

Southerner could vote or not was decided arbitrarily by his local board, from whose decision there was no appeal. Another supplementary act set up the machinery by which the Southern people were to establish what Old Thad had once spoken of as their "model Republics," which is to say their new Radical governments.

Such was Radical Reconstruction in law. What it was in fact is an often-told tale and not a very pleasant one. There began for most of the South an era of unrest and violence and corruption in government. Without meaning to simplify the procedures by which Radical Reconstruction was overthrown, it can be said that long before the compromise of 1877, which gave the Republicans the White House and returned home rule to the entire South, the whole shabby structure was beginning to fall of its own weight, condemned and disavowed by the American people, North and South alike.

At the close of the war there were in the South about 260,000 Negroes who had lived in freedom all or most of their lives and to whom, therefore, the privileges and responsibilities of freedom were no novelty. Louisiana alone had at least 30,000 such Negroes. Descendants of the original French and Spanish settlers, many of them could point to ancestors who had fought in the war of 1812 under Andrew Jackson. All but a thousand of them were literate; many were highly cultured. A few were already voters due to special legislative acts. Some owned plantations and the group as a whole owned fifteen million dollars worth of property.

Had the Southern states, shortly after the war, seen fit to introduce Negro suffrage gradually by first enfranchising the free Negroes, it is hard to believe that Radical Reconstruction would ever have materialized. When it did materialize, its quantitative effect on the Negroes was startling. During the summer of 1867—overnight, so to speak—703,000 Southern Negroes were registered as voters.

Some of them became delegates to the conventions which framed the new state constitutions—constitutions which, for the most part, were excellent. Soon thousands of them were occupying such minor local offices as constable, justice of the peace and superintendent of education. One was elevated to the bench of a state supreme court. Two became Lieutenant Governors, one of them eventually occupying the Governor's chair after his superior had been impeached and removed. Some were elected to the new state legislatures, their numbers varying from one in the legislature of Tennessee to a majority in some sessions of the legislatures of South Carolina and Louisiana. In due time, as the states were readmitted to the Union, twenty-eight of them were sent to Washington as Representatives and Senators.

Many of the Negro officeholders and law-makers were competent and turned in good performances. But those who were born and bred in slavery had been kept in illiteracy and were unprepared. And since history is not so much what we remember as how we remember it, later generations would often speak of Radical Reconstruction as "Negro rule." But when one considers the circumstances under which the Negroes were so abruptly called upon to vote and hold office, the term becomes a misnomer and a cruel jest.

It was Radical rule of course. Many groups in the South were hurt by it, but no single group was more seriously or lastingly damaged than the Negroes. There is no satisfactory evidence that if Radical Reconstruction had been averted, the Negro would have had an easy time of it. On the contrary the passage of the Black Codes, long before Radical Reconstruction was even dreamed of, suggests that at no time were Southern leaders interested in helping the Negro to achieve full citizenship. The fact remains that Radical Reconstruction only worsened the situation. All the Negro got out of it was increased enmity on the part of the white South. In after years the memory of "Negro rule" would serve as an excuse for the passage of the Jim Crow laws, the "grandfather clauses" and the other devices by which the progress of the Negro was made difficult, if not impossible. Granted that Andrew Johnson was no real champion of the former slaves, the Southern Negroes might have fared better under the President than they did under their Congress.

The foremost idea in the minds of the string-pullers in Washington, irrespective of how much true humanitarianism was operative, was the vote. "I know that I love thee because you can vote," ran a contemporary parody on Radical thinking. In the beginning, however, the freedmen did not have the voting habit. Many a freedman at this juncture would have welcomed "40 acres and a mule" or any economic assistance aimed at alleviating poverty and disease. But as a group the former slaves were not too interested in the franchise for the reason that they did not yet fully understand its value. In a frenzied effort to get indifferent Negroes to the polls, General John Pope, commander of the Third district, paid registrars as much as 40 cents for every name obtained. Highly effective as a vote-getter was the Union League, the Northern Republican organization that had been imported into the South where its branches were usually spoken of as Loyal Leagues. These Leagues and similar groups were instrumental in getting thousands of Negroes to the polls to vote the Republican ticket.

At the beginning of Radical Reconstruction the procedures under which a state could gain readmission to the Union were intricate and slow-moving. As time went on the Radicals eased the process, impelled by concerns having to do with the Presidential election coming up in the fall of 1868. In the North the Democrats were gaining strength and there was some fear among Republican leaders that their candidate could not win without the electoral votes of the Southern states. So those states had to be pulled back into the Union and fast. In all the Radicals passed four Reconstruction laws. The second provided that in any Southern election for the purpose of ratifying a state constitution at least one half of the registered voters must participate. The fourth law repealed this provision. The laws were eased in other ways and in some instances their stricter provisions were simply ignored. The result was that in June of 1868, well in advance of the election and only a few weeks before the Fourteenth Amendment became part of the Constitution, seven more Southern states were readmitted to the Union.

The most dramatic development of Andrew Johnson's administration, the attempt of his enemies to remove him from office by impeachment, raises a tantalizing question. Why did the leaders of Congress go to the enormous bother of trying to depose a President who had long since, and irretrievably, lost all ability to interfere in a substantial way with their legislative programs?

On the surface of it, their purpose was to halt his stubborn and persistent opposition to their reconstruction plans. But they did not have to remove Johnson to have their way about reconstruction. They already had their way. By 1868, when they finally got around to impeaching him, they had scuttled his reconstruction program and substituted their own. One way or another they had made it difficult for him to exercise many of his constitutional powers, hamstringing him to the point where even if they failed to oust him, he would still be unable to wrest control of the South from their hands.

There was the further fact that his term of office was almost over. Nor was there any reason to believe that he could be elected to another. True, his presence in the White House was annoying and sheer hatred of the man may have played a role in the flow of events. Yet the fact remains that the Radical leaders had only to bide their time in patience for a few months and Andrew Johnson would be out of their way. They did not wait, and for this they had compelling reasons.

PART THREE

The Victory

XVIII

FIRST IMPEACHMENT ATTEMPT

In essence, of course, to impeach a civic official is to indict him. It is to accuse him of acts which, if he be found guilty, make him unfit to continue in office. We know from James Madison's account of the debates in the Federal Convention in Philadelphia in the spring and summer of 1787 that the Founding Fathers gave long and earnest thought to the question of impeachment.

Some of the Constitution-makers, notably Gouverneur Morris of Pennsylvania, thought the President should not be subject to impeachment at all. Some body of men, Morris reasoned, would have to be given the authority to impeach. What was to prevent this body from using its power to make a creature of the Chief Magistrate, thus destroying the independence of the Executive? Later Morris bowed to the arguments of the other side. History, he agreed, showed many examples of countries suffering because they could not rid themselves of corrupt or oppressive rulers. Then, too, impeachment was a safety valve. Given a legal way to depose the President the people would be less inclined to try to do so by armed revolt.

Once the delegates had agreed that impeachment was necessary, there arose the problem of how its dangers were to be avoided.

Who should have the authority to bring the charge? Serious consideration was given to lodging this power with the states, to be exercised through their legislatures, their chief judges or their executives. Only after lengthy discussion was there almost unanimous agreement that the safest depository for such power was the lower, most numerous and most representative House of Congress.

Once an official was impeached, who should try him—the Federal courts, some special court, or the Senate? Again considerable discussion preceded the decision to select the Senate.

Most important of all, what sort of acts justified removal from office? From the beginning there was agreement that no officer should be ousted for trivial reasons. The mildest words used in debate were "malpractice" and "neglect of duty." Toward the end of the session it was proposed that an officer be impeached "for treason, bribery or maladministration." Then "maladministration" was stricken as too broad. In the end the clause provided impeachment for "Treason, Bribery, or other High Crimes and Misdemeanors." In after years it would be the weight of legal opinion that the key words were "treason" and "bribery," that "High Crimes and Misdemeanors" meant acts of equal seriousness.

A reading of the debates settles one question beyond quibble. It was not the intent of the Founding Fathers that impeachment should be a political weapon. A President was not to be removed simply because his views differed from those of the Congressional majority.

In its final form the Constitution contained six clauses relevant to impeachment. One declared that a Federal official could be removed only if two-thirds of the Senators voted him "guilty" of the charges framed by the House. Another ruled that when the President was tried the presiding officer of the Senate, sitting as a court for the trial of impeachment, was not to be its regular chairman but the Chief Justice of the Supreme Court. Still another provided that if an official were convicted by the Senate he could be punished only by removal from office, although he would then be liable to "Indictment, Trial, Judgment and Punishment" by a regular court.

If the Founding Fathers did not wish impeachment to be used often, they did their work well. During the first 170 years of the life of the Constitution, only eleven individuals were impeached: a Senator, a Cabinet officer, eight Federal judges including an Associate Justice of the Supreme Court, and a President. The Senator was expelled but the impeachment case was dismissed on the grounds that he was not a civil officer within the meaning of the Constitution. Of the judges five, among them the Associate Justice, were acquitted. The President, of course, was Andrew Johnson.

Impeachment talk was in the air from the start of his administration. In February of 1866 there was a flurry of it after his veto of the Freedmen's Bureau bill, and his unfortunate Washington's Birthday address in front of the White House. In Chicago the Radical *Tribune* suggested that Congress force Johnson into an impeachable act by hedging him in "with law" and then removing "him from his office if he attempts to . . . break through or defy it."

In New York City George Templeton Strong, indefatigably keeping his wonderful diary, anticipated action to remove the Executive "within thirty days!!!" Once an admirer of Johnson, Strong was fast losing faith. His guess was that the charge on which the President would be brought to book was intoxication. In this contention he had the support of his friend, Dr. Cornelius Rea Agnew, who claimed that thanks to his "acquaintance with toxicology" he could tell just from reading the Washington's Birthday speech that Johnson was "more or less *drunk*" when he delivered it.

Ben Butler came onto the scene again during the election campaign in the fall of 1866. Throughout the early months of Johnson's regime Butler had laid low. Still hopeful of a post in the Cabinet, he kept in touch with the President, placing before him sundry proposals concerning the South. Only after it became unmistakably clear that Johnson did not intend to change course—or to make use of Butler's talents—did he join hands with his Radical friends in a large and open way.

When Butler decided to run for what would be the first of his four terms in the House of Representatives he encountered a snag. His own district, which was Middlesex, was represented by George S. Boutwell, who was running to succeed himself. Butler was averse to displacing Boutwell. For one thing the two were friends. For another Boutwell, a machine politician of mediocre abilities, was a tried-and-true Radical.

Butler solved the problem with his usual inventiveness. It so happened that there was a vacancy in the neighboring district of Essex. It also so happened that in 1863 Butler had purchased a plot of land near Gloucester in Essex for vacationing purposes— his "tent on the beach," he called it. Since there was nothing in the Massachusetts Constitution to prohibit such an expedient, he declared the tent his home for the time being and threw his hat into the Essex ring.

Sure of victory and never one to do things on a small scale, Butler wasted little time on the local gentry. Far and wide he roamed over the country, assuring his auditors everywhere that the minute he assumed his seat in the upcoming 40th Congress he would take steps to eliminate Andrew Johnson from public life. In Middlesex, Boutwell followed the same tack. They caused *Harper's Weekly* to assert that although Johnson's Presidency was "a national misfortune," so far he had given no cause for impeachment.

With or without cause, a strong impeachment sentiment was coursing through the halls of Congress long before March 4, 1867, when the gavel fell on the last meeting of the 39th only to fall again seconds later on the first of the 40th. A few weeks earlier the impeachment movement had gained recruits when Andrew Johnson exercised another of his monotonous vetoes. This time he disapproved a bill to give the vote to the Negroes of the District

of Columbia. Although Secretary Welles purported to see constitutional flaws in this measure, Johnson did not assume this high
ground in his veto message. He said it was unfair to compel the
District to engage in an experiment in Negro suffrage when most
of the states from which the sponsors of the bill came had refused
to do so. He thought it unfair to force Negro suffrage on the District when in a recent referendum the white citizens of its two communities, Washington and Georgetown, had voted 7663 to 36
against it. Ignoring the presence in the District, as in Louisiana, of
a substantial and educated body of free Negroes, the President
pointed to the fact that since the war thousands of former slaves
had poured into the national capital. Finally he predicted that
enfranchising the Negroes would lead to a war of races.

Congress, of course, passed the bill over Johnson's veto. Time
would prove his objections to it ill-grounded. The first District
municipal elections in which the Negroes participated were orderly
and without incident. In connection with the elections of 1868
and 1869, there were riotings of an undetermined and never-
properly-documented extent. But these were troubled years throughout the country. During this period there were also riotings in
connection with municipal elections in New York and San Francisco where almost no Negroes had voted. In 1871 Congress did
away with the mayor-council system in the District and substituted
a Territorial Legislature. In 1874 even this limited form of representative government was abolished and the District placed under
direct control of Congress. A twentieth-century study shows that
at the time of the abandonment of Home Rule, Negro suffrage was
working out well in the District, and that its abandonment was a
setback to the cause of democratic government.*

The initial move in the direction of the impeachment of
Andrew Johnson was made December 17, 1866, at the opening
of the 2d Session of the 39th when Congressman Ashley offered a

---

* See James H. Whyte, *The Uncivil War*, New York, 1958, p. 278-284
et passim.

resolution calling for an investigation of the President's conduct. Nothing came of this. The time was not ripe, but it would be soon.

James Mitchel Ashley, Representative from Ohio, was Secretary Stanton's friend. A resident of Toledo, where he had engaged for some years in the wholesale drug business, Congressman Ashley was short and fat with the face of a peevish cherub and a mass of unruly curls. There were no lengths to which he would not go in his effort to bring before Congress proof that Andrew Johnson was a traitor and a murderer. Not that he himself needed proof. In the words of the author of an unpublished biographical sketch, to Ashley "suspicion was evidence."* He was a headstrong man, and somewhat vain, blessed with the "courage of ignorance." He once gave serious thought to making a trip to Russia for the purpose of persuading the Greek Orthodox leaders to "challenge the western supremacy of Roman Catholicism."

To his warfare with Andrew Johnson he brought the accumulated passions of a picaresque life. Born near Pittsburgh in 1824, he grew up in a deeply religious atmosphere. His father was an itinerant Campbellite preacher, a man fashioned in the mould of the prophets of the Old Testament, who labored in the Lord's vineyard without compensation. At sixteen the boy ran away from a home too strict even for his ascetic inclinations. He got a job as a boot-black on an Ohio River steamer, saved his pennies—and spent them on a journey to the Old Homestead in Tennessee where the idol of his youth, Andrew Jackson, was still living. Hero-worshipping was one of Ashley's traits. In later years Salmon Portland Chase and Charles Sumner occupied his shrines. For some years he followed a variety of occupations; he edited first one and then another newspaper; and he studied law and medicine, neither of

---

* The unpublished sketch mentioned is part of a Master's thesis, "An Ohio Congressman in Reconstruction," prepared in 1916 for the Faculty of Political Science at Columbia University by Margaret Ashley (later Mrs. Paddock), granddaughter of James Mitchel Ashley. Mrs. Paddock's thesis is on file in the Special Collections room of the Columbia Library.

which he ever practiced. Elected to Congress for the first of five terms in 1858, he busied himself throughout the war in forwarding the good cause. He was demanding that the rebel states be treated as territories before Thaddeus Stevens. He was the first Radical in the House to seek legislation aimed at confiscating Confederate property on a wide scale. He introduced the bill which abolished slavery in the District of Columbia, was the first to propose what eventually became the Thirteenth Amendment and helped frame the Wade-Davis bill, the Radicals' first official pronunciamento on Reconstruction.

At his Toledo home at the time of the assassination, his reaction to Johnson's accession was that of the Radicals generally. Within hours after Lincoln's death he was writing the new President, offering his good wishes and prayers, suggesting the Honorable Daniel S. Dickinson of New York as successor to Secretary of State Seward. As chairman of the House Committee on Territories, he assured a San Francisco audience that Johnson was entitled to the respect of the country and that "It does not seem to me possible in view of the fact that the slave barons always feared him [Johnson] . . . that he can now hesitate to follow the logic of events."

En route from the Pacific Coast Ashley learned belatedly that not only had Johnson embraced Lincolnian reconstruction, but that the Federal Collector of Customs in San Francisco had been dismissed for presiding over a Radical meeting. Ashley was stunned and bewildered, but not for long. By the time the 39th Congress convened, Ashley had become a vessel of wrath.

Other Radicals might assume that Johnson had merely suffered a change of mind; not Ashley. He was certain that in 1864 the Republicans had unwittingly raised to the vice presidency a Democrat with whom the rebel leaders had quickly ingratiated themselves, knowing Johnson's "vanity, his unscrupulousness, his love of power, and his capacities as a demagogue." Playing upon these weaknesses, the Rebels had whispered sweet temptation in Johnson's ear and a bargain had been struck. The rebels would maneuver the murder of Lincoln and the elevation of Johnson. In return Johnson was to shield the rebels "from punishment and restore them to political power."

Once this vision took form in the mind of J. M. Ashley he became a dedicated man, determined, as he put it, to deliver the American people from the "loathsome incubus" in the White House, this "acting President" who had "blotted our country's history" with its "foulest blot." To Ashley the impeachment movement was no political maneuver; it was a holy crusade.

By Saturday, January 5, 1867 it was common knowledge in Washington that Johnson was about to veto the District Suffrage bill. That night Stevens summoned his followers to a caucus. Although the meeting was behind closed doors, the Daily *National Intelligencer* was able to report that about 70 Radicals attended and that there was a "spirited debate" marked by "a want of harmony." One faction, led by Stevens and Boutwell, was for an immediate impeachment attempt; the other, led by Bingham and Spalding of Ohio, counselled delay.

On Monday morning the President's veto of Negro suffrage in the District was received and tumultuously overridden. No sooner was this action completed than two Missouri Radicals—Benjamin F. Loan and John R. Kelso—were on their feet, demanding impeachment. Somehow their resolutions got sidetracked by technicalities.

In the midst of the furor James Mitchel Ashley got up. "I rise to perform a painful but, nevertheless, to me an imperative duty," he began and devoted considerable wordage to his reluctance to do what must be done. Impatient colleagues urged him to get to the point. Finally he directed the Clerk to read the resolution he wished to propose. It ran:

I do impeach Andrew Jackson, Vice President and acting President of the United States, of high crimes and misdemeanors.
I charge him with a usurpation of power and violation of law:
In that he has corruptly used the appointing power;
In that he has corruptly used the pardoning power;

In that he has corruptly used the veto power;

In that he has corruptly disposed of public property of the United States;

In that he has corruptly interfered in elections . . .

Therefore,

Be it resolved, That the Committee on the Judiciary be . . . authorized to investigate the official conduct of Andrew Johnson, Vice President of the United States . . . and to report to this house whether . . . the said Andrew Johnson . . . has been guilty of acts which are designed or calculated to overthrow, subvert or corrupt the Government of the United States.

Thaddeus Stevens promptly blocked all attempts by the opposition to postpone a ballot. The vote was taken; the resolution passed by 107 to 39, with 45 not voting.

The first impeachment attempt was under way.

XIX

THE CONGRESSIONAL
INVESTIGATION

The task of investigating the Executive was assigned to a sub-committee of the House Judiciary headed by James F. ("Tama Jim") Wilson of Iowa and consisting of seven Republicans and two Democrats. Although all of the Republicans were Radicals, Wilson and Frederick E. Woodbridge of Vermont were fair-minded men, bent on seeing to it that the Committee did not recommend impeachment unless the probe turned up "High Crimes and Misdemeanors" within the meaning of the Constitution.

Of the remaining Radicals the most determined impeacher was Boutwell of Massachusetts. Primly handsome with his neat white beard and mustache and his steely eyes, Boutwell was a man of enormous energy. He amused the reporters with his "prayer-meeting tones," his flights of fancy and intemperance. Fanatic, calculating, and unreasoning he was as convinced as Ashley, and always would be, that Andrew Johnson had engineered the murder of his predecessor.

Of the two Democrats, Charles Augustus Eldridge was the more persevering in the President's cause. Virile and full-bearded with a strong acquiline nose, this New England-born Congressman from

Fond du Lac, Wisconsin brought to the investigation a penetrating mind illuminated by a passion to see justice done.

Ashley was not one of the official probers, but his plump and bouncy figure was frequently visible in the Committee Room and from time to time, with Committee permission, he questioned witnesses.

In late February of 1867 the Committee reported that it would not be able to complete its work during the life of the 39th Congress and early the next month, the 40th authorized it to continue. Intermittently then, throughout most of the year, the Committee held hearings. Its activities were not confined to Washington. Its agents traveled about the country. In after years, in Greeneville, Tennessee a certain Squire Self enjoyed relating an incident presumably connected with the visit of a Committee investigator to the President's home town.

Was not Johnson, the Squire was asked, "in the habit of getting drunk and making a spectacle of himself?" The Squire thought that over. "Well," he drawled, "I'll tell you this: he never got too drunk to disremember his friends."

Into the Committee Room trouped eighty-eight witnesses from all walks of life and all parts of the country. At least a million words of testimony were taken and by the time the Committee was ready to report to the House, Andrew Johnson had been subjected to the most thoroughgoing investigation ever given to an elected official of the United States government.

The first and for a time the star witness was LaFayette C. Baker, proprietor of a Washington detective agency. Born in a New York village and reared in Michigan, Baker in his early manhood had migrated to the Pacific Coast where he had acquired his first lessons in detecting as Number 208 in the California Vigilance Committee. At the onset of the war he had hastened to Washington where his talents were soon rewarded with the rank of Brigadier General and the directorship of the Bureau of the National Detective Police, set up by Stanton in the War Department and a forerunner of the F.B.I. Lincoln, occasionally thrown into touch with the Detective

Chief, rapidly sized him up. Hearing the complaint of a Washington resident that a man with a hand organ was disturbing him by playing in front of his house, the President offered a solution. "I'll tell you what to do," he said. "Speak to Stanton about it, and tell him to send Baker after the man. Baker will steal the organ and throw its owner into Old Capitol [prison], and you'll never be troubled with his noise again."

In 1867 the General still cut a dashing figure. It is assumed that he approached the witness stand eagerly. He had a score to settle with Andrew Johnson thanks to a series of incidents connected with the Mrs. Lucy Cobb whose name the Radical scandal mill had long since linked with the President.

Like Baker himself Mrs. Cobb had for years been a town character. She had haunted the White House in Lincoln's day. Following Johnson's accession she continued to do so, and it appears that the lady was not unwilling, in return for a fee, to obtain pardons for former rebels. This sort of activity was frowned on, of course. Johnson's instruction to his aides was to report such cases and when this was done the President took action to see to it that those eligible for pardons received them without payment of money.

Discouraging pardon brokers by legitimate means was one thing; deceit and trickery were another, and when Baker's underhanded methods became a matter of public knowledge, the President was angry. What Baker had done was lay a trap for Mrs. Cobb by having one of his operatives pose as a former rebel in need of a pardon and seek the lady's services. Then when Mrs. Cobb got the pardon, Baker stepped in and arrested her as she was in the act of receiving the final installment of the agreed-on-fee—$200 in previously pin-pricked bills.

The incident became a staple of Washington gossip when Mrs. Cobb's husband haled the General into court where he was convicted of false arrest and imprisonment. In retaliation Baker ordered some detectives he had placed on duty at the White House to deny Mrs. Cobb access to the building. Evading the detective who sought to prevent her from entering, Mrs. Cobb slipped in by another door and reported the incident to a White House policeman. The policeman brought the matter to the attention of the President, who summoned Baker, asked him by what authority he was prohibiting citizens from visiting the Executive mansion, told him to remove his sleuths from the premises and subsequently had him dismissed from the government service.

It was a disgruntled General then who, on February 6, 1867, seated himself at the long table in the committee room of the House Judiciary. During this and two later appearances, Baker unravelled a hair-raising tale. He testified that in 1864 a Negro employed by a son of Governor Brownlow of Tennessee sneaked into the house of Andrew Johnson in Nashville and took from a desk there a letter that Johnson had written and signed but had not yet mailed to Jefferson Davis. Baker was vague as to the contents of the purloined letter, but he managed to convey the impression that Johnson had offered to reveal to the Confederate President the number of troops on hand in the capital. The letter itself was not produced. Baker said that it had been brought to him by a Mr. John W. Adamson of Nashville, that Mr. Adamson had let him keep it "for two or three weeks" and had then taken it back. Baker also mentioned a conversation with a Mrs. Sallie Harris of Philadelphia, saying that Mrs. Harris claimed to know the contents of the letter.

The investigators lost no time in following up these revelations. John Corson of the Capitol Police was dispatched post haste to Nashville with a subpoena for the John W. Adamson mentioned by the General. There Corson was informed by the Postmaster and a number of long-time residents that there was no John W. Adamson in the city and hadn't been for twenty years. Following a trail that led him from Philadelphia to Boston, Corson encountered several ladies who claimed to be Mrs. Sallie Harris but who in every case turned out to be somebody else. Reporting back to the Committee in July, Corson was impelled to the conclusion that both Mr. Adamson and Mrs. Harris were figments of General Baker's imagination. As for the purloined letter, it was never located for the reason that it had never been written.

The pattern set by the "Case of the Purloined Letter" was the pattern of the entire investigation. Over and over witnesses laid tongue to damaging revelations which withered into nothingness as soon as more reliable witnesses were called.

The "Case," for example, of the two Tennessee railroads, the Nashville and Chattanooga and the Nashville and Northwestern. In his days as military governor Johnson had taken over these roads for the Union, had improved and extended them at government expense, and had then returned them to their original owners after the war. These facts were spread on the record in the hope of showing that Johnson, who owned some Tennessee-guaranteed bonds of one of the carriers, had benefited financially from its return to its stockholders. These disclosures had a sinister sound until they were demolished by none other than Edwin McMasters Stanton. He testified that it was he who had recommended the return of the roads to their owners as the only practical way of getting them quickly into interstate operation and of relieving the government of the costs of maintaining them.

Still convinced that Johnson must have made some money from the transactions, the investigators summoned William S. Huntington, cashier of the First National Bank of Washington. A look at the President's personal account, it was assumed, would reveal considerable income from his Tennessee railroad holdings. Asked to produce a transcript of the account, Mr. Huntington demurred, pleading that such things were confidential. Reminded that the Committee held powers of subpoena, the cashier brought in the requested documents, showing that the bulk of the President's modest balance, about $60,000, came not from his railroad bonds but from securities of the United States government. Eldridge asked the reluctant witness a pertinent question. Did Johnson know that his personal account was being shown to the Committee? The banker said yes, he had called at the White House and had so informed Mr. Johnson. "The President," Eldridge went on, "did not make any objections?" The banker said, "None whatever. He smiled and said he had no earthly objection to have any of his transactions looked into; that he had done nothing clandestinely . . ."

Nothing was overlooked. At the slightest hint of action on the part of the President that might be construed as even remotely suspicious, the more rabid members of the Committee were in full cry. Was it not a known fact that Johnson had actually driven government employees from their posts because their political views were dissimilar from his own? It was indeed a fact, testified Postmaster-General Randall. To be statistical about it, at the start of the unsuccessful Third Party movement, the President had removed 1,283 office holders. Whatever shouts of joy were forthcoming in the Committee Room at this admission were choked back when Randall added what every man present knew, that the same thing was done under Lincoln and was a "common practice."

Much was made of the fact that Johnson utilized the writing skills of other men in preparing his state papers, as if a procedure followed by every President from Washington on became reprehensible when practiced by Andrew Johnson. Former Attorney-General Jeremiah S. Black was summoned. Asked if he had written the message vetoing the first of the Radical Reconstruction bills, he answered that yes, he had penned some of it but that "after being submitted to the President," Johnson or someone toned it down. "If I had written the message," the lawyer continued, ". . . it would have been a much more objectionable document to the Majority of Congress than it is."

General Baker took advantage of the limelight surrounding the witness chair to advertise the fact that his recently ghost-written autobiography was now available in print. The General let it be known that prior to the book's appearance, an attempt had been made to suppress it by a man close to the President, namely William H. Seward. Requested to testify, the Secretary of State helped himself to a pinch of snuff and made his urbane answer. To the best of his knowledge, the Secretary said, he had never interfered with any literary enterprise except that of a New Yorker who, during the war, had threatened to print and distribute copies of the Constitution of the Confederate States of America.

If much of the investigation was comedy, more of it was melodrama. Within the four walls of the Committee Room and in the world outside, some of the investigators and other members of Congress devoted much of 1867 to a frenzied search for evidence that would link Andrew Johnson to the murder of Lincoln.

To the witness stand was summoned the actor John Mathews, one of the performers in the play Lincoln was watching on the night of his assassination. To nervous John Mathews the memory of that tragic Good Friday was a living nightmare. That afternoon, in front of Willards, he encountered his friend, J. Wilkes Booth. Booth handed him a sealed letter with the request that on the morrow Mathews deliver it to the editors of the *National Intelligencer.*

At the time of the assassination that night Mathews recognized Booth but gave no thought to their meeting of the afternoon. It was not till he got to his hotel room and Booth's letter fell from the pocket of his frock coat that he remembered. He opened it then. Its contents horrified him, for it was Booth's confession. It came to Mathews that if he fulfilled the assassin's request and carried this letter to the *Intelligencer* he would be implicated in the terrible crime. With public feeling at fever pitch he might even be lynched. He read the letter twice and burned it. Later, during the trial of the Lincoln conspirators, he made known what he had done, but not until now had Mathews ever discussed the contents of Booth's letter from a witness stand.

Boutwell questioned him. Was it not true that in his letter Booth revealed the names of his accomplices? It was true, Mathews said; he remembered their names vividly. He remembered the name of the accomplice Payne because he (Mathews) was an admirer of John Howard Payne, actor, dramatist, poet and author of *Home Sweet Home.* He remembered the name of Atzerodt "because it was written hurriedly," that of Herold because he knew him. Were any other people listed in Booth's letter? Boutwell put this question repeatedly, clinging to the end to the vain hope that the witness would suddenly remember one more name—Andrew Johnson.

It will be recalled that during the trial of the Lincoln conspirators the diary taken from J. Wilkes Booth as he lay dying was suppressed. It was now much in evidence. Interest was intense, not because of what the diary said but because of what it did not say. A portion of it—three, four, twelve or fifteen pages (testimony varied)—had been removed, sliced out by a sharp instrument. What was written on those missing pages? Had Booth removed them before his death, or had someone else done so afterwards? Everyone who had handled the diary was questioned: the officers who had taken it from Booth's body; Secretary Stanton who had thumbed through it one spring morning; and Judge Advocate General Holt who had secreted it in his safe during the Conspirators' Trial. Boutwell and Ashley would go to their graves convinced that somewhere along the line those pages had been removed because they implicated—Andrew Johnson!

During the investigation any number of unimportant individuals played minor roles in the drama. There was W. P. Matchett, for example—the Reverend Matchett he called himself. He began to figure prominently when one summer morning a naval petty officer, emerging from his Washington boarding house, noticed some scraps of paper on the ground. Picking them up and putting them together the sailor discovered that he held in his hand a letter from Matchett to Judge Holt. The record is not clear as to the contents of Matchett's letter but it is known that he purported to be acquainted with two gentlemen of "excellent characters" who had first-hand knowledge that J. Wilkes Booth was in personal communication with Andrew Johnson sometime prior to the assassination. Of course efforts were made to unearth the "two gentlemen of 'excellent characters' " and of course they were never located because like General Baker's purloined letter they existed only in the mind of their inventor.

An even more spectacular participant was Sanford Conover whom we last encountered in the act of laying before Stanton and

Judge Holt evidence that the assassination was plotted by Jefferson Davis and other reputable Southerners. Conover, it will be remembered, headed up a little gang of professional witnesses. In 1866 the House Judiciary looked into the charges against Davis and in the course of these proceedings two of Conover's accomplices—his "unimpeached witnesses" as he called them—confessed that the testimony they had given in connection with the trial of the Lincoln conspirators was made of whole cloth by Conover himself. Conover denied everything, was arrested, tried, convicted of perjury and placed in Old Capitol pending his removal to the Federal Penitentiary.

Among his more frequent visitors was Congressman Ashley, who made several trips to the jail, sometimes by day, sometimes late at night. The local press had it that he was not always alone, and that occasionally Ben Butler came along. Whatever efforts Ashley made to cloak his visits with secrecy were unavailing. The doctor at the jail was a friend of the President and Johnson was well informed. What Ashley and Conover talked about can never be known. Ashley's version of their secret meetings was the product of an obsessed mind, Conover's the word of a convicted perjurer. According to Conover he and the Ohio Congressman had an understanding. Ashley was to obtain a pardon for the convict. In return for this Conover was to manufacture testimony linking Johnson to Lincoln's murder and then suborn witnesses and see to it that they parroted this testimony under oath.

Whatever the arrangement, its results were negative. Discovering that no pardon was forthcoming and that he was about to be shipped off, Conover switched sides and in anger sent a long letter to Johnson, exposing the whole scheme.*

The removal of Conover from Washington did not deflect James Mitchel Ashley from his self-imposed rounds. He was on leave of absence during the summer, too busy seeking evidence against the

---

* During the trial of John H. Surratt (see page 76) Conover provided the prosecution with useful information and for this reason he was pardoned in February, 1869, by Andrew Johnson.

"traitor in the White House" to tend to his legislative duties. Butler and Boutwell were equally active. The *National Intelligencer* quoted Butler as admitting that he had paid Conover's wife "$50 to produce certain evidence on which to impeach the President," evidence which never materialized. Boutwell was quoted as admitting that he was cognizant of Ashley's efforts to obtain testimony from Sanford Conover.

At long last, on Saturday November 23, the investigating subcommittee of the Judiciary held its final hearing. It was a pathetic scene with Congressman Ashley on the witness stand and most of the questions coming from Congressman Eldridge:

Q. Have you not stated to members of the House of Representatives that you had evidence in your possession which would implicate Mr. Johnson in the assassination of Mr. Lincoln?

A. Yes, I certainly have.

Q. Then I ask you why you did not produce this evidence to the committee?

A. It was not that kind of evidence which would satisfy the great mass of men, especially the men who do not concur with me in my theory about this matter . . . I have always believed that President Harrison and President Taylor and President Buchanan were poisoned . . . for the express purpose of putting the Vice Presidents in the Presidential office. In the first two instances, it was successful. It was attempted with Mr. Buchanan, and failed . . . Then Mr. Lincoln was assassinated, and from my stand-point I could come to a conclusion which impartial men, holding different views, could not come.

A few days later the findings of the Committee were before the House. There were two dissenting reports. One, signed by Chairman Wilson and Woodbridge, censured Johnson's policies but asserted that in the mass of testimony procured by the Judiciary there was not an iota of evidence justifying impeachment. The other, signed by the two Democrats, declared Johnson guilty of nothing but a determination to protect the Republic against its enemies. The majority report, signed by Boutwell and the other four Radicals of the investigating subcommittee, leveled seventeen charges at the President. Boiled down to their essence, these charges said the President had vetoed legislation he should have approved, had restored large amounts of Southern property to its rightful owners and had pardoned Southerners he should not have pardoned. In short, the President had pursued a reconstruction policy contrary to the wishes of Congress, and for this high crime and misdemeanor the Committee presented, with its blessing, a resolution to impeach him.

On December 7, 1867, a ballot was taken on the resolution. Fifty-seven members of the House voted for it but 108, most of them Radicals, voted against it.

Thus was conducted and thus laid to rest the first attempt to depose Andrew Johnson. Tawdry and incredible—how otherwise can the investigation be described?

XX

SUBVERSION OF THE FEDERAL
SYSTEM

After the Republican Moderates joined hands with the Radicals, early in 1866, Andrew Johnson's administration became one long quarrel with the Congressional majority. In the beginning this quarrel revolved around Reconstruction, but in the 1866 elections this issue was settled for the remainder of the administration. It became so unimportant that speeches on the subject in Congress were often delivered to empty chambers since it was known that whatever Congress decided to do about the South would be done, the President's objections notwithstanding.

To be sure, during the autumn elections of the following year the Radicals got a scare. The voters went to the polls in eleven states, some choosing Governors and legislatures, others minor officials. The over-all results were adverse to the Republicans. This outcome suggested growing public dissatisfaction with Radical Reconstruction. It served notice that the Democrats would be hard to beat in the 1868 Presidential election. But it was not an endorsement of Johnson. He remained practically powerless, and it is certain that if Congress had not been in the hands of extreme men it would simply have passed its bills, repassed them over the vetoes of the Executive and ignored him.

The extremists were not inclined to proceed in this manner, however. Organizing in March of 1867, the Senate of the 40th Congress named Ben Wade of Ohio as President *pro tem,* thus putting one of their own in line for the Presidency in the event Johnson could be thrown out. Unchastened by the collapse of the first impeachment attempt, the Radicals persisted in their efforts. It was their will that the quarrel go on, but it now revolved around a new issue. The question was no longer who was to control the South, Congress or the Executive; the question was who was to control the government.

The determination of the Radicals to remove from office a President who had ceased to be an obstacle to them was a revolutionary movement. True, some of the dunderheads of the group—Ashley and Boutwell, for instance—remained convinced not only that Johnson was secretly plotting with the Rebels to overthrow the government but that he had the strength, sooner or later, to accomplish it. But it is difficult to believe that the impeachment leaders—men of the caliber of Stevens and Butler, Sumner and Wade—entertained such misapprehensions. Far from seeing a danger in Johnson's strength, these men saw an opportunity in his weakness. Here was a President cut off from organized political support, repudiated by the people and opposed by at least sixty per cent of the press. Here, in other words, was an Executive who probably could be removed. The proximity of the end of his term in office, instead of being a deterrent was a spur, since it might be many years before another President, so defenseless and so vulnerable, came along—a fact of which Thad Stevens, old and sick, was poignantly aware.

The anvil was hot; the time to strike now. If the 40th Congress could oust a President because he disagreed with them, what was to prevent future Congresses from ousting other Presidents for the same reason? The result was certain to be a gradual erosion of the federal system of government and its replacement by something akin to the parliamentary system of Great Britain, a system in which

Congress would rule supreme, with the Executive and the Judiciary in satellite positions.

Later on it would be the consensus of most historians and political scientists that had Congress managed to remove Johnson after impeaching him for purely political reasons, some change in the structure of the American government would have ensued. "Had the impeachment succeeded," a twentieth-century commentator* would write, "had Congress tasted blood by putting one of its own [Ben Wade] . . . into the White House, who can say what would have happened to the presidential office? What remained of the theoretical powers of the French President after the expulsion of MacMahon from the Elysée? . . . It can be said that the failure of the Republicans to carry the impeachment shows that they had no chance of recasting the form of government."

In January of 1867 *Harper's Weekly* was quoting the assertion of the London *Times* "that the scheme of impeachment looks like a fatal blow at the Constitution." Many American observers had come or were about to come to the same conclusion. In a letter to General Sherman a Cincinnati friend labeled the Radical program as a whole "a virtual abrogation of the government we had before the war . . . an attempt by mere politicians to make a new government."

It is certain that the Radicals had little regard for the Constitution. It was their disregard for it that had given rise to their bitter battle with Lincoln, who although compelled to high-handed measures by the exigencies of the war was as determined as his successor to see the basic law preserved. It is worth remembering Lincoln's epitaph on his Radical foes, words spoken at his last Cabinet meeting: "These humanitarians [stand ready to trample on] all state rights and constitutional rights."

Sumner's views were a hangover from his Abolitionist days. While not quite ready to agree with William Lloyd Garrison's denunciation of the Constitution as a "league with death and a

---

* D. W. Brogan, *Government of the People: A Study in the American Political System,* new ed., New York, 1943, p. 123.

covenant with hell," the Massachusetts Senator looked upon it as a document of secondary importance. The country, in his opinion, could rock along nicely with the Declaration of Independence supplemented by whatever laws Congress saw fit to pass. In a lecture in 1867, he declared that it was a distortion of history and fact to speak of the United States government as "federal"; the proper term was "national." In public Thaddeus Stevens was willing to make an occasional obeisance in the direction of the Constitution, but in private conversation with Confederate General Richard Taylor he called it "a worthless bit of old parchment."

It was a belief of the Radicals that the outcome of the war had spelled the end of all states rights. Some of them were for obliterating state boundaries. Sumner was for treating the states "as conveniences rather than essential organs of national life," for reducing "them almost to the level of counties and towns." Not that the Radicals were willing to settle for the centralization of all governmental power in Washington. Their ultimate aim, repeatedly professed, was its centralization in only one branch of the federal government.

The supremacy of Congress was a major tenet of their creed. "Congress is the sovereign power," said Stevens in a campaign speech. In the House the old warhorse declared that "though the President is Commander-in-Chief, Congress is his commander, and God willing, he shall obey!" Senator John Sherman, moderate-turned-Radical, summed up the doctrine when in his memoirs he asserted: "The executive department of a republic like ours should be subordinate to the legislative department. The President should obey and enforce the laws, leaving to the people the duty of correcting any errors committed by their representatives in Congress."

Men's words, of course, can shield as well as point to their motives. Their deeds are a more trustworthy criterion, and here we move on even firmer ground. Some of the major legislation passed by the 39th and 40th Congresses was designed to strip from the Presidential office powers imparted to it by the Constitution. The 39th amended a wartime law in such a way as to deprive the President of his right to grant pardons, a right so explicitly stated in the Constitution that Johnson simply ignored the enactment. He kept right on granting pardons and Congress never challenged his right to do so in an official way.

The last month of 1866 found Congressman Boutwell fussing up the stairs of the War Department building to confer with Old Mars behind the closed door of his private office. Stanton, who had sent for the Massachusetts Radical, poured into his receptive ears a tale rife with alarums and horrible imaginings. He was certain that Johnson was about to put the rebels in control of the government by forcibly assembling a Congress made up of Southern Democrats. He had come to this conclusion because recently Johnson had issued orders directly to some military officers without first consulting him, as Secretary of War, or Grant in his capacity as General of the Army!

Something must be done, Stanton said. Boutwell agreed. So then and there, with Stanton dictating and Boutwell scratching it down, a bill was framed, making it a misdemeanor for a military officer to take orders directly from the President or for the President to issue such orders directly except through the General of the Army! This conference ended, Boutwell fussed back down the stairs and across town to look up Thaddeus Stevens, who could be counted on to get the bill converted into legislation.

It was slickly done. When this flagrant attempt to strip the President of his prerogatives as Commander-in-Chief reached Johnson's desk, it was in the form of a rider to the Army Appropriation Bill covering the year ending June 30, 1868. Rather than leave the military without funds, Johnson signed it, taking care to state in his return message that the rider was unconstitutional.

Congress not only chipped away at the powers of the Executive; it applied its chisel also to the foundations of the Supreme Court. The Court was more vulnerable than the President for the reason that its powers are not so clearly defined in the Constitution. Article III requires Congress to establish a Supreme Court, but the size of the court and the sort of cases over which it can exercise appellate jurisdiction are subject to the discretion of the legislature. Since 1863 the high court had consisted of nine justices. When two of them died in 1866 Congress, in a reversal of the famous "court-packing" episode of the 1930's, prevented their replacement with Johnson appointees by limiting membership in the Court to seven.

The real attack began to shape up when, in the celebrated case of *ex parte Milligan,* the high court handed down a decision widely viewed as a threat to Radical plans for reconstruction. During the war Lincoln, with the consent of Congress, had suspended the writ of *habeas corpus* in cases where military officers arrested persons for offenses against the armed services. In 1864, Lambden P. Milligan, an Indiana civilian, was accused of instigating insurrection, tried by a military commission, convicted and condemned to death. Milligan petitioned for a writ of *habeas corpus.* The matter came before the Supreme Court and a majority of the justices ruled that a civilian could not be tried by the military if the civil courts were operating in his locality. Since the regular Indiana courts were open at the time of Milligan's trial, his sentence was set aside and he was freed.

The decision in the Milligan case troubled the President's opponents. The first of the Radical Reconstruction acts contained a provision authorizing the district commanders in the South, where the regular courts were in operation, to try civilians accused of crimes before military commissions. It was a foregone conclusion that sooner or later this provision would be challenged by Southerners, mindful of *ex parte Milligan.*

A case involving a Mississippi newspaper editor named William H. McCardle provided the test. In the fall of 1867 McCardle, formerly a colonel in the Confederate army, angered the commander of the district embracing his state by publishing editorials critical of Radical Reconstruction. Arrested and jailed pending trial by a military commission, McCardle tried to obtain his freedom by applying for a writ of *habeas corpus* from the United States Circuit Court for Mississippi. When this application was denied,

McCardle's lawyer took another tack. Earlier in the year Congress had passed what was known as the Habeas Corpus act, a clause of which authorized an appeal from the United States Circuit Court to the United States Supreme Court "in all cases where any person may be restrained in his or her liberty, in violation of the Constitution. . . ." Seizing upon this clause, actually intended to protect only so-called "loyal men" in the South, McCardle's lawyer contrived to bring his client's plea before the high court.

When the Justices agreed to hear the case, panic seized the Radicals. Here for all practical purposes was another *ex parte Milligan*. It mattered not what happened to the obstreperous Mississippi editor, Mr. McCardle; but if the Supreme Court ruled in his favor, its decision would have the effect of wrecking Radical Reconstruction by declaring unconstitutional a substantial portion of the laws on which it rested. There was furious activity both in and out of Congress. For a period the Radical propaganda guns were turned not on the "unrepentant Rebels" of the South or on "the bad man in the White House" but on the "old men" on the high bench. "The Reconstruction acts," fumed the Indianapolis *Journal*, "are full of the rights and liberties of millions of men; and to have these stricken down by the decision of some old fossil on the Supreme Bench whose political opinion belongs to a past era would be an outrage on humanity."

In the House Thaddeus Stevens proposed a bill simply forbidding the Supreme Court to take jurisdiction in any case arising from the Reconstruction acts. This was going too far even for the impetuous Congressmen. They chose instead to consider a bill narrowing the Court's authority to declare an act of Congress unconstitutional by directing that any decision to this effect must be concurred in by two-thirds of the justices. Hastily passed by the House, this measure failed in the Senate.

But the Radicals, having rendered the Executive helpless to block their schemes, had no intention of letting the Judiciary do it for him. Only a few days before the ruling in the McCardle Case was scheduled to be handed down, they achieved their ends. This they accomplished by repealing the law under which the case had been brought before the court, thus removing the matter from its jurisdiction.

Appalled by this maneuver, Secretary Welles concluded that the attempt to depose Johnson was only a phase in a larger scheme. "It is evident," he decided, "that the Radicals in Congress are in a conspiracy to overthrow not only the President but the government."

It was on March 14, 1868, that Welles penned these words. Time and again he had poured the same sombre thought into his diary. As early as 1866 he wrote: "If the Southern states should be put to the ban by Congress and declared Territories, the Radicals will not have even then accomplished their purpose . . . Andrew Johnson must be disposed of and impeachment must be effected. This the less radical portion are not yet prepared for, but when they have gone so far as to break down the Constitution and the States, they will follow the violent leaders the rest of the way."

On January 12, 1867: "We are living in a revolutionary period, and the character of the government is undergoing a strain which may transform it into a different character."

On the following October 1: "Congress is disposed to . . . take into its own hands not only the making but the execution of the laws."

On February 4, 1868: "There is a conspiracy maturing for the overthrow of the Administration and the subversion of . . . our federal system."

Welles' diary has aptly been called the Greek Chorus of the drama which he records. The clarity of his insight will become increasingly apparent as we follow the events leading up to the drama's climax.

XXI

THE DISMISSAL OF STANTON

For more than two years Johnson permitted Edwin McMasters Stanton to remain in office. The President knew that his Cabinet officer was working with his enemies. Everybody knew it, and Johnson's failure to do anything about it was a topic of avid speculation. In Washington, where whispered slander was the salt of social life, hundreds of people believed the published rumor that the President was afraid to act because Stanton had evidence tying him to Lincoln's murder.

Repeatedly Johnson's advisers, notably the Blairs, impressed upon him the importance of replacing Stanton with someone he could trust. At the conclusion of the Conservative soldiers-and-sailors convention at Cleveland in 1866, nine prominent generals put their names to a round-robin calling for the Secretary's ouster.

As time passed and Stanton continued to sit at the Cabinet table, Welles was beside himself with the prophetic conviction that Johnson's failure to act in Stanton's case would prove to be his most fatal error. Welles attributed the President's procrastination to a fear that the removal of the darling of the Radicals would so increase the wrath of his foes that they "would break down his Administration." One must add to this surmise Johnson's deep-seated reluctance to dismiss from high office anyone appointed by Lincoln, the "greatest man of all." It was a reluctance peculiarly applicable to Stanton, whose manifest abilities Lincoln had admired and whose crotchets he had patiently endured.

Frequently, at Cabinet meetings and elsewhere, Johnson tried in vain to smoke out Old Mars, assuming that once Stanton had shown his hand he would do the decent thing and resign. Had Johnson been a better reader of character he would have known that these efforts were a waste of time. Stanton had no intention of relinquishing a position that gave such wide scope to his dictatorial nature, and no intention of treating Andrew Johnson decently.

Johnson was no sooner in office than Stanton was planting detectives at the White House to spy and report on the President's activities. Behind the scenes he encouraged the Radical convention in Philadelphia in 1866. We have seen him in the act of dictating the rider to the Army Appropriations bill with the intent of depriving Johnson of his prerogatives as Commander-in-Chief. These and other hostile moves by Stanton came to Johnson's attention. Still he hesitated, and as usual, while the President pondered and forbore, his enemies acted, rapidly bringing to fruition the fateful Tenure of Office Act, one objective of which was to prevent Johnson from firing Edwin McMasters Stanton.

In its final form the Tenure of Office Act prohibited the President from dismissing any official holding his position by presidential appointment and at presidential discretion without the consent of the Senate, except under circumstances so vaguely described as to be open to contradictory interpretations. The doctrine thus set forth was at odds with what had been established practice for almost eighty years. The Constitution empowers the chief executive to appoint a variety of federal officers "by and with the advice and consent of the Senate." As to how such officers can be removed the Constitution is silent, but from Washington's day on down it had been assumed that whenever a President saw fit to remove an appointed official whose tenure was not fixed by law, he could do so without consulting anyone.

Sanction for this construction of the basic law was found in the act setting up the State Department and passed by the 1st Congress, thirteen members of which had also been members of the convention which had framed the basic law. John Marshall, fourth Chief Justice of the Supreme Court, had declared this action by the 1st Congress strictly in line with the intent of the Founding Fathers. It had the imprimatur of James Madison who, in a letter penned toward the end of his life, had said that for the Senate to have "a share in removal as well as appointment of officers . . . would not only vary essentially the existing balance of power, but expose the Executive occasionally to a total inaction."

The Radicals, far from being averse to reducing Johnson to "total inaction," had no lesser goal in mind. The developments responsible for the passage of the Tenure of Office bill were freighted with their most cherished dreams: the ouster of the President and the establishment of a Congressional dictatorship. Speaking for the bill in the House the Pennsylvania Radical, Thomas Williams, pointed out that if "you would impeach successfully," some way must be found to take control of the patronage out of the President's hands. No attempt to depose the chief executive stood much chance, Williams warned, so long as Johnson could surround himself with an "army of stipendiaries" dependent "upon his will."

The bill was framed and introduced during the first session of the 39th Congress, cursorily debated and referred to committee. As matters stood at this point the Radicals, thanks to the "advise and consent" powers of the Senate, could keep the President from putting his friends in office but they could not keep him from putting his enemies out. Pressure for acting on the measure increased when during his Swing around the Circle, Johnson bluntly threatened "to kick them out."

Debate on the measure began in the Senate on January 10, 1867. In the form in which the bill came from committee, the members of the President's cabinet were excluded from its operation. When Edmunds of Vermont, reporting for the committee, was asked why this was, he made the obvious reply. He pointed out that the Cabinet members were the President's personal advisers. Whenever the relationship between President and Secretary ceased to be one of mutual "confidence and trust and personal esteem," the President should "be allowed to dispense with the services of that officer." Howe of Wisconsin disagreed. He said the Secretaries were not members of the Cabinet of the President but of "the Cabinet of the people." From this position even the most ardent Radicals dissented at first, only to change their minds some days later and join Howe in a concentrated effort to have the Cabinet members included in the bill.

Sumner defended this stand in a three-day oration, ingenuously entitled "Protection against the President." This verbal marathon waxed in eloquence as it grew in length. By the second day the Massachusetts Radical's words were those of a man firmly convinced that the Senators should barricade themselves lest Andrew Johnson march in and take them over. No previous Senate, he said, had been in such danger because never before had a "President of the United States . . . become an enemy of his country." On the third day Sumner's theme was "treason" at the other end of the Avenue. He called Johnson "the successor of Jefferson Davis . . . a terror to the good and a support to the wicked."

Howe, taking up where Sumner left off, let the cat out of the bag. He reminded his fellow-Senators that there was "a probability" that one of these days Johnson would ask for the resignation of Secretary Stanton. He charged that the Senators would be assuming "a grave responsibility" if, realizing that this might come to pass, they failed to prevent it by including the cabinet officers in the bill under consideration. But respect for the Presidential office, if not its incumbent, was by no means dead in the upper House. An amendment to put the Cabinet officers into the bill failed and they were still excluded when the measure was passed and sent to the House.

In the House, in the face of considerable opposition, the Radicals contrived to strike out the exclusion clause. When the measure returned to the Senate, the Cabinet officers were "included." Once again the Senate "excluded" them and the bill went to a committee representing both Houses for conference. From this maneuver the Tenure of Office Act emerged in its final form.

It declared that while Congress was in session the President must get the consent of the Senate to remove a civil officer. While Congress was in recess he could suspend an officer and commission another man to act in his place, but within twenty days after Congress reconvened he must put the matter before the Senate. In any event, whenever the Senate refused to concur in the President's judgment, the individual he had suspended was to be reinstated immediately.

As for the Cabinet officers, the Radicals carried the day. They were included under a compromise clause that was oddly worded. It provided that the members of the Cabinet "shall hold their offices respectively for and during the term of the President by whom they may have been appointed, and for one month thereafter, subject to removal by and with the advice and consent of the Senate."

What was the meaning of this fuzzy verbiage? Did it or did it not furnish Edwin McMasters Stanton with "Protection against the President"? Stanton was a holdover from Lincoln's cabinet. Lincoln not Johnson had appointed him; or rather, in effect, Johnson had reappointed him. Whose term then was Stanton serving—Lincoln's or Johnson's? In short, was Johnson still free to fire Stanton at will, or must he have the consent of the Senate to do so? Legal minds, the most competent in the country, would disagree. In the near future the debate over this little section of the bill would be part of the great spectacle of the era, for in passing the Tenure of Office Act, Congress had laid the groundwork for impeachment.

On February 18 the bill went to the President. Eight days later, at the regular Tuesday cabinet meeting, Johnson took it up with his advisers. At various later moments three of the men present at the meeting—Welles, Secretary of Interior Browning and the President's confidential secretary, Colonel Moore—would record in their diaries a bit of information that was ironic under the circumstances. While all of the Secretaries urged Johnson to veto the bill as unconstitutional, none was more emphatic than the Secretary it was intended to keep in office.

"No man of a proper sense of honor," Stanton declared, "would remain in the Cabinet when invited to resign."

The President's reaction to these words was to intimate that since Stanton felt that way, it would be seemly of him to turn in his own portfolio. If Stanton caught this broad hint, as Colonel Moore characterized it, he gave no sign. Johnson pressed on. Since Henry Stanbery, the Attorney General, was too busy to draft the necessary veto message, perhaps the Secretary of War would be good enough to do so. Old Mars squirmed out of that. He would be delighted, he said, to help but as for drafting it himself he must decline, owing to a touch of rheumatism in his writing arm. So Johnson turned the enterprise over to Seward with the understanding that Stanton and Browning would assist him. Presumably the resulting message, like many of Johnson's state papers, received the attention of several members of the Cabinet, although Secretary McCulloch, who was on close terms with Stanton, later asserted that it was the latter's work.

Its fate in Congress came as a surprise to no one, since passing bills over the Presidential veto had become a reflex action. Congress had agreed to adjourn on Saturday March 2, and that turned out to be a fruitful day for the President's enemies—and a long one. So heavy was the schedule that the clock was turned back and several of the most turbulent sessions of "March 2" were actually held on Sunday and Monday, March 3 and 4. When at noon Monday the tap of the gavel put a period to the never-to-be-forgotten 39th Congress, the first of the Radical Reconstruction laws was on the statute books and so was the Tenure of Office Act.

Ordinarily the incoming Congress would not have met until the following winter, but at this juncture the Republican leaders were averse to long recesses. Contending that "Andrew Johnson was a bad man, and that this House and the Senate should sit here and take care of his acts," the members of the 39th had decreed that the new Congress was to meet immediately after the old one closed. It was so done. Convening a few seconds after noon, March 4, the 40th Congress remained in session until March 30. The Senate met in special session April 1-20 and both Houses returned to Washington for an extra session July 3-20. At this point, still reluctant to leave the government too long to the tender mercies of the "bad man" in the White House, Congress voted to reconvene on the following November 21.

During this interval Stanton, assuming himself to be cemented to his post by the Tenure of Office Act, grew bolder. The principal business of the extra session of Congress in July was to pass the second supplementary Reconstruction Act, a section of which conferred certain powers of appointment and removal on the General of the Army and in effect denied those powers to the President. When, shortly after Congress recessed, Johnson learned that this new attack on his constitutional rights had been authored by his Secretary of War, he did what he should have done long before. From the White House to the War Department, on August 5, went this curt note to Stanton:

Sir: Public considerations of a high character constrain me to say that your resignation as Secretary of War will be accepted.
Very respectfully yours,
ANDREW JOHNSON

Welles, calling at the White House that Monday morning and learning what the President had done, was half fearful that Johnson had waited too long, and that the attempt to relieve Stanton at this point would do more harm than good; half hopeful that Old Mars, true to his own statement that "no man of a proper sense of honor" would remain where he wasn't wanted, would bow to the President's wishes.

Stanton's reply, dated the previous day, was in Johnson's hands at 11:45 the next morning:

Sir: Your note this day has been received, stating that public considerations of a high character constrain you to say that my resignation as Secretary of War will be accepted.
In reply, I have the honor to say that public considerations of a

high character, which alone have induced me to continue at the head of this department, constrain me not to resign the office of Secretary of War before the next meeting of Congress.

EDWIN M. STANTON
Secretary of War

Colonel Moore got the impression that Johnson was neither surprised nor upset at Stanton's answer but Welles, observing the President closely as the matter was discussed at next day's Cabinet meeting, got the impression that momentarily Johnson was not quite certain of his next step. Whatever the state of the President's mind that Tuesday, he had determined on his course sometime prior to the end of the week.

On Sunday morning he summoned General Grant to the White House for a lengthy talk. On the following day, which was August 12, he sent another note to Stanton, informing him that he was "hereby suspended from office" and that Grant was to take his place with the title of Secretary of War *ad interim.*

Stanton's reply was more insolent than his previous note. Denying the right of the President to suspend him "without the advice and consent of the Senate and without any legal cause," he added that "inasmuch as the General Commanding the armies of the United States has been appointed *ad interim,* and has notified me that he has accepted the appointment, I have no alternative but to submit, under protest, to superior force."

Colonel Moore was with Johnson when Stanton's note was delivered. There was a frown on the President's face as he read it, but as he put it down and turned to Moore, there was an unmistakable expression of relief in his dark eyes and in his voice.

"The turning point has at last come," he said. "The Rubicon is crossed."

XXII

THE PRESIDENT

AND THE GENERALS

The heroes of the people of the North after the war were those generals who had led them to victory, and in the political battles of Reconstruction no effort was spared by either side to attract to its ranks such lustrous names as Sherman and Grant.

From first to last Sherman was sympathetic with the President's policies. He took a proprietary pride in them, pointing out to his brother John, the Senator, the similarity in spirit between what Johnson was doing and what Sherman had tried to do in drawing up his surrender pact with Confederate General Johnston—the pact that the President and his Cabinet had rejected and on which Stanton had seized in his futile effort to sully a great soldier's reputation.

When the President vetoed the first Freedmen's Bureau bill, Sherman wrote brother John that "as I am a man of peace, I go for Johnson and the veto." Even at this early date the astute General perceived the conspiratorial pattern of Radical activity. "If we do not design to make a complete revolution in our form of government," he told John, "but rather to preserve it, you must, sooner or later, allow representation from the South, and the longer it is deferred, the worse will be its effect." Even more pointed were his observations in a letter to Chief Justice Chase. Attacking the Radical plan for keeping Southern states out of the Union until they fulfilled certain stipulated conditions, the General reminded the jurist that the Constitution required the Federal government to guarantee each state "a republican form of government" and that if "now we go outside the Constitution for a means of change we rather justify the rebels in their late attempt."

But penetrating as was Sherman's understanding of Johnson's policies, he had no intention of permitting himself to become involved officially in Johnson's feud with Congress. In part this determination was dictated by an aversion to politics, a type of warfare less damaging to the flesh than that Sherman knew so well but infinitely more damaging, in his opinion, to the spirit. In part it was dictated by his conclusion, after watching the President in action, that Johnson's methods were faulty. He also felt that the President was as much an extremist as his Radical enemies. Lloyd Lewis, in his excellent biography of Sherman, describes as "prose poetry" the General's thoughts on the blunders of the President. Johnson, the General averred, "never heeds any advice. He attempts to govern after he has lost the means to govern. He's like a General fighting without an army—he is like Lear roaring at the wild storm, bareheaded and helpless."

Headquartering in St. Louis, after the war, Sherman was content with the relatively simple task of pacifying the Indians throughout the vast Division of the Mississippi over which he held command. He let it be known in no uncertain terms that any place was pleasant to him so long as it was far from Washington which he considered "corrupt as hell," and "the focus of intrigue, gossip and slander."

General Grant chose a different course. Of compact figure and stern and bearded visage, he had little talent for politics for reasons embedded in his singular nature and in the experience which had conditioned it.

As General of the Army, Washington became his home after the war. Honors and presents were heaped upon him. The town of

Galena, where he had once tramped the streets a man forgotten except by his creditors, gave him a house worth $16,000 with a photograph of Lincoln on the parlor wall and a "Big Acorn," the latest thing in cooking stoves, in the kitchen. Philadelphia gave him an even more expensive house. New York City gave him one hundred thousand dollars in cash and Boston a library worth five thousand. Grant was pleased with these things.

In the squabble over Reconstruction he held one deeply felt view—the determination to preserve his personal honor by seeing to it that the government stood behind the promises of lenient treatment that he had made to General Lee and his soldiers at Appomattox. Otherwise he harbored no firm views as to how the South should be treated. For a time he gave his support to Johnson, largely because he was a good soldier and the President was his Commander-in-Chief. When after the Arm-in-Arm Convention in the summer of 1866, the Committee of Seventy called at the White House to present the convention resolutions, Grant was there, standing symbolically at the President's right. He accompanied Johnson on his Swing Around the Circle, although by this time Gideon Welles, that peerer into dark corners, was of the opinion that Grant was beginning to move towards the Radicals.

They had been cultivating the General all along. Johnson was aware of this and went to some pains in an effort to keep the great hero in his camp. On the same April evening in 1866 that the Senate passed the Civil Rights bill over the President's veto, the Grants gave their last reception of the season. The Radicals made a bee-line for the affair for the purpose of courting the General and under the assumption that Johnson, no social butterfly, would not be around to cramp their style. Welles, suffering from a headache, attended only because his son was out of town and there was no one to accompany his wife. The Secretary of the Navy was struck by the miscellaneous nature of the crowd. Present were such prominent conservatives as Alexander H. Stephens of Georgia and Montgomery Blair. In the swarm of admirers buzzing about the General were such prominent Radicals as Thaddeus Stevens and Theodore

Tilton. It was a most interesting affair, and it became more so when a servant appeared to announce:

"The President of the United States!"

Johnson entered accompanied by his two daughters, Mrs. Patterson and the blond and statuesque Mrs. Stover. Welles recorded his pleasure in seeing Thad Stevens, "brave old stager" that he was, "discomfited" for once and unable to hide it.

Any advantage Johnson may have gained was wiped out by the November elections of 1866. Unhampered by profound political convictions, Grant naturally leaned toward the winning side. In October *Harper's Weekly* observed that he was becoming less fervent in his support of Johnson. It was common knowledge that the Radicals had baited their hook with irresistible lure, the strong probability that the General would be the Republican choice for President in 1868.

As Johnson's tussle with Stanton came to a head, as he prepared to "cross the Rubicon," it became increasingly important to him to know just where Grant stood. Johnson knew what his projected removal of Stanton could lead to. If the Senate, taking advantage of the Tenure of Office Act, refused to go along and if Johnson defied the Senate, another and no doubt successful attempt to impeach was certain to follow. There was only one way by which this hurdle might be leaped and that was to replace Stanton with a man so strong with the people that the Senate would hesitate to stand in his way.

Before acting on Stanton then, Johnson, on August 1, 1867, summoned Grant to the White House. From the standpoint of the President, the interview was inconclusive. Johnson revealed his intention to dismiss Stanton and said he would like to appoint Grant to the Cabinet. Grant said that firing Stanton would be "impolitic," that most of the people eager to see Old Mars out were "persons who had opposed the war." The President said that no one was more eager than himself, that "it could not be said that *he* had opposed the war," and reiterated his desire to put Grant in Stanton's place. Grant said he "would not shrink" from any public duty "imposed upon him" and reiterated his belief that firing Stanton would be "impolitic."

Still uncertain what to think, the President on the third of August, had a little talk about Grant with Secretary Welles. Hinting that he was giving thought to removing Stanton, Johnson showed the Secretary a letter that Grant had written him in his official capacity as General of the Army—a letter the President thought unfriendly in tone. Welles, having perused the letter, minced no words.

"Grant is going over," he declared, meaning of course to the Radicals.

"Yes," agreed the troubled President. "I am aware of it."

After Stanton refused to resign, Johnson again summoned Grant. In this interview the President asked the General point blank, "Is there anything between us? I have heard it intimated that there was." Grant replied that he had not agreed with Johnson's opposition to the Fourteenth Amendment and the Reconstruction acts, but that beyond this difference of opinion there was "nothing personal" between them. Once more Johnson asked Grant if he would be willing to serve in Stanton's post. Once more the General replied that he would "obey orders." The following day Stanton was suspended and Grant took over as Secretary of War *ad interim*.

Coming in the summer of 1867 this action was one of the most commendable of Johnson's administration. Granted that the Radical attack on the President's powers might have been fended off if Johnson had got rid of Stanton earlier. Granted Secretary Welles' judgment that had Johnson "been less yielding, less hesitating, more prompt and decided, met Radical error and misrule at the threshold, checked the first innovations on his prerogative, dismissed at once faithless public officers, he would have saved himself and the country many difficulties." The fact remains that Johnson's removal of Stanton was decidedly a case of better late than never.

By the summer of 1867 the President's alternatives had become painfully clear. He could stand by, do nothing, wring his hands and fade ignominiously but comfortably out of the picture as James Buchanan had done on the eve of the Civil War. Or he could challenge his enemies and put to the test their most dramatic attack on his prerogatives, the Tenure of Office Act, by dismissing Stanton. In choosing to fight, of course, he risked impeachment, but that was a risk Johnson had already decided to take. He had made this clear to his Cabinet shortly after the passage of the first Reconstruction Act. Urging the President to execute the act promptly, Secretary McCulloch argued that to do so "would tend to prevent impeachment."

Ordinarily, at Cabinet meetings, Johnson's manner was calm but on this occasion he threw control to the winds. He informed McCulloch that "he was tired of being threatened—that he would not be influenced by any such considerations, but would go forward in the conscientious discharge of his duty without reference to Congress, and meet all the consequences." In recording the President's words in his diary, Secretary Browning took refuge in the delicate spelling habits of the day. Johnson was very angry. "Let them impeach," he roared, "and be d-m-d!"

Stanton's removal occasioned surprisingly little furor. Even among the enemies of the President mourning was muted and superficial. As Radicals they appreciated Stanton's services to their cause but, as men, many of them found him difficult to admire. Not that the impeachment movement slackened or that the President's troubles were at an end.

Many of them revolved around the administration of the South under military rule. For a time there was hope in Radical circles that Johnson, believing the Reconstruction acts unconstitutional, would refuse to execute them and thus make himself eligible for impeachment. But the President had no such intentions. His hatred of the laws never abated; he did everything he could to mitigate the damage they imposed upon the South; but his execution of them was scrupulous.

One of his first tasks was to appoint commanders for the five military districts into which Congress had divided the ten unrepresented states. In making his selections Johnson tried not to offend his enemies. In fact some of the districts were ruled for varying periods by Generals of pronounced Radical leanings. Falling into this category, among others, were Philip H. Sheridan and David E. Sickles, both of whom in the eyes of the President were guilty of high-handed and oppressive measures within their commands. Shortly after Stanton's suspension, Johnson replaced first Sheridan and then Sickles, and in both instances Grant not only objected to the removal of these Generals from their Southern posts but pushed his objections to the point of being almost insubordinate. The result was a series of run-ins, from which neither President nor Secretary of War *ad interim* emerged umblemished. Johnson was tactless and Grant's arguments reflected coaching by his Radical friends and a woeful ignorance of where his authority ended and that of the Chief Executive began.

These arguments with Grant were worrisome to the President. In the wake of the fall, 1867, elections, with Democratic victories chalked up at several points, the impeachment movement gained momentum. There was a rumor, one that later showed brief signs of materializing, that the Radicals were scheming to deprive Johnson of his position even before he could be placed on trial in the Senate. This was to be done by arresting and suspending him from office the minute an impeachment resolution passed the House. No sanction for such action existed in the Constitution and most of Johnson's advisers were of the opinion that if such an attempt were made he would be duty-bound to resist it. But what of the Secretary of War *ad interim?* It was plain by this time that Grant, pleased at the prospect of being the next occupant of the White House, was deferring more and more to the powerful Radical leaders. If Congress passed a law suspending the President pending trial, what would Grant do? Would he take the position that constitutional or not, the law was a law, and order the Army to see that it was executed, or would he stand by the President?

In mid-October Johnson, at the urging of Secretary Welles, called on Grant at the War Office. Once more the President's purpose was to make certain that he and the General understood one another.

Johnson opened the interview with a résumé of the situation confronting him. He assumed that Grant was aware of the fact that the rights of the Presidential office were under fire and that Johnson had no choice but to defend those rights and do all he could to vindicate the dignity and independence of the executive. Once these general propositions had been aired, Johnson presented to Grant a hypothetical situation and a question.

The President, as he would later point out in so many words to Grant, did not believe that Secretary Stanton was covered by the Tenure of Office Act. He realized that Congress might take a contrary view. Quite likely the Senate, soon to be in session, would refuse to concur in the suspension of Stanton; but whatever the Senate did, Johnson was not going to reinstate Stanton. The question then: If the Senate acted as anticipated and Stanton then wished to regain possession of the War Office, what steps would he have to take?

Grant's answer was prompt. He said his view of the matter was the same as the one he had expressed in connection with a recent dispute in Baltimore. The Governor of Maryland had ordered the removal of the Baltimore police commissioners and their replacement by new men. The old commissioners had refused to get out, and Grant's view had been that technically the Governor had a right to order them out, but since they were *in* the only way the Governor could assert his right was by an appeal to the courts. By the same token, Grant reasoned, Stanton would still be *out* even after the Senate voted in his favor; and to get back *in* he would have to appeal to the courts.

Johnson was pleased with this response. It corresponded with the plans he had in mind in case the Senate sought to reinstate Stanton. The President's hope was that Stanton would be forced to go to the local courts, whereupon the matter could be carried up to the United States Supreme Court. The high bench could then pass on the constitutionality of the Tenure of Office Act.

There was a little further conversation and the President departed under the impression that he and Grant had arrived at an understanding. If the Senate ordered Stanton reinstated, Grant was to do one of two things. He was to remain on as Secretary of War *ad interim,* thus compelling Stanton to appeal to the courts. Of, if he decided that he would rather not be involved in the necessary judicial proceedings, he was to resign and turn the War Office over to Johnson sufficiently ahead of time to enable Johnson to place the office in the hands of another man until such time as Stanton's appeal could be settled. Grant revealed that he had not as yet given the Tenure of Office Act careful study; "but what I have stated," he said, "is the general principle and if I should change my mind in this particular case I will inform you of the fact."

Such was the agreement between Johnson and Grant in October of 1867. Had matters worked out along these lines, Congress would have found it difficult, perhaps impossible, to impeach the President. But as we will shortly see, matters did not work out this way.

On November 21 Congress reconvened and on December 12 Johnson sent to the Senate a formal notification of his suspension of Stanton along with an able and tempered explanation of his reasons for doing so. The President's major argument was that the relationship of President and Cabinet minister was "analogous to that of principal and agent." The President was under oath to execute the laws and he should not be compelled to retain as his agent and confidential adviser anyone who consistently and deliberately hampered him in the fulfillment of these duties.

The Senate did not act quickly. The matter was referred to the Committee on Military Affairs. The holidays had come and gone when on Friday, January 10, 1868, the Committee reported, recommending that the Senate refuse to concur in the suspension. The Democrats went into action immediately in an effort to stave off a ballot. The Radicals did not even bother to reply. On Saturday and until late Monday afternoon they listened in silence, confident that as soon as the opposition tired of talking the Senate would pass the recommended resolution.

Some weeks earlier, Johnson had summoned General Sherman to Washington on temporary duty. An incurable optimist, the President was still hopeful of preventing Grant from "going over" completely to the Radicals and he believed Sherman might be able to pound some sense into his fellow-general's head. Secretary Welles was dubious. His guess, confided to his diary shortly before Sherman's arrival in October, was that "the stubborn will and selfishness of Grant will overpower the yielding genius and generous impulses of Sherman . . . That Sherman has a mortal antipathy to Stanton and is really in sympathy with the President, I can well suppose, but when he associates with Grant, I apprehend from what I have seen and understood he will be powerless. Had he been here for the last fifteen months, his influence upon Grant, who is subordinated by Stanton, whom he dislikes, might have been salutary. He can now do but little."

Welles' doubts were to prove well founded. Earlier Sherman had recognized the revolutionary intent of the Radical attack on Johnson, but somehow he failed to grasp the fact that the crisis over Stanton was the moment at which this attack might be halted. He made no effort to lure Grant away from his new associates. On the contrary he believed his old soldier friend when Grant told him that he had not accepted the Cabinet post to be useful to Johnson but to protect the Army against Johnson—a statement which Grant later made to the President himself and which shows how thoroughly he had imbibed the doctrines of Thaddeus Stevens and followers.

On the same day—Friday, January 10—that the Senate received the committee report disapproving of Stanton's suspension, Grant informed Sherman that if the Senate voted as anticipated he was going to resign as Secretary of War *ad interim*. Sherman urged Grant to convey his decision to the President at once and Grant called at the White House the following afternoon.

Once more President and General stood face to face. Grant said that if the Senate refused to concur in the suspension, he had no choice but to resign. Recently he had studied the Tenure of Office Act. He had discovered in it a punitive clause, under which he could be imprisoned for five years and fined $10,000 if he persisted in retaining his office in defiance of its terms. Johnson waved these fears aside. He said he had not appointed Grant under the Tenure of Office Act. He had done so under the Constitution, and he had informed the Senate of Stanton's suspension merely as a matter of courtesy. As far as that went, Johnson said, he would be happy to serve any prison terms or pay any fines that might befall the General.

The two men talked for more than an hour. They arrived at no conclusions, but when they parted, the President was under the impression that Grant had promised to return to the White House on Monday to let Johnson know what he was going to do. If such was the General's promise, he broke it. Late Monday afternoon the Democrats ran out of speeches and the Senate passed the resolution which in effect ordered the reinstatement of Stanton. That night there was a ball at the White House. Grant was present but he made no effort to communicate with the President concerning the Senate's vote.

Tuesday morning, which was January 14, Grant was a busy man. During the preceding evening he had received from the Senate an official notice of its action on Stanton. Stuffing this document into an envelope, Grant had one of his aides carry it to the President along with a note declaring that "according to the provisions of Section 2" of the Tenure of Office Act, "my functions as Secretary of War *ad interim* ceased from the moment of the receipt of the enclosed notice."

The understanding had clearly been that at this point Grant was to turn the Secretaryship over to the President. But Grant did not proceed in this manner. He turned the office over to Stanton. He did this by bolting one door of the war office on the inside, locking the other on the outside and handing the key to the Assistant Adjutant, General E. D. Townsend, better known in the Army as "Aunt Nancy." A few minutes later, having picked up the key from Townsend, Edwin McMasters Stanton was once more ensconced as Secretary of War.

XXIII

"THE MOST DANGEROUS SPOT

ON EARTH"

Colonel Moore was with the President when Grant's resignation arrived at the White House. Johnson made no effort to disguise his feelings. Grant's behavior, he declared, was "duplicity." On that day, Tuesday January 14, there was a Cabinet meeting and the President sent word to Army headquarters, whence Grant had retreated, that he hoped the General would attend.

The General arrived and the scene in the council room was a distressing one. Present, in addition to Grant and the President, were Secretaries Seward, McCulloch, Stanbery, Welles, Randall and Browning. Johnson asked several sharp questions. Subsequently, when Grant's answers became a matter of public dispute, Stanbery urged the President to protect himself. The Attorney General's suggestion was that Johnson solicit from each of the other five Cabinet ministers a letter detailing his recollection of Grant's responses. Although Secretary Seward gave Grant the benefit of the doubt on some minor points, all five letters were in agreement on essentials.

The first of Johnson's questions had to do with his talk with Grant at the War Department some months before. At that time, had the General not agreed that should the Senate refuse to concur in Stanton's suspension, he (Grant) would either remain on as Secretary of War *ad interim* or resign sufficiently ahead of Senate action to permit Johnson to name someone else to the post? The President's other questions referred to his talk with Grant at the White House on the previous Saturday. At that time had Grant not assured the President that their agreement still held, and had he not promised to confer again with Johnson on Monday?

The recollection of four of the Cabinet members was that Grant's answers to all three questions was an unmistakable yes. Seward characterized Grant's replies as neither "denying nor . . . explicitly admitting" anything, but agreed with the others that General Grant had never "distinctly or finally advised you [Johnson] of his determination to retire from the charge of the War Department otherwise than under your own subsequent direction." Welles was struck by the General's "humble" and "hesitating" manner. He took it to mean that Grant was suffering from bad conscience. Another interpretation is possible. It was galling to the hero of Appomattox to be called on the carpet and lectured like a school-boy, galling to hear his word questioned. Grant was obtuse about political matters. It is conceivable that, face to face with a roomful of sharp minds, he said things he did not quite mean. In any event, during a later exchange of acrimonious letters with Johnson he presented a different version of what had happened. He denied admitting anything at the Cabinet meeting, insisted he had broken no promises and asserted that any "understanding" between him and Johnson existed only in Johnson's mind.

Frankly, what Grant said at the Cabinet meeting of January 14, 1868, or in his letters is not too important. The facts speak for themselves. General Grant was suffering from an affliction easily recognized in Washington: Presidentitis. Eager to keep in the good graces of the Republican leaders, he let Andrew Johnson down. Thanks to the General's defection, Johnson could not now force Stanton into the courts. The President was in a tight spot. He could give up the battle and leave Stanton where he was, an intolerable situation. Or he could continue to seek a court test of the Tenure of Office Act by taking the only step by which that could now be achieved. He could defy the act by appointing another Secretary of War and demanding that Stanton turn over the office to the appointee.

The procrastinating Andrew Johnson of an earlier date had disappeared. He moved as swiftly as he could. For weeks he cast about in a frenzied effort to find someone who would take the Cabinet post, no easy task since whoever accepted was certain to become a sacrificial lamb. Twice Johnson offered the office to General Sherman. Twice Sherman refused, pleading his desire to remain aloof from politics. Johnson offered the post to the chief clerk of the War Department who begged off. He tried in vain to give it to General George H. Thomas, the "Rock of Chickamaugua." In the end he was compelled to lean on another General Thomas, a frail reed, a man whom Johnson himself realized carried no weight. This man was Major-General Lorenzo Thomas of Delaware. Lorenzo Thomas was something of a gay dog, convivial, vain and a conservative in politics. Member of a military family and educated at West Point he had behind him a long and impeccable professional career.

Many of the President's friends, cognizant of Johnson's predicament, urged him to abandon the effort. But the President's mind was made up; Stanton must go. "If the people," he told Colonel Moore, "do not entertain sufficient respect for their Chief Magistrate to uphold me in such a measure, then I ought to resign." He summoned Lorenzo Thomas and sounded out the old general on his willingness to accept appointment. Then he had Moore prepare three documents. One was a message to Stanton, dismissing him from his office and ordering him to turn it over to Thomas. The other was Thomas' appointment, making him Secretary of War *ad interim*. The third was a message to the Senate, informing that body of what the President was doing.

Thomas, hastening to the White House at Johnson's bidding, was delighted. The white-haired Adjutant-General knew what he was in for, but for the moment he could think of nothing but the glory surrounding the post to which he was being elevated. Johnson's instructions were for Thomas, armed with the proper documents and accompanied by a witness, to go at once to the War Office and demand it from Stanton. Taking a fellow officer along with him, Thomas was off like a shot.

Stanton's manner was pleasant, fond and patronizing, the manner most men automatically adopted toward the amiable Adjutant-General. "Do you wish me to vacate at once," he asked Thomas, "or will you give me time to take away my private property?" Thomas told Stanton to "act your pleasure," to take his time, he would return on the morrow and take over. Stanton's manner was the velvet glove over the iron fist throughout. His last words were as soft as a pillow. "I do not know," he said, "whether I will obey your instructions or resist them."

Back to the White House went Thomas, happy as a lark, to give the President a report of progress. But the old warrior might not have stepped across President's Park with such martial briskness had he been able to witness the scenes he was leaving behind.

No sooner was Thomas gone than Stanton was in action. He dispatched to the Senate a formal notice of what Johnson was trying to do. He followed this with a barrage of notes to individual Senators. To Fessenden, Howard and Edmunds, jointly: "Adjutant-General Thomas is boasting . . . that he intends to take possession of the War Department at nine o'clock tomorrow morning. If the Senate does not declare its opinion of the laws, how am I to hold possession?" To John Conness of California: "I am at the War Department and mean to continue in possession until expelled by force."

By this time Johnson's formal message had reached Capitol Hill and the Radicals were in a state of delirium tremens. At 2:30 the Senate went into executive session for the purpose of framing a resolution. Rapidly voted at the conclusion of the huddle, it asserted that "under the Constitution and the laws" the President had "no power to remove the Secretary of War and to designate any other officer to perform" his duties.

Some of the Radicals rushed to the War Department to implore Stanton to stand his ground. Tears flowed from their eyes as they clustered about Old Mars. Touched, he fell to weeping with them. It was a damp occasion. One of the Senators brought along the most incredibly brief message its author ever wrote:

United States Senate
Hon. Edwin H. [sic] Stanton:
Stick!

CHARLES SUMNER

Old Mars assured his sodden supporters that he would. He did. For the next several weeks, except for short walks under guard, he would never set foot outside of the War Office. He would sleep on the old sofa, and eat the meals brought in by his guards or Mrs. Stanton. General Sherman, paying the self-imprisoned minister a visit, discovered that not only were the doors of the War Office locked but also all but one of those of the building itself. The General went chuckling to the White House to report his findings to Colonel Moore. "Why," he declared, "the Secretary takes more precautions . . . than I thought of when traveling through the Indian country . . . is surrounded by bayonets and locked in by bolts and bars." To the General this was confirmation of his contention that Washington was "the most dangerous spot on earth."

During the fortnight beginning Friday, February 21, it was certainly one of the most jittery. Attending a party Friday night, Edgar Welles, son of the Secretary of the Navy, noticed something that he passed on to his father who passed it on to Johnson. Twice during the party orders had arrived calling on certain army officers present to report to headquarters. Could this mean, Johnson wondered, that Congress was about to make good on its threat to arrest him? The President promptly summoned Major-General William Helmsley Emory, commander of the department of Washington.

What passed between them would be one of the highlights of the testimony at the forthcoming impeachment trial.

Rumors coursed through the city. One was that the President had called up the marines to eject Stanton. Speaker Colfax of the House received an agitated message from the police chief of New York. A shipment of nitroglycerine had mysteriously disappeared from the city; destination unknown but presumably Washington. Additional police were flung around the Capitol. Even so some Congressmen considered the place unsafe and were clamoring for immediate adjournment. Old Thad quieted them with one of his favorite words, "Humbug!" he snorted. The impression in some circles was that the President, backed by the army, was about to take over Congress; in others that Congress, ditto, was about to take over the President. In the popular mind the stretch of Pennsylvania Avenue twixt White House and Capitol Hill had become a no-man's land.

Secretary Welles' son was not the only party-goer on the night of Friday, February 21. General Lorenzo Thomas accompanied his daughter and one of her little girl friends to a masquerade ball, at which the General donned a mask of memorable grotesqueness. In his mind's eye Thomas was already Secretary of War. At the ball, and going to and fro, he was accosted by sundry friends and reporters, told of Stanton's determination to "stick," asked how he planned to proceed. The General assured his questioners that he had everything under control. He would be taking over the War Office tomorrow; if Stanton barred the doors, he would simply break them down!

The night was far spent when Thomas returned to his H Street home, aglow with pride and spirits and blissfully unaware of the shoals ahead. Sometime between two and three o'clock Saturday morning the venerable Return J. Meigs, clerk of the supreme court of the District of Columbia, was routed from his slumbers to affix his seal to a warrant, signed by Stanton, charging that contrary to the Tenure of Office Act General Thomas had attempted to seize the war office and calling for the General's arrest. At 7 A.M. David

S. Gooding, United States marshal for the District of Columbia, was routed from his slumbers to execute the warrant. At 8 A.M. a startled General Thomas was taken in custody by Gooding, another marshal and a constable.

En route to court Thomas asked permission to stop by the White House to tell the President what had happened. To Andrew Johnson this not altogether unexpected development was the answer to a prayer. Here, at long last, was the opportunity for which he had been hoping. Now perhaps, by some legal device, the troublesome matter could be brought before the United States Supreme Court and the Tenure of Office Act declared unconstitutional. "Very well," he said to Thomas, "we want it in the courts."

Following instructions received at the White House, Thomas, completing his journey to court, gave bail and promised to return for trial on the following Wednesday.

Leaving court, he made another brief stop at the White House. Then he marched to the War Department to assume the duties of his new office. Stanton was not alone. Several friends were with him and their later description of what Thomas said to Stanton and *vice versa* would provide the spectators at the impeachment trial with some of their most entertaining moments. Thomas demanded the office. Stanton refused and ordered Thomas back to his post as Adjutant-General. Thomas refused to go, demanded the office again and was refused again. More talk, and considerable moving about from room to room before General Thomas, thoroughly perplexed, hurried back to the White House to report this latest turn of events to his anxious chief.

Early that afternoon two flags were hoisted above the House wing of the Capitol. The Senate stood adjourned. Most of its members were on the other side of the building, watching an unprecedented event: the impeachment of a President of the United States.

XXIV

IMPEACHMENT

Impeachment was put through with amazing haste. To its prime mover, Thaddeus Stevens, speed was of the essence. During the preceding September Old Thad had suffered a serious breakdown. A reporter for a Boston newspaper, visiting him the following month, was shocked at what he described as "the total wreck" of a once "powerful and athletic frame." It was a dying man who on Friday, February 21, 1868, lumbered to his feet in the House at 2:30 P.M. when the news arrived that the President had defied the Tenure of Office Act. One hand grasping a cane, the other resting on the arm of Representative Bingham of Ohio, he moved about the chamber, saying: "Didn't I tell you so? If you don't kill the beast it will kill you."

To bulky John Covode of Pennsylvania fell the honor of offering the appropriate resolution. Boutwell performed the next parliamentary duty, moving that the resolution be referred to the Joint Committee on Reconstruction with orders to report back fast. By the time adjournment came, shortly before 5 P.M., it was common knowledge throughout the city that the House of Representatives was going to try to impeach the seventeenth President on the birthday of the first.

Saturday, February 22 dawned cold with a wet snow draining from a dismal sky. Early in the morning masses of people were trudging through the slush of the Capitol grounds en route to the House galleries. By ten not only the galleries but the corridors leading to them were filled. As noon approached and with it the opening of the session, the police, locking arms in front of the outer doors, were having trouble keeping latecomers from pushing in. There was a move to open the cloakrooms to the overflow, but the motion was shouted down. Reporters, fighting their way to the press gallery, found their chairs occupied by ladies who refused to be dislodged.

The Senate met, heard its chaplain intone a prayer beginning "Thou settest up one and puttest down another," and adjourned. Its members then filed into the House where President *pro tem* Ben Wade, who would be put up if Johnson was put down, was given a seat on the rostrum alongside Speaker Colfax.

The House chaplain stumbled over his words. The spectators, damp and odoriferous in the jammed galleries, were restless. Stevens and the other House members of the Joint Committee, meeting at 10:30 that morning, were still out, working behind closed doors elsewhere in the building. There was nothing to watch, nothing to listen to but languid debate over routine bills. Congressman Eldridge, Wisconsin's alert Democrat, provided a diversion by calling on the House to honor an annual custom by having the Clerk read Washington's Farewell Address. Colfax banged him out of order. A heckler in the gallery shouted, "How about Johnson's farewell address!" and whoops of glee all but drowned out another and repeated banging of the gavel. Eldridge said he would propose a reading of the Constitution but he assumed that, too, would be out of order.

At 2:20 there was a craning of necks in the gallery, a muttered "There he is! There he is!", then a hush as a door near the rostrum opened and Thaddeus Stevens, leaning heavily on his cane, came in, followed by the other committee members. The old man did not speak from the floor. He took a chair on the left of the Speaker and there he remained throughout the debate, standing or slouched in his seat and occasionally retiring to one of the cloakrooms to lie down.

He presented the committee report. It was a simple resolution to impeach the President. He saw no reason for debate but if the Democrats wanted to say something and the Republicans wished to reply, he would yield, with the understanding that he was to have the last word. Later he arranged for stringent rules: no one to speak for more than half an hour, all speeches other than his own to end at 4:30 the following Monday afternoon.

James Brooks of New York led off for the Democrats. He characterized the impeachment movement as an attempt by Congress to seize "sole control of the Government . . . I solemnly bid them beware. . . ." If it succeeded, he warned, future Congresses could impeach a President "for the hat he wears or for the color of his coat." The impeachers, Brooks contended, were moved by a fear that the people were with the Democratic party. "The sacrifice of two of the three branches of Government," he charged, "is deemed indispensably necessary to keep the Republican party in power." Other Democrats spoke, often pointedly but in vain. On the majority side of the House nobody wanted to listen, everybody wanted to talk. For hours on Saturday and again on Monday the chamber reverberated with vituperation.

John F. Farnsworth of Illinois: "Sir, this nation has been too long disgraced by this man, this accidental President. . . . Let him be removed."

William D. ("Pig Iron") Kelley of Pennsylvania: "The great criminal whom the American people arraign for thousands of crimes."

John A. Logan of Illinois: "[He] has done every act a man can conceive of, not only . . . to degrade himself, but to destroy the rights of the American people."

Henry L. Cake of Pennsylvania: "To the work of debauching the departments Andrew Johnson has brought all the cunning of the practical demagogue."

Elihu B. Washburne of Illinois: "His personal and official character has made him the opprobrium of both hemispheres . . . As mendacious as he is malignant . . . Surrounded by red-handed rebels, advised and counseled by the worst men that ever crawled like filthy reptiles at the footstool of power, the President has used all the vast authority of the Government to prevent the reunion of the States, the restoration of harmony and peace and happiness to the country."

On and on it went, a spectacle that the public of Washington, accustomed though it was to the bizarre ways of Congress, would not soon forget. These were not thinking men, and the House of Representatives for the time being was not a deliberative body but a mob. Its Republican members were not speaking for the people they represented. They were speaking only for the ears of the strange, dying old man who sat up there, slumped in his chair, to the left of the Speaker.

It was Old Thad's show. This was the moment for which he had lived and struggled and labored and schemed since the opening of the 39th Congress two years before. Twice, during the last twelve months, he had seen full-scale attempts at impeachment fall by the wayside. The first had collapsed in the closing weeks of 1867, amidst the mocking laughter of the public when the ridiculous "findings" of the Congressional investigation came to light. The second had occurred briefly only a few weeks before when the Joint Committee had requested the correspondence between Johnson and Grant, only to discover that there was nothing in it pointing to executive criminality.

Old Thad spoke few words during the debate. By quiet signals to the Speaker—a lift of the eyebrows, a small movement of the hands—he guided the proceedings. Late Saturday night a second effort was made to mark the birthday of the first President in the traditional manner by having Washington's Farewell Address read. This time the motion was put by William S. Holman, Democrat of Indiana. John A. Peters, Republican of Maine, objected that the address was not germane to the question under debate. Another Republican, William Lawrence of Ohio, quipped that it was germane; it had to do with retirement from office. The famous James Gillespie Blaine of Maine was spelling Colfax in the chair. He ruled it was *not* germane. But then came the quiet signal from Stevens, a signal saying in effect "the public might not like this insult to the first President." Whereupon the majority changed its mind and the House voted not to hear the Address but to let it appear in the records as part of the debate.

Late Saturday night the House recessed. The clock was set back and the session of Saturday 22 was completed Monday morning. Outside a storm wind tore at the still-falling snow. Inside angry voices rose and fell in the hot and foul-smelling chamber. At 11:59 A.M. the House went through the formalities of adjourning the session of February 22 and opening the session of February 24.

The hours strode on, speech following speech. At 4:30 the gavel fell. Old Thad, who had been resting in a cloakroom, hobbled in and up to the rostrum to say the last word. The scene that followed, according to *Harper's Weekly*, was "one of the most interesting ever witnessed in the House. When Stevens said in a clear and emphatic voice, 'Never was a great malefactor so gently treated as Andrew Johnson,' even the noisy galleries became quiet, and a deathlike stillness reigned." According to *Harper's* correspondent the silence

was broken a moment afterward, but for a moment only, by the movement of persons in the rear seats of the gallery rising to lean forward and by the general movement on the floor of the House of the members who, walking on tip-toe, approached the Speaker [Stevens] and gazed up into his face while he spoke.

Even the pages ceased their noiseless movement about the room, and gathered near the old man, perhaps more to gaze upon than to hear him. The Chairman, too, left his chair and stood before the Clerk's desk, to hear and watch the old "leader of the House." This speech, the last on Impeachment in the House, will probably also be the last great effort of Mr. Stevens, as he is very weak and aged and has been warned by his friends of an early end to his earthly career.

Old Thad spoke as always, wasting no words, every sentence a hammer blow. Conceding that for the time being the impeachment proceedings rested on Johnson's defiance of the Tenure of Office Act, Stevens contended that they had been made necessary by a host of flagrant misdeeds. There was Johnson's attitude toward the Negro. Ignoring the fact that the President's position was that regulation of suffrage belonged to the states and not to the Federal Government, Stevens characterized Johnson as one who believed it "undemocratic to legislate for unrepresented whites, but not for unrepresented blacks; that though Congress may not rule whites against their will, whites may rule blacks against their will . . . Color in Mr. Johnson's mind is evidently an essential political distinction, and not an incidental or artificial one." He reviewed Johnson's correspondence with Grant, finding in the President's desire to bring the Tenure of Office Act before the courts "a high official misdemeanor," an "effort to prevent the execution of the law." Once more he declared that "the sovereign power of the nation rests in Congress, who have been placed around the President . . . as watchmen to enforce his obedience to the law and the Constitution."

It was all over. By a straight-party vote, 126 to 47, the President was impeached.

XXV

THE SENATE AS A COURT

All was quiet at the White House that Monday morning. There were no police at the doors, no excitement within. The President asked his confidential secretary to stay for dinner in the evening. Colonel William George Moore was 37, an energetic and quick-moving man who had entered the war as a private and risen in the ranks. Easy-going and affable, he was probably closer to the President than anyone outside of Johnson's immediate family. He and the President were at table, talking contentedly of small matters, when the news arrived. Johnson received it calmly. "I think," he said, "many of those who have voted for impeachment feel more uneasy as to the position in which they have thus placed themselves than I do as to the situation in which they have put me."

At his home on the north side of Lafayette Square, Secretary Welles pondered events and dropped an arresting comment into his diary. "I have sometimes," he wrote, "been almost tempted to listen to the accusation of his [Johnson's] enemies that he desired and courted impeachment. Yet such is not the fact."

It most certainly was not. Johnson suffered from occasional failures of nerve, from bouts of terrible unsureness; but one searches his actions in vain for any symptoms of an appetite for

[275]

martyrdom. He had defied the Senate only because he realized that unless the line were drawn somewhere, the Presidential office would shortly be reduced to a mockery. At this point, moreover, he still had hopes of pulling the rug out from under the impeachers by bringing the Tenure of Office Act before the United States Supreme Court.

The critical moment in that development was reached on Wednesday when the jaunty Adjutant-General, free on $5000 bail since the preceding Saturday, stepped into a District of Columbia courtroom to stand trial in the case number 5711, *The United States* v. *Lorenzo Thomas*. Two lawyers accompanied Thomas, one of them employed by himself, the other by the President. At the White House, conferring with Johnson, the attorneys had matured their plans. They were not going to ask for further bail. They were going to surrender their client into custody and then sue for a writ of *habeas corpus* with a view to obtaining a quick Supreme Court hearing.

But the President's foes knew better than to let this happen and they had the means to stop it. The District court judge, David K. Cartter, was a close friend of Stanton, one of his "creatures," according to Secretary Welles. When Thomas' attorneys approached the bench and made plain their intentions, Judge Cartter grinned. No one, he said in effect, would dream of putting a nice man like Lorenzo Thomas in jail; case dismissed!

Actually, technically, the case was not dismissed. It was merely dropped, forgotten, swept under the rug. According to the New York *Commercial Advertiser* Judge Cartter's action was "based upon previous consultation" with the Radicals. It "was an implied admission," the newspaper editorialized, "that Congress dare not submit its acts to a judicial interpretation . . . apprehensive that even so partial a judge as Mr. Chase [of the Supreme Court] would be compelled to decide the tenure-of-office bill unconstitutional." So fell to the ground Andrew Johnson's final attempt to remove from the books the law on which his impeachment rested.

On Capitol Hill preparations for the trial of the President moved steadily forward. The House elected seven of its members to serve as managers. Although the nominal head of this body was John A. Bingham of Ohio, Ben Butler contrived to nab for himself the role of chief prosecuting attorney. The other House managers were Stevens, Wilson of Iowa, Thomas Williams of Pennsylvania and John A. Logan of Illinois. All were Republicans and confirmed Radicals.

Over on the other side of the building the Senate voted twenty-five rules to govern its conduct as a court of impeachment. This action drew a rebuke from Salmon Portland Chase who, as Chief Justice of the Supreme Court, would preside at the trial. Chase charged the Senators with being premature. The Senate, sitting as a legislative body, was one thing; sitting as a court with each of its members under special oath, it was something else. The Chief Justice argued that until the Senate organized as a court it had no right to lay down rules for its behavior as such.

Chase's unsolicited advice gave rise to no end of speculation. What was happening to the man whom a Southern newspaper had once described as the "high priest of radicalism"? Was he drawing away from the Radicals? He was—reluctantly and with what inner turmoil it is not difficult to imagine. Chase still had his eyes on the White House, and the New York *Herald* was predicting that he, rather than Grant, would be the Republican nominee in 1868.

The Chief Justice was a large man, over six feet. Bland-faced and clean-shaven prior to the impeachment trial, during which he began growing a beard, he was the possessor of a physical grandeur beyond the ability of a mere human to live up to, a fact of which no one was more aware than Salmon Portland Chase himself. Intermittently and disloyally, as Lincoln's Secretary of the Treasury during the war, he had striven to discredit his chief so as to succeed him in the White House. There was that about Chase—the heavy good looks, the orotund voice—that made him a natural target for witticisms. It was said that as he lathered for his daily shave he invariably addressed his mirror with the words, "Good morning, Mr.

President." Another quip, originating with Ben Wade, had it that he regarded himself as "the fourth member of the Trinity."

Some observers, smitten by Chase's awesome façade, thought the Chief Justice cold. Impassive on the outside, he was ablaze within like a smokeless volcano. A devout Methodist, his mind was a battleground between grasping ambition on the one hand and adherence to the Christian ethic with its emphasis on humility on the other. His intellectual attainments were great, but humor was seldom apparent among them. During his secretaryship he had devised for United States coins and bills the legend, "In God we trust." The government was in financial straits at the time, its coffers empty, its debts mountainous. When Lincoln suggested that under the circumstances a more appropriate legend would be the words of Saints Peter and John, "Silver and gold have I none, but such as I have I give thee," Chase was shocked by what he considered unseemly levity in the face of national disaster.

If a certain pomposity bespoke the outer Chase, a goodness of heart and a devotion to principle bespoke the inner. He had everything to gain from going along with the Radicals; everything, that is, except peace of mind. All that was honest behind that stonily handsome façade rebelled at the subversion of the Judiciary under Radical Reconstruction. "I do not believe in military government for American states," he said; "nor in military commissions for the trial of American citizens, nor in the subversion of the executive and judicial departments of the general government by Congress, no matter how patriotic the motive may be."

Radical dissatisfaction with the Chief Justice increased when on Wednesday night he gave a reception at his home at Sixth and E Streets and the President, accompanied by his daughters, made a brief but dramatic appearance. It increased tenfold when the Chief Justice contended that as presiding officer of the Senate, sitting as a Court, he must be allowed to vote in cases of tie, a position that was later sustained. As the opening of the trial drew near, it became clear that the Chief Justice intended to conduct it fairly. He was going to do everything in his power to keep it from degenerating into a mere political inquest. Salmon Portland Chase had become the first political casualty of the forthcoming battle; he had crossed a little Rubicon of his own.

At the White House Johnson was busy with the tasks connected with readying his own side of the case. He was cast down by his failure to invoke a Supreme Court test of the Tenure of Office Act, buoyed up by an avalanche of friendly letters and telegrams.

From Social Hall on Fayette Street in Baltimore came the tender of seventy-five well-drilled men. Just "telegraph to say where and when we can serve you," wrote Captain Hugh O'Brien. Signing himself "Dick Singleton, colored voter," a Charleston Negro wrote: "Hold fast, there are One Hundred thousand Loyal Colored men in South Carolina who stand by the man that supports the Constitution and the laws of our country." Another document of similar import bore the signatures of almost a thousand South Carolina Negroes. From Greeneville, from the President's old friend Sam Milligan, came a note to be "calm and firm" no matter what, a reminder that in the long pull "accused and accusers, thank God," would have to be tried before the great tribunal of history.

The members of the President's official household closed ranks. An emissary of the Radicals approached Secretary Seward with a proposition. Let Seward put no obstacles in the path of impeachment and Ben Wade, who would succeed Johnson following his conviction, would retain the little New Yorker as Secretary of State. "I will see you damned first," was Seward's rejoinder. "The impeachment of the President is the impeachment of his Cabinet."

Attorney General Stanbery, chosen to head the President's counsel, resigned his Cabinet post to give full time to the job. A mild-appearing man with his heavy sideburns and humorous face, "courteous, gentlemanly and dignified," Stanbery was in very poor health—a fact which gave point to his statement to Johnson: "Mr. President if I can only keep well for this trial, I will be willing to be sick during the balance of my life."

Thus encouraged, the President went ahead with the preparation of his defense. Stanbery and all the other members of his counsel, among them some of the finest legal minds in the country, donated their services.

Among the other lawyers selected by the President was the Jeremiah Sullivan Black whom we last encountered in the act of giving the House a piece of his mind during the Congressional investigation. Judge Black was singularly able; no doubt he would have been a pillar of strength to Johnson had the two of them not come to a parting of the ways during the third week of March. It had to do with the small Caribbean island of Alta Vela, whose title was in dispute. The Dominican Republic claimed it; so did the United States. The island was valuable for its guano deposits, and the Dominican Republic had leased the rights to some Americans who were working them. It so happened that the Pennsylvania law firm headed by Judge Black and his son Chauncey had among its clients a Baltimore firm known as Patterson, Murguindo and Company. The Baltimore company claimed title to the guano deposits and wanted the United States to enable it to assert its rights to work them by seizing the island.

Long before the impeachment proceedings came into view Judge Black, acting in the interest of his Baltimore client, asked the President to send a warship into the Caribbean to take possession of Alta Vela. There was nothing off-color about this request. The President was inclined to think it just, but when he submitted the matter to Secretary of State Seward an ironic discovery was made. Some years before, a similar guano island title case had arisen and Judge Black, then Attorney General of the United States, had ruled that the government had no right to press its claim. Seward informed the President that, according to the precedent established by Judge Black himself, the United States could not seize Alta Vela and the President so informed the Judge.

But Jere Black and his son Chauncey were not men who gave up easily. Nor was their determination to see Alta Vela seized retarded when their Baltimore client assigned to them and their law partners "one and one-half per cent on all their rights, title and interest in, and to the deposit of guano on the Island of Alta Vela

in trust, to disburse . . . in aid in prosecution of the claim."
When Judge Black accepted with thanks Johnson's invitation to
become one of his defense counsel, his Baltimore client saw an
opportunity and urged the Judge to make the most of it. The suggestion was that Black have some of the impeachment leaders put
a little pressure on the chief executive.

The pressure was brought. Black submitted to the President a
petition, urging the seizure of Alta Vela, and the President was
understandably astonished to find this document signed by no less
than four of the House impeachment managers, including Thaddeus Stevens and Ben Butler!

Johnson was not slow to realize the spot into which Black had
boxed him. If he went along with the petition, he would be giving
in to a veiled bribe since the implication was that if he did so things
would be easier for him at the impeachment trial. If he refused,
Black was certain to resign as one of his counsel and this action
would be widely interpreted as meaning that the eminent Judge was
convinced that the President could not be acquitted.

Johnson remained in character. As he put it to Colonel Moore,
"Thus four of the seven men selected by the House to prosecute
me come to me to ask me to prosecute an award, doubtless that
each might secure to himself a half million, or, it may be, a million,
of dollars. The whole land seems to be rank with corruption. *Judge
Black won't do!*" He informed the Judge that the petition was
denied and the Judge resigned.

As finally selected, the President's counsel consisted of Stanbery
and four other prominent attorneys. The star of this aggregation
was William M. Evarts of New York. A Radical by inclination,
Evarts had never held political office, preferring to confine himself
to legal practice, at which he had few peers. Thin and wiry, his wit
was razor-edged. At a dinner in his honor a friend observed that
he was drinking the potations served with every course. "Mr.
Evarts," he remonstrated, "it will hurt you to drink so many different wines." Evarts smiled. "It isn't different wines that hurt me,"
he said, "it's indifferent wines." Chided for working for Johnson

on a Sunday, he had recourse to Holy Writ. "Is it not written," he queried, "that if thine ass falleth into a pit, it is lawful to pull him out on the Sabbath day?" Evarts brought to the President's legal battery a mind described by *Harper's Weekly* as "lucid, precise and cogent," the mind of a man who was never in haste, but who never hesitated.

The other members of the President's counsel were Benjamin Robbin Curtis of Boston, a man of impeccable character who had served for a time on the Supreme Court where he had won merited fame for his dissenting opinion in the Dred Scot case; Judge Thomas A. R. Nelson of Johnson's home town in Tennessee, and William S. Groesbeck of Ohio, who was chosen to replace Judge Black.

One of the early decisions of counsel was that Johnson should not appear in person before the bar of the Senate, a wise decision in view of the President's somewhat impetuous nature when confronted with a crowd. Johnson was dubious about this move, complained of it bitterly throughout the trial; but he acceded to it and abided by it.

The trial proper began at 1 P.M. March 5, 1868, but the opening sessions were of a technical nature. The chief incident of the first day had to do with Ben Wade. When his name was reached in the roll call, a Democratic Senator protested. He pointed out that if Johnson were convicted, Wade would become President. He argued that Wade should not be allowed to participate in the trial since he had a personal interest in the outcome. All this was mere stalling and formality. The Radicals easily carried the day and on the following afternoon Senator Wade, having promised to "do impartial justice according to the Constitution and the laws; so help me God," was sworn in for the purpose of passing judgment on the chief executive.

On the afternoon of March 7 Johnson was served with the proper papers by George T. Brown, the Senate Sergeant-at-Arms. The President received Brown in his office, standing beside his table, alone except for Colonel Moore. Brown handed over the summons, the President took it, said he "would attend to the matter," and *Harper's Weekly* devoted the front page of its March 28 issue to an elaborate engraving of the scene by its artist.

On the thirteenth the President's counsel asked for forty days in which to prepare their answer to the charges framed by the House. The request was denied. They were given ten days, a short period in view of the length and variety of the charges and the numerous points of fact and law involved.

In a hurried series of committee meetings and debates on the floor the House had formulated a "bill of particulars" against Johnson, consisting of eleven Articles of Impeachment. Although the President was accused of everything from using harsh language to making public speeches "in a loud voice," most of the articles dealt with his alleged violations of the Tenure of Office Act.

The first three articles accused the President of defying the Tenure of Office Act by dismissing Stanton, by issuing a letter authorizing Lorenzo Thomas to take over Stanton's post and by appointing Thomas to the post. Articles IV through VIII accused the President of conspiring with Thomas and unknown "others" to use "intimidation and threats" for the purpose of preventing Stanton from holding his office, of preventing the execution of the tenure act, of seizing property of the United States in the War Department and of controlling the money appropriated to the department and Military Service. Article IX charged that Johnson had endeavored to issue orders directly to Major-General William H. Emory, commander of the military forces in Washington, thus violating that section of the Army Appropriations Act of March 2, 1867, forbidding the President to issue such orders except through the General of the Armies.

Ben Butler was not a member of the House committee assigned to formulate these charges; but Ben got his oar in. He fathered Article X, which was a cataract of words. It quoted portions of speeches made by Johnson in Washington and during the Swing Around the Circle and asserted that in these utterances Johnson had held Congress up to ridicule in an attempt to set aside its "rightful authority."

When Old Thad examined these ten articles, he was disgusted. With characteristic perspicacity he declared them "paltry" and insisted on adding the famous eleventh or "Omnibus Article." This article was intended to be all things to all men. Succinctly it recited practically all of the charges made in the first ten articles and accused the President of deliberately scheming to violate the tenure act, that section of the Army Appropriations Act limiting his powers as Commander-in-Chief, and the first Reconstruction Act.

Such were the "high crimes and misdemeanors" with which Andrew Johnson was charged as the prosecution made ready to put its first witness on the stand and the great trial got under way in dead earnest.

XXVI

THE UNITED STATES VS.

THE PRESIDENT

It is not altogether clear yet whether the Congress will impeach the President, or the President impeach the Congress; or both, indeed. According to present appearances it will be just about nip-and-tuck. The brilliant array of counsel retained by the President are not likely to come before the Senate in any very apologetic . . . attitude . . . It must be borne in mind that the strict rules of legal trial do not apply in impeachment trials. New Testimony can be brought in at any time; special pleading is allowable. . . . It is a sort of loose and popular court, consisting of 50 or 60 judges . . . Counsel accordingly cannot be tied down to petty technicalities, must have a free range over the whole field. Just think of it. Somebody will get impeached badly. There is little doubt about that.

—Springfield (Mass.) *Republican*—Radical

PRESIDENT JOHNSON INSANE. It is a relief to those who are best acquainted with the circumstances of Andrew Johnson's conduct, and it will be a relief to the country to believe that an explanation of his eccentricities may be found, short of the contention that he is guilty of a deliberate, wilful, wicked attempt to overthrow the government. That explanation is furnished by the theory that he is, and long has been, partially insane. Many facts tend to establish this as the true interpretation of his tortuous course.

—New York *Sun*—Independent

A bidder in a horse auction in Nashville last week mounted a mare to try her speed and was so well satisfied that he has not yet returned.

—Washington *Intelligencer*—Conservative

Why take names second hand from abroad, when we have good healthy excitement of domestic growth to organize our shopping nomenclature? Is not Impeachment blue as good as Bismarck brown?

Frank Leslie's Illustrated Newspaper

For eleven and a half weeks, beginning March 5, 1868, the trial of the President absorbed the attention of the country and kept it in an uproar. The members of the lower House, aware that they had a "hit" on their hands, ruled that admission to the Senate galleries during the trial was to be by ticket only. A thousand were printed for each day, good for that day only. Distribution was according to protocol: 40 to the diplomatic corps, 20 to the President, 4 to each Senator, 4 to the Chief Justice, 2 to each Representative, and so on. So great was the clamor for tickets that on the eve of the trial Ben Wade received 400 requests in person, thousands more by mail. The home of Senator Anthony, who had dreamed up the ticket idea, was besieged by such throngs that he had to call in the police.

In the packed galleries on opening day reporters recorded the presence of such luminaries as Anthony Trollope, the British novelist; John Russell Young, managing editor of the New York *Tribune;* Postmaster-General Randall; Mr. Thornton, the British minister; James Gordon Bennett of the New York *Herald;* and stout and venerable Thomas Ewing of Ohio, father-in-law of General Sherman.

Henry Adams found the scene hard to take and even harder to believe. He conceded that the egotistic antics of the Senators were a comedy, but a sad one certain to do "permanent and terrible mischief" to the Republic. Robert Henry Newell put tongue in cheek before placing impressions on paper. He found the trial "the most brilliant scene in our distracted national history." Personally he was compelled to view it through smoked glasses; the dazzle being too much for "eyes not thus protected." The women were responsible for this, according to Newell. It was their "organdy and grenadine" and the fact that this season's dresses "are so low that they are virtually a take-off of everything our mothers used to wear." Newell suggested a program for the trial to be headed "Theatre of War," as follows:

Impeachment;
or
The Man Without a Friend

Man without a friend .... A. Johnson
Macbeth .... B. Wade
Mephistopheles .... Thaddeus S.
First Supernumerary .... S. P. Chase
Corps de Bully .... Butler & Co.
To be followed by the ever popular farce of
"Reconstruction"
To Which has Recently Been Added an Alabama Breakdown.*

Thousands of words were bestowed on the dramatic opening of each day's session. At noon or thereabouts the Senate adjourned as a legislative body, reconvening shortly as a court. At 12:30 or 1 P.M., the hour varying, Chief Justice Chase entered the chamber, resplendent in his official robes and escorted by Senator Pomeroy, head of the committee appointed for that purpose. Chase having seated himself at the President's desk on the rostrum, the sergeant-at-arms made proclamation: "Hear ye! Hear ye! Hear ye! All persons are commanded to keep silence on pain of imprisonment while the Senate of the United States is sitting for the trial of the articles of impeachment against Andrew Johnson, President of the United States." Next, as a rule, the members of the House were announced and the Representatives marched in and took the seats set aside for them. Then, with fanfare, came the House impeachment managers,

* By popular vote Alabama had recently rejected the state constitution that would have restored her to representation in Congress.

walking arm-in-arm. Thaddeus Stevens was not always among them. Ailing badly he was more and more confined to his plain brick house on nearby B street. On those days when he could attend he was brought across the public grounds and up the broad stairs of the Capitol in a large arm-chair carried by two officers of the House. "Who will be so good to me," he asked these young huskies "and take me up in their strong arms when you two mighty men are gone?" Last of all, unannounced, the President's counsel came in.

For the duration of the trial the chamber took on a special appearance. On the floor, to the left of the rostrum, a plain oak table was set up and lined with comfortable arm chairs for the seven House impeachment managers. On the other side a similar setup served the President's five counsel. The Senators confined themselves to the two inner tiers of seats, leaving the two outer tiers to the visiting Representatives along with a miscellany of chairs and sofas set up in the open space at the rear of the room. At first the witnesses stood on the lower level of the rostrum on the managers' side. But then came complaints that they could not be heard and it was found that this could be remedied by shifting them to the other side. On good days the sun, pouring through the skylight provided the illumination; on cloudy ones and in the late afternoon the reddish yellow of flickering gas jets bathed the scene.

The newspapers fed the public an endless series of vignettes, word-pictures of participants and spectators: Old Thad dispatching a plate of oysters at the managers' tables; Ben Butler, chief prosecutor, scratching his bald pate and yelling at witnesses, prompting one newspaper to coin a new nickname for him—"Buzfuss"; bad-tempered and unkempt Chairman Bingham of the managers, reminding one of his colleagues of a "singed cat"; Congressman Ashley with his "ambrosial curls," limping a little for some unannounced reason; General Sherman on the floor, seated beside his tall and slender Senator-brother; ladies in the gallery reading novels during the long technical moments; the pale intellectual face of William M. Evarts of the President's counsel; Chief Justice Chase removing his glasses and twirling them absently in his hand, streaks of white in his newly grown beard; the elegant Senator Sumner declaring in a firm voice, "This proceeding is political in character—before a political body—and with a political object," a statement as honest as it was superfluous.

Ben Butler assumed the task of presenting the opening argument for the prosecution. During the course of a meeting of the House managers behind closed doors on Friday, March 27, to schedule events for the remainder of the trial, it was immediately agreed that Old Thad was to have the last word. Then "who," Butler made haste to inquire, "is to make the opening argument, and put the case in form for presentation in the Senate?" The silence that greeted his query was just what Butler had hoped for. "And thus," to quote Butler's own words, "I became the leading figure of the impeachment, for better or worse."

The speech was delivered on Monday, March 30. Butler would always remember the event as the most dramatic in his life. "When I entered the Senate chamber from the Vice President's room," he would write twenty years later, "the scene was almost appalling to one who had to address such an audience. The floor of the Senate chamber was filled because the House attended [the trial] in committee of the whole; the galleries were also crowded . . . and the ladies' gallery shone . . . with bright, beautiful women in the most gorgeous apparel. I came as near running away then as I ever did on any occasion in my life. But summoning up such courage as I could, I stuck to my post and addressed the Senate in a speech of two hours' length." (It was three hours, less a ten-minute recess, according to the official record.)

He was noticeably nervous, especially during the opening passages; and his nervousness was not exclusively attributable to weariness. Butler was too good a lawyer not to know that the case against the President was thin to the point of being non-existent. A year earlier he himself had intimated that the Tenure of Office Act was unconstitutional, expressing the opinion that it would not be criminal of the President to seek a test of the measure before the

Supreme Court. Some time later he would admit to Evarts of the President's counsel that as an attorney he would have preferred being on the other side of the case.

But speaking in the crowded Senate chamber that March afternoon he struggled manfully "to sustain the cause of the people against the President." He asked, "What are impeachable offenses under the provisions of our Constitution?" His answer was so broad as to suggest that mere opposition by the President to the majority in Congress constituted "high crimes and misdemeanors." He made no bones about the obviously political nature of the proceedings. They were not a trial, he argued, subject to the rules of evidence and in support of this position he cited any number of precedents. Among these was the famous impeachment trial by the British House of Lords of Warren Hastings for "high crimes and misdemeanors" allegedly committed during his governorship of India in the late eighteenth century—a rather unfortunate choice, perhaps, since after seven years of argument and testimony-taking Hastings was acquitted. Butler heaped scorn on those who had concluded that the trial of Andrew Johnson was unfair because most of the Senators had already decided that he was guilty. The current proceedings, Butler insisted, were "but an inquest . . . always partaking, more or less, of political considerations." Under the circumstances it was "impossible that Senators should not have opinions and convictions upon the subject-matter more or less decidedly formed before the case reaches them." The audiences in the crowded galleries were disappointed in the speech. "Quite a number of persons," the *Intelligencer* reported with satisfaction, "left the galleries before the end of the speech, in good order, a little fagged."

On the following afternoon, Tuesday, March 31, the taking of testimony began, to continue for almost three weeks. There were 25 prosecution and 16 defense witnesses. Under the regulations ordered by the Senate, the Chief Justice was permitted to rule on a point of law, but if so much as one Senator objected to his decision the matter was put to a vote and the Senate given the last word. On 17 different occasions the decisions of the Chief Justice were overruled by the Senate in an attempt, usually although not always successful, to suppress evidence favorable to the President.

In their answer to the eleven Articles of Impeachment, the attorneys for the President set forth two major contentions. One was that Johnson's only purpose in appointing Lorenzo Thomas as Secretary of War *ad interim* was to test the constitutionality of the Tenure of Office Act. One proof of this—so ran the Defense argument—was the fact that on the heels of Thomas' appointment Johnson had sent to the Senate the name of the eminent Thomas Ewing of Ohio with the request that he be given the War portfolio on a permanent basis. The other major contention of the President's counsel was that in firing Stanton, Johnson had proceeded on the assumption that the Tenure of Office Act, whether constitutional or not, did not apply to Stanton since the act exempted from its terms any Cabinet officer appointed not by Johnson but by Lincoln.

From first to last the prosecution pounded away at these contentions. In his opening argument Butler described as "a subterfuge" the President's plea that he had removed Stanton to test the tenure act. "We shall show you," Butler declared, "that he [Johnson] has taken no step to submit the question to any court although more than a year has elapsed since passage of the act." Repeatedly Butler and the other impeachers dismissed as an afterthought Johnson's belief that the tenure act did not apply to Stanton. They charged that the President had made that up *after* he was impeached.

To show that from the beginning Johnson had viewed the tenure act as unconstitutional and inapplicable to Stanton, the defense summoned several witnesses. Over and over again the prosecutors sought to keep these witnesses from being heard.

Sometimes they succeeded. Their most notable victory occurred when the defense put Johnson's close friend and adviser, Gideon Welles, on the stand. The diary-keeping Secretary of the Navy was in a position to testify that at two Cabinet meetings *prior* to impeachment Johnson had voiced the conviction that the Tenure Act was unconstitutional and that it did not apply to Stanton. Welles was ready, also, to testify that all of Johnson's advisers, including Stanton himself, had agreed with him on both points.

But the Secretary's account of those two Cabinet meetings was not to be heard. For two days prosecution and defense wrangled. Butler blustered down the corridors of legal history and quoted from everything including de Tocqueville's *Democracy in America* in an attempt to show that what Johnson had said to his advisers and *vice versa* should not be admitted as evidence. Chase ruled that it should be admitted. The Chief Justice's argument was eminently reasonable. The prosecution, he pointed out, had offered to prove that prior to impeachment Johnson had *not* intended to test the constitutionality of the Tenure Act and had *not* believed Stanton to be exempt from its terms. Surely the defense had a right to prove that Johnson *had* so intended and so believed. The Senate voted 26 to 18 to suppress Welles' testimony concerning the two Cabinet meetings.

The impeachers did not always fare so well. The second witness placed on the stand by the defense was General Sherman. Twice, during the preceding January, the President had asked Sherman to accept the post of Secretary of War. During those two conversations Johnson had revealed to Sherman exactly what he thought about the Tenure of Office Act. As the drift of Sherman's testimony became apparent a barrage of objections arose at the managers' table. The usual formalities were raced through. Chase ruled that the General should be allowed to speak his piece and the Senate voted that he couldn't. Twice more Stanbery, who was conducting the interrogation for the defense, sought to elicit Sherman's testimony by putting his questions in a different form. Twice more the Senate silenced the witness. Sherman was still on the stand when the Senate adjourned as a court at 4:45 P.M. on Saturday, April 11.

On the following Monday Sherman was recalled. The Democratic Senator from Maryland, Reverdy Johnson, had sent up a question for him in writing. The question was: "When the President tendered to you the office of Secretary of War *ad interim* . . . did he, at the very time of making such tender, state to you what his purpose in so doing was?" In essence this was the very question Stanbery had asked in vain on the preceding Saturday. The Senate had refused to listen then. Would it listen now? It is plain that the Conservatives had been doing some earbending over the weekend, for the Senate reversed itself and Sherman was permitted to relate what Johnson had said to him some weeks prior to impeachment.

The President, General Sherman testified, had made it clear that he not only wanted to test the constitutionality of the Tenure Act but that he was confident the act "would not stand half an hour" once it was brought before the Supreme Court. As Sherman was speaking Senator John B. Henderson of Missouri sent up another question in writing and after some argument Sherman was permitted to answer it.

Henderson's question: "Did the President . . . express to you a fixed resolution or determination to remove Stanton from his office?"

The General's answer: "If by removal is meant a removal by force, he never conveyed to my mind such an impression; but he did most unmistakably say that he could have no more intercourse with him [Stanton] in the relation of President and Secretary of War."

The tenth Article of Impeachment turned out to be an embarrassment to its makers. This was the article Butler himself had fathered. It quoted from some of the President's speeches, including two of those made during the Swing Around the Circle, to show that Johnson had held Congress up to ridicule. The House managers put on the stand several of the reporters who had accompanied Johnson on the Swing. So long as Butler was questioning these gentlemen, all went smoothly; but when the defense began its cross-examination, Article X blew sky high.

There were hilarious arguments over such questions as whether the President had pronounced the word "yes" in the usual manner or whether he had drawled it, making it come out "y-e-s." The impeachers were counting heavily on the widespread impression that the President was a sot and there were frowns on Radical faces when the reporters, under cross-examination, said that during the Swing Johnson had done no drinking of consequence.

The President's attorneys did not have to exert much oratorical skill to show that in making the speeches cited in Article X Johnson had been guilty of only one crime: he had exercised his right of free speech. Was this right to be denied him, his attorneys asked, because some people thought his remarks in bad taste? Robert Newell concluded that all Article X alleged, in essence, was that "he, Andrew Johnson, did make public speeches which . . . are calculated to produce the impression that Congress has at least a competitor in the art of political vituperation, and to destroy that confidence in the superior vulgarity of Congressional oratory which is one of the elements of our national complacency."

Since a major charge of the prosecution was that Johnson and General Lorenzo Thomas had tried to seize the War Office by force, it is of essence to have a look at some of the testimony relevant to this point. Congressman Burt Van Horn of New York, blithe and blasé of manner, testified* as follows:

By Mr. Manager Butler:

Q. Will you state whether you were present at the War Department when Major General Lorenzo Thomas, Adjutant General of the United States, was there to make demand for the office, property, books and records?
A. I was.
Q. When was it?
A. It was on Saturday, the 22d of February, 1868, I believe.
Q. About what time in the day?
A. Perhaps a few minutes after 11 o'clock.

---

* All trial testimony, excerpts from speeches, etc., are taken from the official record (United States Congress, *Trial of Andrew Johnson*, 3 volumes). In adding clarifying words and such stage directions as "laughter" the editors of the record used parentheses and brackets indiscriminately, so for the purpose of distinguishing their additions from those of the author, the following procedure has been followed: All additions by the editors are enclosed in parentheses; all additions by the author in brackets.

Q. Who were present?

A. General Charles H. Van Wyck of New York; General G. M. Dodge of Iowa; Hon. Freeman Clarke of New York; Hon. J. K. Morehead* of Pennsylvania; Hon. Columbus Delano of Ohio; Hon. W. D. Kelley of Pennsylvania; Hon. Thomas W. Ferry of Michigan and myself.** The Secretary of War, Mr. Stanton, and his son were also present.

Q. Please state what took place.

A. The gentlemen mentioned and myself were in the office the Secretary of War usually occupies, holding conversation. General Thomas came in; . . . he said, "Good morning, Mr. Secretary," and "Good morning, gentlemen"; the Secretary replied, "Good morning," and I believe we all did; then began this conversation as follows: (referring to a printed document) "I am Secretary of War *ad interim* and am ordered by the President of the United States to take charge of the office;" Mr. Stanton then replied, "I order you to repair to your room and exercise your functions as Adjutant General of the Army;" Mr. Thomas replied to this, "I am Secretary of War *ad interim* and I shall not obey your orders; but I shall obey the orders of the President, who has ordered me to take charge of the War Office;" Mr. Stanton replied to this as follows: "As Secretary of War, I order you to repair to your place as Adjutant General;" Mr. Thomas replied, "I shall not do so;" Mr. Stanton then said in reply, "Then you may stand there, if you please," pointing to Mr. Thomas, "but you cannot act as Secretary of War; if you do, you do so at your peril;" Mr. Thomas replied to this, "I shall act as Secretary of War". . . .

Cross-examined by Mr. Stanbery:

Q. You say that when that conversation began between General Thomas and the Secretary you were ready to take notes?

A. . . . I had a large white envelope in my pocket, and I had a pencil also . . .

Q. Are you in the habit, generally, in conversations of that kind, of making memoranda of what is said?

A. I do not know that I am . . .

Q. Did any one request you to take memoranda?

---

* Correct spelling is Moorhead.
** All Republican Congressmen.

A. No, sir.

Q. It was on your own motion?

A. On my own responsibility, supposing I had a perfect right to do so.

Q. Undoubtedly . . .

Re-examined by Mr. Manager Butler:

Q. You said, if I understood you, that there was a single remark of Thomas that you did not write down that now occurred to you, in answer to the counsel for the President; what was that remark?

A. . . . I recollect now General Thomas saying he did not wish any *"on*pleasantness.". . . .

Representative Moorhead of Pennsylvania testified:

By Mr. Manager Butler:

Q. We have learned from the testimony of the last witness that you were present at Mr. Secretary Stanton's office when General Thomas came in there to make some demand; will you state now in your own way . . . what took place. . . ?

A. . . . The testimony of Mr. Van Horn is correct as to what passed. . . .

Cross-examined by Mr. Stanbery:

Q. How long had you been at the office before General Thomas came in?

A. I think about half an hour.

Q. Did you see him coming?

A. Yes, sir; I saw him coming. The windows opened out toward the White House, and it was announced by some person near the window that General Thomas was coming; and I, with some others, got up and looked out of the window, and saw him coming along the walk, and we expected somewhat of a scene then.

Q. When he came in, did he come in attended, or was he alone?

A. He was alone.

Q. Was he armed in any way?

A. I did not notice any arms.

Q. Side arms or other?

A. I did not notice anything except what the Almighty had given him.

One Karsner, the very caricature of a country bumpkin, was brought to the witness stand by the Managers. His testimony in part:

By Mr. Manager Butler:

Q. What is your full name?
A. George Washington Karsner.
Q. Of what place are you a citizen?
A. Of Delaware.
Q. What county?
A. New Castle county.
Q. Do you know Major General Lorenzo Thomas?
A. Yes, sir.
Q. How long have you known him?
A. I have known him a great while; I think I have known him since a short time after his graduation from West Point.
Q. Was he originally from the same county with you?
A. Yes, sir.
Q. Did you see him in Washington somewhere about the 1st of March of this year?
A. I think it was about the 9th of March I first recollect seeing him here. . . . I saw him in the President's house; in the East Room of the President's house. . . . It was, perhaps, a quarter past ten o'clock . . . on a Monday evening.
Q. Was the President holding a levee that evening?
A. Yes, sir.
Q. Did you have any conversation with him?
A. Yes, sir.
Q. Please state how the conversation began; . . .
Mr. Evarts (of the President's counsel). With General Thomas?
Mr. Manager Butler. With General Thomas.

A (by witness). Well, it commenced by my approaching him [Thomas] and mentioning that I was a Delawarean, and I supposed he would recognize me, which I think he did, but could not remember my name. I then gave him my name and told him I knew him a great many years ago, and knew his father and brother and all the family. I gave him my hand, and he talked. He said he was a Delaware boy, which I very well knew; and he asked me what we were doing in Delaware. I do not remember the answer I gave to him, but said I to him, "General, the eyes of Delaware are on you." (Laughter)

The Chief Justice. Order!

The Witness. I gave my advice to him. I told him I thought Delaware would require him to stand firm. "Stand firm, general," said I. He said he would; he was standing firm, and he would not disappoint his friends; and in two days, or two or three days, or a short time, he would kick that fellow out. (Laughter) . . . .

Q. When he said he would "kick that fellow out," did he in any way indicate to you to whom he referred?

A. He did not mention any name.

Q. The question was whether he indicated to whom he referred.

A. Well, I think he referred to the Secretary of War. I did not have any doubt on my mind.

Mr. Evarts. That was not the question.

Mr. Manager Butler. It answers all I desire. The witness is yours, gentlemen.

By nightfall the phrase, "the eyes of Delaware are on you," had become a part of the national vocabulary.

When the prosecution completed its case, Benjamin R. Curtis presented the opening argument for the defense, concluding with the words: "It must be apparent to every one . . . that this . . . will be the most conspicuous instance which ever has been . . . of that justice which Mr. Burke* says is the great standing policy of all civilized states, or of that injustice which . . . makes even the wise man mad."

There was a rustle in the galleries as the counsel for the President summoned their first witness, General Lorenzo Thomas. His testimony in part:

By Mr. Stanbery:

Q. What first happened to you the next morning? [the morning of Saturday, February 22, 1868]

A. The first thing that happened to me next morning was the appearance at my house of the marshal of the District . . . and he arrested me.

Q. What time in the morning was that?

---

* The reference, of course, is to Edmund Burke (1729-97), English statesman and political writer.

A. About eight o'clock, before I had my breakfast. The command was to appear forthwith. I asked if he would permit me to see the President; I simply wanted to inform him that I had been arrested. To that he kindly assented, though he said he must not lose sight of me for a moment. I told him certainly; I did not wish to be out of his sight. He went with me to the President's and went into the room where the President was. I stated that I had been arrested . . . [and] he [the President] said "Very well, that is the place I want it in—the courts." . . . .

Mr. Stanbery (to the witness.) Did you go to court?

A. I was presented by the marshal to Judge Cartter . . . [and] I was required to give bail in $5,000.

Q. After you were admitted to bail, did you go again to the War Department that day? . . . .

A. I went immediately . . . , first stopping at the President's on my way, and stating to him that I had given bail. He made the same answer, "Very well; we want it in the courts." I then went over to the War Office. . . . up to Mr. Stanton's room. . . . I found him there with some six or eight gentlemen, some of whom I recognized and I understood afterward that they were all members of Congress. They were all sitting in a semi-ellipsis, the Secretary of War at the apex. I came in the door. I stated that I came in to demand the office. He refused to give it to me, and ordered me to my room as Adjutant General. . . . I made the demand a second and a third time. He as often refused, and as often ordered me to my room. . . . I saw nothing further was to be done, and I left the room and went into General Schriver's office, sat down and had a chat with him, he being an old friend. Mr. Stanton followed me in there, and Governor Moorhead, member of Congress from Pittsburgh. He told Governor Moorhead to note the conversation, and I think he took notes at a side table. . . . Then there was some little chat with the Secretary himself.

Q. Between you and the Secretary?

A. Between me and the Secretary.

Q. Had these members of Congress withdrawn then?

A. Yes, sir.

Q. Now, tell us what happened between you and the Secretary after they withdrew.

A. I do not recollect what first occurred, but I said to him, "The next time you have me arrested". . . .

Mr. Manager Butler. Stop a moment. I propose, Mr. President [the Chief Justice], to object to the conversation between the

Secretary and General Thomas at a time which we have not put in, because we put in only the conversation while the other gentlemen were there. This is something that took place after they had withdrawn.

Mr. Stanbery. What is the difference? They did not stay to hear the whole.

The Chief Justice. It appears to have been immediately afterward and part of the same conversation. . . .

Mr. Manager Butler. Go on, then, sir.

The Witness. I said, "The next time you have me arrested, please do not do it before I get something to eat." I said I had had nothing to eat or drink that day. He [Stanton] put his hand around my neck, as he sometimes does, and ran his hand through my hair, and turned to General Schriver and said, "Schriver, you have got a bottle here; bring it out." (Laughter)

By Mr. Stanbery:

Q. What then took place?

A. Schriver unlocked his case and brought out a small vial, containing I suppose about a spoonful of whiskey, and stated at the same time that he occasionally took a little for dyspepsia. (Laughter) Mr. Stanton took that and poured it into a tumbler and divided it equally and we drank together.

Q. A fair division?

A. A fair division, because he held up the glasses to the light and saw that they each had about the same, and we each drank. (Laughter) Presently a messenger came in with a bottle of whiskey, a full bottle; the cork was drawn, and he and I took a drink together. "Now," said he, "this at least is neutral ground." (Laughter)

Q. Was that all the force exhibited that day?

A. That was all.

Q. Have you ever at any time attempted to exercise any force to get into that office?

A. At no time.

Q. Have you ever had any instructions or directions from the President to use force, intimidation, or threats at any time?

Butler and company interposed an objection at this point but after a brief legal battle Thomas was permitted to place on the record the fact that Johnson had never authorized or directed him to use force of any sort; whereupon Stanbery directed the attention of the general to his now-famous encounter with his fellow-Delawarean "on the west side . . . of the East Room" of the White House during the President's levee on the night of the previous March 9th.

Q. What was the conversation you had with Mr. Karsener [*sic*] . . . ?

A. It was towards the end of the President's reception, and I was . . . about going out of the door when I found that this person rushed forward and seized me by the hand. I looked surprised, because I did not know him. He mentioned his name, but I could not recollect it. I understood him to say that he was from New Castle, my native village. . . . I tried to get away from him, and he then said . . . "The eyes of all Delaware are upon you (Laughter), and they expect you to stand fast." I said: "Certainly I shall stand fast," and I was about leaving, when he seized my hand again and asked me a second time the same question, saying he expected me to stand fast. Said I: "Certainly I will stand fast." I was smiling all the time. I got away from his hand a second time, and he seized it again and drew me further in the room and asked the same question. I was a little amused, when I raised myself up on my toes in this way (standing on tiptoes) and said: "Why, don't you see I am standing firm?" Then he put this in my mouth: "When are you going to kick that fellow out," or something of that kind. "Oh," said I, "we will kick him out by and by."

Q. Are you certain the "kicking out" came from him?

A. Yes, sir—oh yes. (Laughter.) I want to say one thing. I did not intend any disrespect to Mr. Stanton at all. On the contrary he has always treated me with kindness, and I would do nothing to treat him with disrespect.

And so it went—a farce and a mummery. As witness followed witness to the stand, millions of words of testimony went into the record, but not one iota of evidence pointing to wrongdoing by the man in the White House.

One by one the eleven Articles of Impeachment fell to the ground. True the Senate refused to hear the highly important testimony of

Secretary Welles, but both General Sherman and General Thomas were permitted to say enough to make clear the President's desire to test the tenure act and his sincere belief that it did not apply to Stanton. Once it was revealed that the "eyes of Delaware" were on General Thomas, all of the articles accusing the President of conspiring with Thomas *et al.* to seize the War Office by force were literally laughed out of court. Ben Butler's article, objecting to some of Johnson's public speeches, suffered the same fate. One of the articles accused Johnson of issuing unlawful orders to General Emory, commander of the armed forces in Washington. The testimony of Emory himself, a prosecution witness, took care of that. It turned out that Johnson had issued no orders to Emory at all; his purpose in summoning the general to the White House had been merely to make sure that the city was being properly protected.

As for Article XI, the "Omnibus Article" devised by Old Thad, the President's counsel did not even dignify it with an answer. Most of its charges were a rehash of the other articles and for those that were different the prosecution offered no evidence either in the article itself or during the trial.

Many thoughtful Americans were appalled and frightened by the proceedings, few more so than Salmon Portland Chase. The Chief Justice wrote his friend, Gerritt Smith, that he was "greatly disappointed and pained" by the refusal of the Senate to hear Secretary Welles, whose testimony would have brought out beyond question the motives which had impelled Johnson to risk impeachment by dismissing Stanton.

The Chief Justice expressed the fear that the failure of the Senate to listen to Welles "indicated a purpose which, if carried into effect, will not satisfy the American people, unless they are prepared to admit that Congress is above the Constitution." He called it the Senate's "greatest and most injurious mistake."

Nothing was more obvious to Chase than that

Acts of Congress, not warranted by the Constitution, are not laws. In case a law believed by the President to be unwarranted by the Constitution, is passed, notwithstanding his veto, it seems to me that it is his duty to execute it precisely as if he had held it to be constitutional, *except in the case where it directly attacks and impairs the Executive power confided to him by the instrument. In that case, it appears to me to be the clear duty of the President to disregard the law, so far at least as it may be necessary to bring the question of its constitutionality before the judiciary tribunals.** . . .

How can the President fulfill his oath to preserve, protect and defend the Constitution, if he has no *right* to *defend* it against an Act of Congress sincerely believed by him to have been passed in violation of it? To me, therefore, it seems perfectly clear that the President has a perfect right, and indeed, was under the highest obligation to remove Mr. Stanton, if he made the removal not in wanton disregard of Constitutional law, but with a sincere belief that the Tenure-of-Office Act was unconstitutional, and for the purpose of bringing the question before the Supreme Court. Plainly it was the proper and peaceful, if not the only proper and peaceful, mode of protecting and defending the Constitution.

Had the Senate heard the testimony of Secretary Welles, the President's counsel no doubt would have summoned the other Cabinet members to corroborate his statements. Under the circumstances the defense had no choice but to wind up its case quickly. Its last witness stood down on April 18 and the Senate as a court then adjourned to April 22 with the understanding that on that day the lawyers on both sides would commence their closing arguments. The end of the trial was in sight, but what that end would be was not yet visible. From his quarters in Washington old Tom Ewing wrote his son that the evidence elicited by the House Managers "was a miserable failure, but it does not therefore follow that there will not be a conviction."

---

* Italics added.

XXVII

THE MAN IN THE WHITE HOUSE

The President this morning visited William Slade, his steward, who has been very ill for some time past with dropsy . . . The tears trickled down Slade's cheeks . . . The dying man could only say: "Mr. President, you have been my friend. I have never sought your aid but it has been freely rendered . . . All the ladies of the house have visited me except Mrs. Johnson whose illness has prevented her from calling." The President then sat on the side of the bed and taking Slade's hand in his, talked very kindly to him. I shall never forget the scene . . .

—Colonel Moore's Diary.

What of the man at the other end of the avenue? He was tending to his duties, going about them with such dignity and forbearance as to suggest that Andrew Johnson with his back to the wall was Andrew Johnson at his best. His mood fluctuated, from bitterness in the early days of the trial to grim and philosophic amusement as it entered its closing phases. "Too bad, too bad!" he would mutter to himself, scowling and shaking his head. Occasionally he sounded off to Colonel Moore: "Impeach *me* for violating the Constitution? Damn them!"

Again: "This is a civil incident. Yet the very body which passed the law which it is alleged I have violated, because I deemed it unconstitutional, is to determine upon my case, or, in other words, to decide so far as they can, the constitutionality of a law of their own making. That, too, after having declared my action unconstitutional and illegal. In such circumstances, could not an appeal be taken to the Supreme Court . . . ? Why, in justice . . . did they [the Radicals] not postpone this trial until after a general decision had been rendered? Their intent is clearly to obtain control of the Union for political purposes, never mind how much they may violate the Constitution or trample upon justice."

When a sympathizer pointed out that the Radicals were not averse to spending money to gain their ends and suggested that he do the same, he shook his head. "How would I feel," he asked, "if my conscience told me I owed my acquittal to bribery? I will do nothing of the kind. I will not seek to use any unfair means for my vindication."

That vindication would be his, somehow, some day, he was certain. He took to reading books on the subject of immortality and startled Frank Cowan, that young member of his secretarial staff who had dubbed him the Grim Presence, by asking him to do a little research into the circumstances surrounding the conviction and execution of Charles I of England. It gratified the President to learn that of the members of the High Court set up by Parliament to condemn the King, all but three came to an untimely end. Cowan got the impression that, if acquitted, the President would be disappointed, so confident was he of the dire fate awaiting the impeachers if they succeeded.

Johnson also took to reading and re-reading and even memorizing sections of one of his favorite pieces of literature, the only play ever written by the eighteenth century British essayist, Joseph Addison—his dramatization of the last days of Cato the Younger, or Cato of Utica, who chose to die by his own hand rather than submit to the dictatorship of Julius Caesar. It was plain to both Cowan and Moore that the President found solace in comparing his own situation with that of the ancient defender of Roman liberty.

He kept close tab on the proceedings on the Hill. W. W. Warden, a member of the White House staff, was given the task of sounding out the Moderates since it was obvious that the final vote would depend on whether or not the erstwhile Conservatives of the Senate strung along with the Radicals to the bitter end. Each evening Warden would come to the White House to make his report and each evening Johnson would open the conversation with a cheerful, "Well, Warden, what are the signs of the zodiac today?"

Spiritualism was in vogue. Caroline E. Colby, medium, informed the President that she and her husband had received messages for him from the spirits of A. Lincoln, A. Jackson, Stephen A. Douglas and Daniel Webster. "Work quietly," A. Jackson urged, "but with strong will and you will meet with success." A. Lincoln's message: "I grieve, not for what I did do but for what I did not do. I should have dismissed the Secretary of War."

The White House was the scene of endless legal conferences. Many a quiet Washington dawn found Martha Patterson, the President's daughter and hostess, brewing coffee and tea in the kitchen while Johnson and his lawyers polished off a night-long session in the big oval library on the second floor. Martha was constantly at her father's side, cheering him when he despaired, watching always for those painful symptoms which preceded what Cowan called his "fits of the gravel."

The President's lawyers found him at times a difficult and temperamental client. He resented their frequent calls on him for assistance and information. Again and again he regretted his agreement to remain in the White House during the trial. Although in the end he would admit that his counsel had done a splendid job, there were times along the way when he was convinced that the case was being mismanaged and that the only solution was for him to march into the Senate and do a little "plain speaking."

In the middle of April Stanbery's health broke and he was forced to his bed for several weeks. His absence put a grave burden

on the other four members of the President's counsel. On April
16, as one of their witnesses stood down, they asked for a slight
delay while they made ready to put another on the stand. This
request brought Ben Butler bellowing to his feet. He said the trial
must not be held up for one second. The economy of the country
was going to pieces. Worse yet, the Ku Klux Klan was terrorizing
the Southland. Men were being murdered in their beds. His own
mail was full of threats of assassination. And all these crimes, Butler
insisted, would go on until such time as that man was removed from
the White House. For twenty minutes the Senator from Massachusetts raged on, waving the bloody shirt. When he sat down Evarts
of the President's counsel said quietly that he had "never heard
such a harangue before in a court of justice," and the Senate
adjourned for the day.

When this episode reached Johnson's ears he did a little raging
of his own, not so much at what Butler had said as at what Evarts
had not said. Had Johnson been in Evarts' shoes he would have
rebuked Butler in a way that would have made that gentleman
regret his meanness all the days of his life. Johnson was unable to
appreciate the fact that Evarts' quiet comment was all the rebuke
necessary, that Butler had damned himself out of his own mouth.

The strain between Johnson and his counsel was the outgrowth
of differing opinions as to just who was trying his case. Understandably enough the lawyers' main objective—their duty indeed—was
to influence the Senate. But Johnson looked upon the Senate as of
secondary importance. In the long pull, as he saw it, his case
would be judged, not by a handful of men in an airless room on
Capitol Hill, but by the American public. Acting on this conviction,
he again took his cause to the people. This time he did not swing
around the circle as he had done on the eve of the 1866 elections.
He granted a series of interviews with reporters representing more
or less friendly newspapers. In doing so he once more broke with
tradition and established precedent. In after years these interviews
at the White House in the spring of 1868 would be regarded as the

genesis of an American institution—the Presidential press conference.

Johnson's lawyers and some of his other advisers took a dim view of them. Welles was disgusted. The Secretary of the Navy noted that Johnson "seems to take pleasure in having these 'talks' of the President with this or that correspondent published. It is in his position hardly a pardonable weakness." During an interview shortly after the trial opened, Johnson mentioned an incident, similar to his dismissal of Stanton, that had occurred during the administration of John Adams.* A few days later, at Cabinet meeting Stanbery scolded him. The retiring Attorney General pointed out that the President's lawyers were planning to cite as a precedent the incident he had revealed. It was part of their case, and they had hoped to spring it as a surprise on the prosecution. Now of course, that was impossible. According to Welles, Johnson "was taken aback" and "attempted some apologetic remark."

Whatever the President's reaction to Stanbery's rebuke, he went on granting interviews—and the student of history is likely to be glad he did. As published in various newspapers, his "talks" were revealing. In an interview with Jerome B. Stillson of the New York *World,* almost two weeks prior to impeachment, he "asserted in positive terms his right under the Constitution and also under the Tenure of Office Act . . . to eject Stanton." Informed by Stillson that some people had "got it into their heads" that he meant to use force to do so, Johnson smiled. "What nonsense!" he exclaimed. "It's very likely that *I* am anxious to start a revolution. No, I'll leave that responsibility with those who have already undertaken it."

A month later, with the trial under way, Stillson was again permitted this interview with the President:

In the cheerful reception room at the White House, the writer of these despatches had on Sunday evening [March 8] the following conversation with the President . . .

---

* The officer dismissed by Adams in 1800 was Timothy Pickering of Massachusetts, then Secretary of State.

"Well, Mr. President, you don't seem to be pining under this infliction."

"No," Mr. Johnson said pleasantly as he invited me to a seat, "I must have lost very little weight, if anything. The rack used to be called in Venice, you know, a great appetizer."

"In that case, Mr. President, one may presume that your dinners will have a lively relish for some weeks . . . I will venture to ask . . . what your own estimate is of the present chances of the trial?"

"Perhaps at this stage," the President replied, "it would be more appropriate for me to ask your opinion. My opportunities of communication with the parties who have impeached the President . . . are not, just now, quite so favorable as yours."

Being thus challenged, I remarked: "Well, sir . . . I believe that if the President should be tried immediately—that is, within a week —the Senate would probably convict him . . . The reasons for this belief are found not only in the previous declarations and temper of a majority of the Senators, but in the lack of opposition to impeachment by the Republican press and party. While most of the leaders of that party would not have favored impeachment upon considerations of justice, they are as well convinced as Congress is, now that Congress has committed itself, that the trial must be gone through with as a measure of party necessity . . ."

"You take . . . a rather gloomy view . . . ," said Mr. Johnson, laughing.

"By no means, sir—because I apprehend that the trial may last long enough to need such a public discussion of its merits as will yet arouse a considerable opposition to the measure in the Radical ranks . . ."

As the President became more engrossed . . . he leaned forward in his chair, and enforced what he said with vigorous gestures. "Congress assumes that the Executive is merely an executive . . . compelled by his oath to execute any law . . . passed . . . over his veto . . . There is a limit to such an assumption as that . . . Suppose Congress should pass a bill abolishing the veto power . . . suppose it should pass a dozen bills of this character—would the President be constitutionally bound to execute them as laws? Would it not be his duty, as in the present instance, to seek immediately judgment in the Supreme Court . . . ?"

Twice, during April, the President gave lengthy interviews to the famous reporter, "Mack" (John B. McCallagh), then with the conservative Cincinnati *Commercial*. Requested to comment on the charge that his speeches during the Swing Around the Circle were undignified, the President did so with spirit. His reply, according to Mack's report, was that at the time of the Swing there "were great questions before the people, and it was more important that they should be understood than that anybody's dignity should be preserved. Besides, he said, 'Did not Mr Lincoln make stump speeches on his way to Washington, and often afterwards . . . ? Do they propose to impeach me on a question of taste and dignity? Is it dignified of Mr. Wade to go around the country, callng me a d—d traitor; and must I be impeached if I say a word in reply?' "

He was equally vehement when asked by Mack to comment on the accusation that he had attempted to usurp the powers of Congress. "The whole course of legislation, for the past two years," the President said, "has been an effort to encroach upon the constitutional powers of the Executive. . . . I have exercised the negative power vested in me to resist those encroachments. This power is, in its nature, conservative; and not aggressive. The aggressions have all come from the other end of the avenue."

Thus, while his enemies sought to depose him from his office, did the President plead his case before the people. To no reporter, of course, did he express himself with as much feeling as he vented in the presence of Colonel Moore one Sunday morning, when taking down a Bible from his bookshelves, he read aloud a pertinent passage from *First Samuel,* Chapter 12, Verse 3:

Here I am; testify against me before the Lord and before his annointed. Whose ox have I taken? Or whose ass have I taken? Or whom have I defrauded? Whom have I oppressed? Or from whose hand have I taken a bribe to blind my eyes with it?

XXVIII

"THE HOLE IN THE SKY"

March 24 [1868] . . . The Constitution-breakers are trying the Constitution-defender; the law-breakers are passing condemnation on the law-supporter; the conspirators are sitting in judgment on the man who would not enter into their conspiracy, who was, and is, faithful to his oath, his country, the Union, and the Constitution. What a spectacle! And if successful, what a blow to free government! What a commentary on popular intelligence and public virtue!
—Secretary Welles' Diary

For almost two weeks, beginning on Wednesday, April 22, 1868, the Senate Chamber was a cave of winds as the impeachment trial huffed through its pentultimate phase—the presentation of the closing arguments by four members of the President's counsel and five of the House Managers.

Groesbeck delivered the most telling defense of the President. The Ohio attorney stuck closely to the legal aspects of the case—safe ground, for legally the prosecution had no case. Evarts' argument took almost four days, prompting Manager Bingham, whose own took almost three, to quip that the brilliant New York lawyer had endeavored to "make his speech immortal by making it eternal."

Sections of Evarts' speech were shot through with mordant

humor. Some of it was at the expense of Manager Boutwell. In his own argument Boutwell had taken the position that Johnson's conviction was certain. There remained but one question: What fate should be meted out to the erring executive; what punishment would fit his crime? Answering his own question Boutwell inadvertently lifted the veil on the space-age to come:

> Travellers and astronomers [he said] inform us that in the southern heavens, near the southern cross, there is a vast space which the uneducated call the hole in the sky. In that dreary, cold, dark region . . . the Great Author of celestial mechanism has left the chaos which was in the beginning.

It was Boutwell's suggestion that once Johnson was formally convicted he be heaved through atmosphere, stratosphere and space to disappear forever into that far-off "hole in the sky." When it came Evarts' turn he could not forbear a passing comment on Manager Boutwell's discovery that that hole in the sky had been "reserved . . . in the final councils of the Almighty, as the place of punishment for convicted and deposed American Presidents." Evarts had a suggestion. When the time came, Boutwell should be given the honor of conveying the great criminal hence. He envisaged the slight Massachusetts Congressman, a struggling Andrew Johnson in his arms, taking off from the dome of the Capitol. Once beyond the pull of Earth's gravity, he and Johnson would become new constellations in the heavens; future generations would indulge in heated argument as to which was sun and which was moon.

By no means all of Evarts' argument was showmanship. Frequently he pierced to the heart of the matter. In the attempt to depose Johnson he saw reflected a great impatience with the federal system. He detected a longing by the Radicals to be done with checks and balances and co-ordinate branches, each possessed of specified but limited powers. Let the Radicals take care, he warned, lest their rosy dream, coming true, turn out to be a nightmare. Let them remember the words of Daniel Webster, spoken in the Senate of 1834: "The first object of a free people is the preservation of their liberty, and liberty is only to be preserved by maintaining constitutional restraints and just division of political power. Nothing is more deceptive or more dangerous than the pretense of a desire to simplify government. The simplest governments are despotisms."

The original plan had been for Stevens to wind up the case for the House managers by speaking last, but the old man had grown too weak to assume this burden. When he arose to deliver his argument on Monday, April 27, there were still two managers to be heard from.

During the preceding weeks of the trial Old Thad had uttered less than a hundred words. The Philadelphia *Press* described him as seated at the managers' table "in his cushioned chair, his elbows resting on the arms, and his long bony fingers interlaced . . . His eyes are dim and apparently the soft light of the chamber hurts them, for they are . . . kept shut for long intervals. At times he leans his head forward, as if buried in deep contemplation, and then raising it, unlaces his right hand from the other, and waving it majestically toward some one of his colleagues, makes a scarcely audible suggestion . . . There is something in his appearance which attracts the gaze . . . with a strange, spellbound sensation, and the idea invariably suggests itself that something supernatural inhabits his weary frame . . . He is the embodiment of all the principles involved in this mighty case; and while he does not absolutely lead or conduct the prosecution because he is too feeble . . . no one imagines that it could be conducted without him."

A hush fell over the thronged gallery as Stevens moved to the rostrum to deliver his argument. Even so a reporter in the press section found his words difficult to catch. The old man was a sight to be seen rather than a voice to be heard. Another reporter had detected in his tones a strange huskiness, "startlingly suggestive of the rattle in the throat of a dying man." Years before Stevens had said that it was his wish to "die hurrahing." In this, almost his last speech, he was hurrahing but feebly, not because his mind had lost its cunning but because his body was whipped with pain.

He stood at the left end of the Secretary's desk, holding in his hand "a roll of manuscript on which had been pasted printed slips of his speech." After a few minutes he asked permission to sit down.

For about half an hour, seated, he struggled on until his voice ceased to have any resonance at all, when he handed the manuscript over to Ben Butler to complete.

His argument had brevity, but little else. No one was more convinced than Old Thad that Andrew Johnson was guilty of something, but even he found it difficult to say what. He made much of a small point that the defense had already battered to nothingness. It will be remembered that one of Johnson's answers to the charges was that he did not believe the Tenure of Office Act applied to Stanton. But in notifying the Senate of Stanton's suspension, Johnson had used the words "in compliance with" the requirements of the tenure act. At the very worst Johnson had made a mistake, one that could not stop him from later asserting his sincere conviction that the act did not cover Stanton. More to the point, the Articles of Impeachment did not rest on his *suspension* of Stanton. They rested on his subsequent appointment of Lorenzo Thomas along with his order to Stanton to vacate. And the President had not taken these actions under the tenure act. He had stood on his constitutional rights and on the 1789 law under which all previous Presidents had removed appointed officials.

Old Thad had other points. He went back to the very beginning of Johnson's administration, the summer and fall of 1865. He reminded his auditors that during that period the President, in the absence of Congress, had not only set up the so-called Johnson Governments in the South but he had also prescribed conditions which the Southern states must fulfill in order to return to the Union. By what right had the President set up those governments? By what right had he made demands of them? Where in the Constitution was there sanction for such acts?

As far as Old Thad was concerned his question was rhetorical; but of course there was an answer, one that had long since been acknowledged. During the period of which the old man was speaking the Civil War was technically still on. As Commander-in-Chief the President not only had the right—but the obligation—to take the steps necessary to preserve order in the defeated states and to make certain that they complied with such obvious outcomes of the war as the repudiation of slavery, of the right of a state to secede and of the Confederate war debt.

Old Thad was straining at gnats. He lingered for some time over the correspondence between the President and Grant; the President's angry charge that Grant had broken a promise when, resigning as Secretary of War, he turned the office over to Stanton instead of to the President; the General's angry insistence that he had made no promise. Old Thad airily dismissed the question of who was lying, Johnson or Grant. It didn't matter. All that mattered was the correspondence itself. It proved beyond doubt that the President had attempted "to prevent the due execution of the tenure-of-office act," going so far as to try to entangle "a gallant soldier" in his schemes. How then, Stevens demanded, could Johnson "escape the just vengeance of the law? Wretched man, standing at bay, surrounded by a cordon of living men, each with the axe of an executioner uplifted for his just punishment."

Not for nothing had Old Thad spent long years cracking the whip over the Republican party. He did not confine his argument to a canvass of the crimes committed by the "wretched man" in the White House. He drew the attention of his audience to another "crime" known as party disloyalty. He issued a warning to any Republican Senator who, when the time came to vote, one by one, on the Articles of Impeachment, might be tempted to declare the President innocent of all eleven charges. "I know," Stevens said, "that senators would venture to any necessary act if endorsed by an honest conscience or an enlightened public opinion; but neither for the sake of the President nor any one else would one of them suffer himself to be tortured on the gibbet of everlasting obloquy. How long and dark would be the track of infamy which must mark his name, and that of his posterity!"

"How long and dark . . . !" Even as the dying Radical dictator was breathing out these words, some of the Republican Senators in his audience were wrestling with their consciences, wondering what it would cost them, politically speaking, if they were to vote "Not Guilty!"

XXIX

SEVEN TALL MEN

April 22 . . . Impeachment trial nears its close. Result duber-
some.

— George Templeton Strong's *Diary*

Speculation on the outcome of the trial was rife and in some
quarters profitable. Betting odds changed repeatedly. At one point
Colonel Moore noticed that some friends of the President, spotting
what looked like sure indications of acquittal, were spreading the
contrary impression, "playing the part of bears." Some people kept
their eye on Senator Ben Wade who, if conviction carried, would
take over the Presidential chair. Signs of confidence on Bluff Ben's
part tended to lift impeachment stock, contrary signs to depreciate it.

Throughout the trial, informed guessers, speculatively polling
the Senate, came to different conclusions from day to day. The
simple arithmetic of the situation, no matter how carefully studied,
yielded no reliable answer. There were 54 Senators. Assuming all
to be on hand when the final balloting began, 36 would have to vote
guilty on at least one of the eleven Articles of Impeachment to convict the President. Nominally 45 were Republicans and nine were
Democrats. Of the Republicans, 29 or 30—estimates varied—were

machine Radicals, certain to go for conviction on some if not all of the Articles. At the other end of the gamut were the nine Democrats and three Administration-Republicans, twelve sure votes for acquittal.

That left twelve or thirteen men, again depending on whose estimate you accepted. In mid-April old Thomas Ewing of Ohio was putting the number of "Doubtful Senators," as they were called, at an even dozen—twelve Republicans, he wrote his son, "too tall to be overawed and driven to judicial perjury by threats or party clamor. . . ."

On May 6 the Senate sitting as a court heard the last of the formal arguments. There was a brief session the following day. Then the court adjourned for several days, during which time the pressures on Doubtful Senators began to assume formidable proportions.

Johnson's supporters were not idle. Evarts, brain of the President's counsel, made a suggestion. He pointed out to Johnson that some of the Conservative Republicans in the Senate, although convinced of his innocence, were hesitant to vote "not guilty" out of a fear that if acquitted the President would renew his war on Congress, creating an unpleasant situation. Evarts urged the President to reassure the Moderates by sending to the Senate, as his choice for permanent successor to Stanton, the name of a man looked upon as a symbol of stability. Johnson had already submitted such a name, that of Tom Ewing. But Ewing, grand old man of American statesmanship, was crowding 80. A younger man, Evarts reasoned, would look better to all concerned.

Johnson agreed, and off to the Senate went a message, withdrawing the name of Ewing and substituting that of General John M. Schofield, a man acceptable to Conservatives and Radicals alike. It was a gesture, of course; it had its anticipated effect on some of the Moderates.

Senator Reverdy Johnson, the President's Maryland friend, was informed that it would be helpful if the President would make a public statement, promising to undertake no rash actions in the event of acquittal. The Senator realized the wisdom of such a move. He realized also that it would be an undignified one for the President to make while the trial was on. But accidents happened, the Senator reflected, and he proceeded to see that one did. He sent to the White House a message, asking the President to call on him the following evening. Simultaneously, without the knowledge of the President, he sent a similar invitation to Conservative Senator Grimes of Iowa.

When Johnson and Grimes were thus brought together at the home of the Maryland Senator, a pleasant conversation ensued. First a little banter about one thing and another. Then a word from the host-catalyst, the statement that he had heard gossip that the President was contemplating some desperate maneuver if sustained by the Senate. The President rose to the bait. There was no warrant "in anything I have said or done," he declared "for believing that the President intends to do any act which is not in strict conformity with the Constitution and laws."

Next day Grimes had something to tell his Conservative associates. "I know Johnson's purposes in the event of acquittal," he said. "You need not fear his behavior will cause you to regret your vote, whichever way cast. He does not dread, personally, a verdict of guilty. He believes such a verdict would be disastrous to the Republic, and hence prays for acquittal. But he has no thought of wrong or rash doings."

Earnest as were the efforts of the President's friends, they were child's play alongside those of his enemies. The Radicals set up an espionage system. The Doubtful Senators were not its only victims. Practically everyone likely to exert some remote influence on the trial, including Chief Justice Chase and General Grant, was subjected to surveillance. Mack of the Cincinnati *Commercial* claimed that protegés of Ben Butler working in the government departments were "spies upon the Cabinet and President." A visitor to the city, having made some critical remark about a Radical leader while ferrying across the Hudson River was reported as startled to discover that his words had preceded him to Washington.

Early in May the Radicals began holding daily and later twice-daily conferences at the home of Senator Samuel C. Pomeroy of Kansas. A score of men made up this caucus, most of them Senators, a few from the House. The fiery and beguiling young editor of the *Independent,* Theodore Tilton, was almost daily in attendance. Nothing was left to chance. The record of every Doubtful Senator was scrutinized in a search for chinks in his political armor.

The Radicals put a question mark alongside the name of Senator Waitman T. Willey of West Virginia—and then took steps to erase it. It so happened that Willey was an active Methodist. Very well, the best procedure was to enlist the services of Bishop Matthew Simpson, Methodist leader and strong anti-Johnsonite. At the General Conference of the Methodist Episcopal Church the Bishop inspired a resolution calling on the members of the Conference to set aside an hour of prayer for the conviction of the President, but it was tabled when an aged delegate pointed out that the Senators were acting under oaths and should not be called on to violate them. On the following day the Bishop achieved his ends with a milder resolution, passed without dissent, providing for an hour of prayer "to save our Senators from error."

Another Republican, regarded as Doubtful, was Sprague, multi-millionaire owner of a Rhode Island textile empire. The Radicals knew just what to ask hard-living, hard-drinking William Sprague, husband of the Chief Justice's older daughter, the beautiful Kate. What would happen to his father-in-law's still-smoldering Presidential ambitions, Sprague was asked, if he failed his party at this critical juncture?

Time would prove these maneuvers highly effective. As the trial drew closer to its end, the number of known "Doubtfuls" grew smaller, levelling off finally to seven "tall" men, to borrow old Tom Ewing's name for them.

Fessenden of Maine, Grimes of Iowa, Trumbull of Illinois. We are familiar with these names and with the mettles of their owners.

Then there is John B. Henderson of Missouri, tall, lithe and full-bearded. The young ladies think him very handsome. He is about to marry Miss Mary Foote, daughter of Johnson's Commissioner of Patents. "Mary," he will shortly be saying, "[i]f I vote for Johnson, it is sure to cost me reelection to the Senate, and I know you will not like that." The young lady will reply: "You go ahead, John. . . . Do what you think is right." The handsome Senator's future is not difficult to read: political tribulations and a happy marriage.

There is Joseph O. Fowler of Tennessee. Once an Ohio school teacher, he is a slow and halting talker. He does not look like a statesman, or very much of anything. Frequently he brushes his hand through wavy red hair, the gesture of a man who would be happier if he could brush his thoughts away.

There is Peter G. Van Winkle of West Virginia. His manner rhymes with his name, one big, jolly twinkle. Nothing about him suggests a capacity for heroism.

There is Edmund G. Ross of Kansas: slight, bearded, with a mild and shrinking manner and run-of-the-mill good looks. Some of the other six remaining "Doubtfuls," if they vote for acquittal, will be adding to their pasts. Ross will be throwing away his future. He is young, devoid of financial resources and a newcomer to the national scene. As he himself will someday put it, he is destined to "be a bigger man dead than . . . alive." He began his adult life as a printer and newspaper editor in Milwaukee. The passage of the Kansas-Nebraska bill in 1854 started him on the great adventure of his life; this bill permitted the settlers of Kansas to decide by vote whether their state was to enter the Union slave or free. Determined to stop the spread of slavery, young Ross organized such a caravan in 1856—the Milwaukee Colony—and headed for Kansas, his wife and little daughter beside him. Settling in Topeka, the members of the Milwaukee Colony found themselves in the midst of Kansas' little Civil War: the anti-slavery Jayhawkers versus the pro-slavery Border Ruffians. Even-tempered, blessed with initiative, a strict teetotaler, Ross rapidly achieved a position of local leadership. For two years, with his brother-in-law, he published the Kansas *Tribune,* a free-soil newspaper. In 1859 he helped shape the constitution under which Kansas became a state a year and a half later. During the war he captained his own company, fought with distinction in the Battle of Prairie Grove. Mustered out in the fall of 1865, he settled down to newspapering in Lawrence, Kansas. In 1866, shortly after the suicide of Senator James Henry Lane, Ross received a message from the Republican leader, Colonel Samuel J. Crawford, asking him to come to Topeka for a conference. Ross knew that one of his townsmen in Lawrence was in line for Lane's post and assumed Crawford wished his opinion of the candidate, but Crawford said: "I saw what you did at [the battle of] Prairie Grove. I want *you* for the Senate." Ross went to Washington. He finished out the few remaining months of Senator Lane's term and then was named by the Kansas legislature to begin his own full term.

On May 1 some of the names of the Seven Tall Men were being bandied about in the Washington press. The *Intelligencer* noted: "Mr. Stanton who holds quite a levee every night at the War Department before retiring to bed, has of late been expressing fears as to the votes of Grimes, Trumbull and Fessenden. . . . Mr. Fowler, of Tennessee, is quite often spoken of, now-a-days, as sure to vote against impeachment; but . . . practically these are the only men concerning whom there is anywhere any serious doubt. They number only four, while a change of seven would be required for Mr. Johnson's escape."

"A change of seven"—and as both the President's supporters and his enemies knew, even if the *Intelligencer* did not, there were still seven "Doubtfuls" with the trial now in its concluding phase.

On Monday May 11, 1868, the Senate sitting as a Court of Impeachment resumed its sessions. In accordance with previously-made rules any Senator who desired to do so was given fifteen minutes in which to reveal how he intended to vote on each of the eleven Articles of Impeachment and the reasons for his decision.

The galleries were cleared and the Senators spoke behind closed doors. But no doors ever made were stout enough to withhold the deliberations of the United States Senate from the ears of those determined to hear them. All day long messengers flew from

Capitol to White House, carrying to the President, waiting in the second-floor library with his lawyers and advisers, the gist of what was being said. By nightfall, with the court still in session, the spirits of the President and his friends were higher than on any day since the beginning of the trial.

Amazing statements were being made in that sealed but porous chamber at the upland end of the Avenue. Senator John Sherman was saying that he could not vote guilty on the first Article, which accused the President of committing a misdemeanor by firing Stanton. At the time of the passage of the Tenure of Office Act Sherman had asserted that a President should not be deprived of the right to dismiss an uncooperative Cabinet officer. Now he could not go back on his own words. Evarts informed the President that if Sherman could not vote guilty on Article I, it followed that he could not vote guilty on any of the others since, if the first Article fell, the other ten fell with it. But—

"Sherman," Secretary Welles scribbled in his diary, "declared himself opposed to the first article, but would vote for the second. In other words the President had the right to remove Stanton, but no right to order another to discharge the duties. Poor Sherman!"

All day long the President and his aides analyzed and re-analyzed the reports coming in from the Capitol. Lawyer Groesbeck and Secretary McCulloch were both convinced that there was "no question of acquittal." Postmaster-General Randall, more noted for optimism than for accuracy, according to the caustic Welles, was saying the President had at least 22 votes, considerably more than the 19 needed for acquittal. Welles wasn't so sure; the Secretary of the Navy was inclined to discount oratory. It was easy enough to talk —the real test would be the voting. Except for the three Administration Republicans (really Democrats in the eyes of their party), where in the present Senate were their seven Republicans with enough moral fibre to defy the party lash?

When late Monday night Court adjourned and the lights faded in the Capitol windows, one thing was certain. Four of the Seven Tall Men were no longer on the Doubtful list. Grimes had made it clear that he could not "agree to destroy the harmonious working of the Constitution for the sake of getting rid of an unacceptable president." Fessenden had said that if Johnson were on trial for "general cussedness" he could vote guilty, but on the Articles of Impeachment his verdict was not guilty. Fowler and Trumbull were also on record, pledged to acquittal. Van Winkle seemed to be; at any rate his remarks had left the Radicals convinced that they could not count on him. Henderson? He had said he would have to go for acquittal on the first eight articles. He had some "doubts" on the eleventh; but before he could discuss Articles IX and X or explain his doubts about the eleventh, his fifteen minutes ended and the gavel of the Chief Justice cut him short. Ross? Silent, and determined to remain so until the time for voting came.

It was near at hand. When court adjourned, it was with the understanding that when it reconvened at 11:30 the next morning the vote would then be taken and the fate of the President decided.

The Radicals were desperate. The best they could come up with was 35 certain votes on some of the Articles of Impeachment—one short of the number necessary to convict. A delaying action was indicated. The court was no sooner under way on Tuesday when to the disappointment of the gallery crowds, Senator Chandler of Michigan was on his feet, pleading for postponement. His colleague, Senator Jacob M. Howard, a Republican wheelhorse, had been taken "suddenly ill, and was delirious yesterday all day, and is very sick, indeed, this morning. He desires to be here . . . but both his physicians protested against his coming, and said it would imperil his life. With that statement I desire to move that the Senate, sitting as a court, adjourn until Saturday at 12 o'clock." It was so moved. A few minutes later the court stood adjourned until Saturday when, if all went as scheduled, the final vote would be taken.

The Radicals devoted the interval—Wednesday, Thursday, Friday and Saturday morning—to an unrelenting effort to add at least one vote to the thirty-five on which they had reason to depend. As chairman of the Republican National Committee Congressman Robert C. Schenck of Ohio dispatched this telegram to scores of party leaders in Maine, Rhode Island, Illinois, Kansas, Iowa, West Virginia and Tennessee: "Great danger to the peace of the country and the Republican cause if impeachment fails. Send to your Senators public opinion by resolutions, letters and delegations."

Senator Fessenden was a special target. One letter to him said: "Any Republican senator who votes against impeachment need never expect to get home alive; so take notice from A RADICAL." The aging Maine Senator ignored this, but he was hurt to the quick by a letter from one of his oldest friends, saying, "You have no right to assume you know more than all the others. If for nothing else, to satisfy those who elected you, you are bound to vote for conviction." More in sorrow than in anger, Fessenden replied, "Do you know how atrocious such a sentiment is, addressed to a judge and juror acting under the solemnity of an oath?"

Pomeroy had dreamed up a bright idea for eliminating Fessenden from the Senate before the voting began. The plan was to have the Maine Senator sent post haste to England as ambassador. It was believed that Fessenden, a sufferer from chronic dyspepsia, would welcome such an assignment as a rest-cure. The suggestion got as far as Fessenden's ears, where it went in one and out the other.

Chicago was buzzing with preparations for the National Republican Convention, set to begin May 21—the convention that would nominate Grant for President with Smiler Colfax as his running mate. On Tuesday night, the twelfth, an orator addressing a pre-Convention group advised Senator Trumbull "not to show himself on the streets" during the Convention lest "the representatives of an indignant people hang him to the most convenient lamp-post." The speaker's sentiments evoked roars of approval.

As for Grimes, Horace Greeley in Wednesday's New York *Tribune* described the Iowa Senator as follows: "We have had Benedict Arnold, Aaron Burr, Jefferson Davis, and now we have James W. Grimes." To Grimes, unwell and already distressed by the maledictions of men he had long regarded as warm friends, this was too much. That afternoon he was carried from the Senate chamber, the victim of a stroke of apoplexy that would leave him partly paralyzed for the few remaining years of his life.

Because Henderson was known to have doubts about the eleventh article, no efforts were being spared to keep him in the Radical column. Even General Grant, eyes on Chicago and the White House, had lent a hand. Grant had whispered sweet words into the ears of the ambitious Missouri Senator. According to the General, the impeachers were so confident of victory that Ben Wade had already selected his Cabinet with Ben Butler heading it as Secretary of State. "These men who are counting on the success of impeachment," the General added, "offer me their influence as the nominee to succeed Wade, in case he becomes President by the removal of Johnson." Grant said the President ought to be deposed "if for nothing else than because he is such an infernal liar." Henderson's reaction to Grant's blatant attempt to influence him was ironic. "On such terms," he retorted, "it would be nearly impossible to find the right sort of man to serve as President," a remark that left the General baffled.

Previously during a visitation by Missouri Congressmen, Henderson's nerve had failed him. He offered to resign, letting the Missouri legislature send a "safe" man to Washington in his place. The Congressmen were not interested in Henderson's resignation; they wanted his vote for conviction. They sent him a letter, a request that "you . . . withhold your vote on any article upon which you cannot vote affirmatively." When the Missourians returned to submit their Senator to another grilling, Henderson met them with more poise. He said he could not accede to their written request that he withhold his vote without "humiliation and shame." He told the Congressmen that he had reason to believe the Radicals could muster 36 votes of guilty on the eleventh article even if he voted to acquit. The delegation shortly withdrew, still in the dark as to what Henderson was going to do.

Wednesday brought a telegram for Henderson from a prominent St. Louis politician: "Can your friends hope that you will vote for the eleventh article? If so, all will be well." With Henderson when this message arrived was Samuel ("Sunset") Cox, former Congress-man from Ohio, now a resident of New York and a stout Johnson supporter. Together they framed Henderson's answer: "Say to my friends that I am sworn to do impartial justice . . . and I will try to do it like an honest man." At midnight a copy of this telegram was shown to Johnson who was greatly heartened by it.

In his self-chosen prison, the bayonet-rimmed War Office, Old Mars labored around the clock. The army list was checked. Every officer known to be friendly to this or that Senator, along with every officer Johnson had relieved of a Southern command was ordered to exert whatever influence he had.

No person was proof against Radical invasion; nor was any place, including the catacomb-like cellars of the Capitol building. What did the Radicals hope to accomplish in the basement of the Capitol? The answer is a case of truth being stranger than fiction.

For the time being a room near the Capitol crypt was being used as a sculptor's studio by Miss Vinnie Ream, a 21-year-old girl with bright brown eyes, an elfin smile, and chestnut ringlets. Vinnie had studied under the American sculptor, Clark Mills. During the war Orville H. Browning had arranged for her to have access to the White House in order to sculpt a head of Lincoln. Praise of the finished head had prompted Congress to award the young lady a $10,000 commission to carve the life-sized marble statue of Lincoln that would later stand in the Capitol rotunda. The statue was to be completed in Italy, but Vinnie was now working on the plaster cast in the Capitol basement room that Congress had lent her for that purpose.

The Radicals had their eyes on the pretty sculptress for two reasons. One was that the North B street cottage where Vinnie lived with her family was the rooming-house of Senator Ross, who had not brought his wife and daughter to Washington. The other was that, during the recent hectic days, Ross and some of his fellow-Doubtfuls had found Vinnie's studio one of the few places where they could confer without interruption. When the Radicals heard rumors that Vinnie was urging Ross to vote for acquittal, there was hob to pay. No less a personage than George W. Julian descended to her Capitol studio. Later the charge was made in the House that the Indiana Congressman told the girl "that if she did not use her influence for conviction, it would be the worst for her." Poor Vinnie! She thought Andrew Johnson "both good and great." She was kicked out of her studio, although she later got it back.

Theodore Tilton, avidly at work for the impeachers, took it upon himself to go to the very fountainhead of "impartial justice"—the home of Salmon Portland Chase. The Chief Justice was understandably indignant when Tilton in his *Independent* published an editorial captioned "A Folded Banner," in which he purported to repeat his conversation with Chase, called the Chief Justice a traitor to the cause, and accused him of befriending the President in an effort to win the Presidential nomination on the Democratic ticket. Chase sent a letter of protest to Tilton and to his friend, Hiram Barney, he wrote: "Think of legislatures, political conventions, even religious bodies, undertaking to instruct Senators how to vote, guilty or not guilty. What would be thought of such attempts to drive the decisions of any other courts?"

Friday came—the day before the scheduled vote. It brought from Leavenworth a telegram addressed jointly to the Kansas Senators, the Radical Pomeroy and the uncommited Ross. "Kansas has heard the evidence," the message read, "and demands the conviction of the President." It was signed, "D. R. Anthony and 1,000 others." Pomeroy received the message at his home and promptly got word to Ross to come around. When Ross arrived, Pomeroy persuaded him to stay for supper and improved the shining hour by pleading with him to vote for conviction.

Shortly after Ross' departure, the Radicals assembled in Pomeroy's library for what was to be their next-to-last pre-vote caucus. The session was in the nature of a celebration. The consensus was that the postponement had been salutary, that some of the "backsliders" had been talked into line, that tomorrow would see Andrew Johnson out of the White House and Ben Wade in. Pomeroy capped the festivities by reporting on his supper-time talk with Ross. He quoted Ross as so far breaking his silence as to say that "he was freer to vote for the eleventh than for any other" article of impeachment.

This welcome information prompted the Radicals to a new maneuver. Under the rules of the court, as set up by the Senators, the vote was to be taken on the articles in strict numerical order. Now that Ross was believed favorable to the eleventh it was the decision of the caucus that the rule must be changed so that tomorrow's first vote could be taken on that article. The wisdom of this proposal was driven home when along toward midnight great news was received. Senator Willey of West Virginia informed a group of Radicals who had spent the evening expostulating with him that he intended to vote guilty on the eleventh.

At a late hour the impeachers, still in caucus, received alarming news. Ross had been sighted in bad company. He had been seen in a downtown restaurant with Henderson and Van Winkle. Stanton was consulted. Stanton was a good man in such crises. He knew just what to do. He summoned General Sickles, one of the Radicals Johnson had removed from his Southern command—the man, moreover, whom Stanton had successfully defended against a murder charge years before.

Sickles made tracks for the Ream home on North B street, intending to buttonhole Ross in his quarters there. But the President's men were also abroad. Learning of Sickles' mission they got word to Vinnie Ream—and the little sculptress waylaid Sickles. The General, a ladies' man to the hilt, was so entranced by her conversation that he never got to Ross.

XXX

"MR. SENATOR, HOW SAY YOU?"

Saturday, May 16, the day of the vote, was one of the "loveliest" mornings, according to a reporter, the city had enjoyed in months. The Radicals were up and about betimes. So was Ross. Seeking privacy he fled to the home of his friend Perry Fuller, an Indian agent. He had breakfast there and prepared a telegram answering the one from "D. R. Anthony and 1,000 others" the day before. "I do not recognize your right to demand that I vote either for or against conviction," he wired. "I have taken an oath to do impartial justice . . . and trust that I shall have the courage to vote according to the dictates of my judgment for the highest good of the country."

Midway of the morning Ross was on his way to the Capitol. Pomeroy was waiting for him near the Senate door. During their supper-time conversation, Pomeroy had been sweet reasonableness; today he was menace. He warned his colleague that a vote for acquittal would not only spell political suicide but would subject Ross to an investigation on a charge of bribery.

The opening hour of the Senate as a legislative body was 10:30. Wade's gavel raised echoes in an almost empty room. Most of the Radicals were absent, locked in final caucus. The galleries were sparsely occupied. When an hour and a half later the rustle of his robes announced the entrance of the Chief Justice to begin court, the chamber was full, fifteen hundred people packed into a room with a seating capacity of one thousand.

General Sickles pushed and shoved his way into the room and headed for Ross, determined to complete the errand interrupted the night before. Scowls wreathed conservative foreheads as Fowler of Tennessee, deserting his usual seat, moved over to sit with a group of Radicals. Smiles replaced the scowls when Van Winkle whispered something to Democratic Senator Hendricks. Scowls again at the sight of Trumbull listening earnestly to words from Radical Senator Drake.

At the front of the chamber everything was as usual: the House managers at their table, all of the President's counsel except Curtis, called back to Boston, at theirs. The Chief Justice removed and then replaced his glasses. For a few seconds his eyes roamed the galleries, a faint smile parting his lips as he located his fashionably-dressed daughter, Mrs. Senator Sprague. At the last minute Senator Howard, whose illness had caused the postponement, was brought as far as the Senate door on a stretcher. Walking the rest of the way, supported by two men, he sank into his seat, a large shawl about his shoulders. Now fifty-three of Andrew Johnson's judges and jurors were on hand—all but the stricken Grimes.

The Radicals encountered no trouble in putting through a change in the rules. Williams, acting as floor manager, made the necessary motion. Democratic attempts to stall a vote withered before a reminder from the Chief Justice: debate was out of order. In a matter of minutes the new arrangement was complete: the Senators would vote first on the eleventh article, immediately after which they would vote on the other ten, one by one, in numerical order.

Senator Fessenden rose, pleading for a half-hour postponement. His old friend from Iowa was not yet present, but he was coming. "I saw Mr. Grimes last evening," he said, "and he told me that he should certainly be here this morning. It was his intention—."

He was interrupted by a cry from Reverdy Johnson. "He is here!"

The half-paralyzed Grimes struggled into the chamber and was guided to his seat by four friends.

The Chief Justice ordered the clerk to read the eleventh article and the voting began. Julian, sitting among the Representatives, was struck by the appearance of some of his fellow-members. Their faces grew "pale and sick under the burden of suspense." Chase had issued a stern warning against demonstrations—a needless order, Julian decided; as the roll was called the stillness was unbelievable. Whenever the name of a doubtful Senator was sounded, a curious thing happened in the galleries: hundreds of people held their breath until the Senator spoke, then vented it simultaneously.

The roll was called alphabetically, each Senator rising in his place to deliver his verdict. First was Henry B. Anthony of Rhode Island. There had been a time when Anthony was being mentioned among the Doubtfuls. He met the gaze of the Chief Justice, said "Guilty" and sat down.

The fourth name called was that of Simon Cameron of Pennsylvania. He shouted "Guilty!" before the Chief Justice could finish propounding the question. Cameron's eagerness provoked a titter, and relieved the tension.

But not for long. It gathered again as Fessenden was called. The Maine Senator got to his feet, slim and straight. "Not Guilty!"

Fowler was next. The Tennessean's speech faltered. It was not clear at first whether he had uttered one word or two. Chase asked him to repeat. This time there was no doubt. "Not Guilty!" rang out.

When the roll call got to Grimes the Chief Justice suggested that he keep his seat. But the sick man rose, painfully lifting himself to his full height. "Not Guilty!"

Soon it was Henderson's turn. The Missouri Senator looked "haggard, weary and over-worn" but his voice was clear: "Not Guilty!"

By the time Ross was reached, there were 14 votes of not guilty. Four more were expected, bringing the total to one less than the 19 necessary to acquit. Everything depended on Ross. He had been nervously playing with the paper on his desk, tearing it into strips, dropping the strips onto his lap. They floated noiselessly to the floor as he rose. His eyes revealed nothing and his stance was firm as he waited for the Chief Justice to finish the lengthily-worded question. Then, "Not Guilty!"

Solemnly the roll call proceeded but the tension was gone. As anticipated, Willey voted with the Radicals and Van Winkle with the Conservatives. The total was 36 to 19, one short of the 36 necessary to convict. The President stood acquitted on the eleventh article.

The minute the roll call was finished, the Chief Justice ordered the clerk to read the first article. But the Radicals were clamoring for adjournment. If at this sitting of the court they could not get a conviction on the eleventh, they could not get it on any article. Only one course would serve their ends, another delay.

Chase ruled the motion to adjourn out of order, pointing out that the court was even now in the process of acting on the existing motion calling for a vote on all the articles. Not for the first time the Chief Justice was overruled. The Radicals did not yet have enough votes to convict, but they easily mustered the simple majority needed to change the rules. Once more the outcome of the trial was left agonizingly in air as the court adjourned until May 26.

For the Radicals it was a ten-day reprieve, another opportunity to bring pressures on the "recusant Senators" as Sumner was now calling the Seven Tall Men. Pomeroy's statement to Ross that if he went for acquittal he would face an investigation on a suspicion of bribery proved to be no idle threat. Within hours after the vote on the eleventh article, Old Thad had persuaded the House to give the impeachment managers extraordinary powers for the purpose of looking into free-wheeling rumors that this or that Republican had received money for voting not guilty. The investigation was headlong, passionate—and embarrassing. Senators' mail was impounded. Monday night found Ben Butler at Jay Cooke's bank, examining private accounts. A Cincinnati lawyer, known to have picked up a tidy sum betting on the trial, was questioned as to what he had done with his winnings; when he balked at answering he was incarcerated temporarily in what used to be Vinnie Ream's studio. One piece of tangible evidence was produced—a copy of a letter (a true copy according to its recipient, Postmaster General Randall) in which a Republican Senator had offered to sell his vote to the President's friends. Unfortunately the letter was not the work of one of the Tall Men. It bore the signature of Pomeroy, moving spirit of the Radical caucus!

Increasingly Radical wrath was concentrated on Ross. His brother William, currently in Washington, was the recipient of a letter offering him $20,000 if he would reveal how the Senator intended to vote. Ben Butler was howling with exasperation. If it's money Ross is after, he told friends, "There is a bushel . . . how much does the damned scoundrel want?" "D. R. Anthony and 1,000 others" sent a second telegram, "Kansas repudiates you as she does all perjurers and skunks." Another Kansas constituent wired, "Unfortunately the rope with which Judas hung himself is mislaid but the pistol with which Jim Lane killed himself is at your service." Ross himself wrote a letter on a piece of Senate stationery: "Don't be discouraged, dear wife, it's all coming out all right. This storm of passion will soon pass away. . . ." The Senator prayed for strength and wisdom.

May 26, 1868, the date of the vote on the remaining ten articles, fell on a Tuesday. Weather: blustery with partly cloudy skies and dust blowing in the streets. Nothing, of course, could keep Washington at home now. Once again the Senate Chamber was jammed to suffocation as Chief Justice Chase strode in at high noon to open the final session of the great trial.

The scene was much the same as that of May 16. There was the same silent, waiting audience and the Radicals once again changed the rules. The Senators agreed to take the initial vote not on the first but on the second article, to be followed by a vote on the third.

The chief clerk read Article II and the roll call began. As the clerk called out the name of each Senator, he stood while the Chief Justice propounded the question:

"Mr. Senator ——, how say you, is the respondent, Andrew Johnson, President of the United States, guilty or not guilty of a high misdemeanor, as charged in this article of impeachment?"

Fessenden, Fowler, Grimes, Henderson, Trumbull and Van Winkle: "Not Guilty."

When Ross rose, there was no sound and hardly any movement. (Years later he would reveal the thoughts coursing through his mind, his feeling that he was "almost literally" looking down "into my open grave. Friends, position, fortune, everything that makes life desirable to an ambitious man, were about to be swept away by the breath of my mouth, perhaps forever.")

"Not Guilty."

The total: 35 to 19. The President was acquitted on Article II.

The clerk read the third article. Individual votes the same, result the same.

Despair among the Radicals. They had pinned their hopes on the eleventh, second and third articles, in that order, and the President had been acquitted on all three. Were the proceedings allowed to continue, there could be only one result—increasingly larger totals for Johnson. Floor-manager Williams threw in the towel: "I move that the Senate, sitting as a court of impeachment, do now adjourn *sine die.*" The vote was 34 to 16, four Senators refraining.

The most important trial in American history was over.

At the White House, according to Colonel Moore:

Sent my orderly to Willard's to bring me dispatches from Capitol addressed to Pres. I received them from orderly as he brought them in and read them to the Cabinet. There was no boisterousness but a quiet excitement . . . Stanton's letter relinquishing charge of War Department received at 3:25 P.M. It was brought to Pres by Townsend who asked orders. Pres declined to give any, seeming to think that a trap was laid into which he might be inveigled into trouble. Many called to congratulate Pres and great joy prevailed throughout the city.

According to Secretary Browning:

We were in telegraphic communication with the Senate, despatches being sent to Willard's and thence to the White House by courier . . . "They have refused to proceed with a vote upon the articles in their order"—"They have resolved to take vote on the second article"—"The vote is being taken"—"Ross stands firm on the third article"—"The vote is closed & the article beaten 35 to 19." "A motion has been made to adjourn the court *sine die.*" "The motion has prevailed & the court is dissolved." All these despatches were brot [sic] in, handed to the President, & read. I watched him. He was calm, dignified, placid & self-possessed with no outward sign of agitation, whatever passions may have glowed in his breast. When the final result was announced, when we knew that the atrocity was ended—that the President was acquitted of all—that the Court was dissolved, without daring to take a vote on the main charge, the removal of Stanton, he received the congratulations of his Cabinet with the same serenity and self-possession which have characterized him throughout this terrible ordeal.

According to William H. Crook (officer of the household who carried the news to Mrs. Johnson in her sickroom):

Tears were in her eyes, but her voice was firm and she did not tremble once as she said, "I knew he'd be acquitted; I knew it . . . Thank you for coming to tell me."

XXXI

DEFENDER OF THE CONSTITUTION

The attempt to depose an American President for political reasons fell to the ground and with the collapse of the trial on May 26, 1868, a great constitutional crisis receded into history.

The fact that Johnson was acquitted by only one vote gave breathless drama to the last moments of his trial, but it cannot be taken as a measure of sentiment in the Senate of 1868. Three months later Johnson was writing his friend Ben Truman that the vote was "not so close as most people think; for Senator Morgan would have cast his vote against impeachment rather than to have seen Ben Wade succeed to the Presidential chair." Still later Henderson revealed that two other Senators, Sprague and Willey, had agreed that they would go for acquittal if their voices were needed.

What the record shows, however, is that Sprague, Willey and Morgan kept their party standing by voting guilty. "The glory of the trial," as the historian James Rhodes has put it, was the action of the Seven Tall Men. "The average Senator who hesitated," wrote Rhodes, "finally gave his voice with the majority, but these seven, in conscientiousness and delicacy of moral fibre, were above any average, and in refusing to sacrifice their ideas of justice to a popular demand . . . , they showed a degree of courage than which we know none higher."

To the roll of honor on which their names belong must be added three others: James Dixon of Connecticut, James Rood Doolittle of Wisconsin, and Daniel S. Norton of Minnesota. In the summer of 1866 these Administration Republicans were read out of their party for participating in the pro-Johnson arm-in-arm convention. Their fate was the same as that of the Seven.

None of them was ever to hold elected office again. The Wisconsin legislature passed resolutions demanding that Doolittle resign. He refused, was rejected for re-election and left the Senate in 1869. Dixon's term—his last—ended at the same time. When Norton died in July of 1870, he was still in the Senate but his successor had already been named.

Trumbull's term had five years to go. When it was over, Illinois retired him to private life. Van Winkle's successor reported for duty during the first year of the Grant administration. Fowler, whose term closed in 1871, spent the rest of his life in Washington where, with no political duties to distract him, he indulged his scholarly tastes, spending long hours browsing in Lowdermilk's famous book store.

During the summer following the trial, Fessenden knew the sweet taste of appreciation. But it did not come from his home state of Maine where his name continued to be anathema in Republican circles. It came from Boston in the form of an invitation to a testimonial dinner in recognition of his "courage and conscientiousness under circumstances of peculiar difficulty." Busy with the heavy duties incident to the closing of Congress, Fessenden was unable to attend. But it must have done the old man's heart good to run his eye down the long list of names, 72 in all, appended to the invitation. Among the signatures were those of Francis Parkman, the historian; James Russell Lowell; Charles Elliot Norton; Asa Gray, America's leading botanist; and Charles Francis Adams, Jr. and Samuel Bowles, editor of the Springfield *Republican.*

Except for the nine months during which he served as Lincoln's

Secretary of the Treasury, Fessenden had been in the Senate since 1854. His term was to expire in 1871, but he was spared the humiliation of certain defeat for re-election. Stricken in August of 1869, "the ablest man of his day," as his friend Grimes lovingly called him, died the next month.

Grimes had already announced that his present term would be his last. Visiting his home in Burlington, Iowa, in the summer of 1868 he was hissed on the street and excoriated in the local newspaper as "Judas Iscariot Grimes." The old Senator sighed: "Perhaps I did wrong not to commit perjury by order of a party, but I cannot see it that way." His doctors sent him to Europe to seek a cure for his paralysis. Instead, while in Paris during the summer of 1869, he suffered a second stroke. "I have the consolation of knowing," he wrote at this time, "that on the subject about which I really made shipwreck of my health, I have daily, hourly, evidence that the intelligent sentiment of the country applauds the course I took, and that that sentiment will increase more and more from year to year." The following December, too ill to go on with his duties, he resigned from the Senate and went home to Burlington where he found the change he had prophesied already in evidence: no hisses on the street, no insults in the press. Death came in December of 1872, and an enormous crowd of mourners made up the procession to Aspen Grove Cemetery.

Henderson, alone among the ten, was publicly forgiven by his party. This turn of the tide occurred in 1884 when he was named permanent chairman of the Republican National Convention in Chicago. When his name was reported, there was a tumult of cheering and foot-stomping, the significance of which was lost on none. Moving to Washington in the 1880's, he made some wise investments in real estate, enjoyed a lucrative law practice and died in 1912, surrounded by affectionate and admiring friends.

Ross suffered most, partly because he had the longest way to go and the least to start with; partly because at the conclusion of his term in 1871 he went back to Kansas, one of the most Radical states in the Union. "Indifference and coolness" were his lot there and his family was "socially ostracised and ignored." He set up a little newspaper and printing shop in Coffeyville and began what for many years was a losing battle for survival. Misfortune dogged him. D. R. Anthony of Leavenworth—he of the "D. R. Anthony and 1,000 others"—came to Coffeyville, invaded the printing shop and subjected Ross to a beating from which he never fully recovered.

In April of 1871 a cyclone swept away his newspaper plant. He returned to his old home in Lawrence, where his family was staying, worked on various newspapers and eventually became publisher of the *Standard*. In February of 1880 he bought the *Press* in Leavenworth, moved the *Standard* there and consolidated the two newspapers.

In 1882 New Mexico invited Ross to attend a fair at Albuquerque to promote the development of the territory. Ross accepted, became interested in the country, sent for his family and settled there. In 1885 President Cleveland named him Governor of New Mexico. He served for four years. Some of the natives were horrified by his refusal to serve wine in the Presidential Palace "even to callers on New Year's Day"; but his administration was vigorous, winning for him the nickname of "Old Montezuma."

Back in Kansas another old man was making preparations for a strange journey of repentance. His name was Hugh Cameron. During the trial General Cameron had presided at a mass meeting held to condemn the Kansas Senator's vote. Later realizing his wrong, he retired to a tree-house on a bluff above the Kaw River, let his hair grow to his waist, and vowed that he would never associate with humanity until the villifiers of Ross admitted their error.

Satisfied in 1907 that the public had come around, Cameron walked to New Mexico. The Lawrence (Kansas) *Journal* called his pilgrimage "sane and righteous," adding that "Time has softened a great many things . . . There is scarcely a man living who does not feel thankfulness that Andrew Johnson was not impeached." When Cameron arrived at the Ross home in Albuquerque, the former Senator voiced the often quoted prediction that he would be "a bigger man dead than . . . alive." Less than two months later Ross was dead, a hero in the eyes of his countrymen.

Senator Sumner's closing years were shadowed by disappointment and loneliness. As Radicalism encountered its inevitable reaction, he lost his preeminence in the Senate. Eventually he was deprived of his chairmanship of the powerful Foreign Relations Committee, the duties of which he had discharged with notable ability for many years. He himself, in due time, parted company with the Radicals and joined the so-called Liberal Republican movement, dedicated to the liquidation of Radical Reconstruction and the redemption of the South. But the leaders of the Liberal forces in his party did not seek his counsel, and what remained of his political life was marked by disquietude. In the Senate, in December of 1872, he offered a proposal which would not be acted on for another thirty years. He suggested that "all names of battles with fellow-citizens"—the Civil War battles—should be removed from American flags and pennants. A civilized nation, he argued, should not perpetuate the memory of civil strife. For this speech he was denounced by Republicans, caricatured and abused in the party press. Toward the end of his life he developed a great hunger for approval. He would ask his friends if they recognized his resemblance to Edmund Burke; three pictures of the great British statesman adorned his study.

Several years after the trial he did a characteristic thing. He issued a dinner invitation to former Senator Henderson, temporarily in Washington to argue a case before the Supreme Court. Henderson accepted. There were other guests, but Sumner asked the Missourian to remain after they had gone. When the two were alone, Sumner spoke his piece. He had been wanting for some time to have a talk with Henderson about the impeachment. "I want to say," he told his startled guest, "that in that matter you were right and I was wrong. I didn't want to die without making this confession . . . But if it is just as convenient to you, I would rather you would say nothing about it until I am dead . . . and I won't live many years." He died March 11, 1874.

Stanton's last official act was his letter to Andrew Johnson on the afternoon of May 26, 1868:

> Sir: The resolution of the Senate of the United States of the 21st of February last, declaring that the President "has no power to remove the Secretary of War and designate any other officer to perform the duties of that office ad interim" having this day failed to be supported by two-thirds of the Senators present and voting on the Articles of Impeachment preferred against you by the House of Representatives, I have relinquished charge of the War Department and have left the same, and the books, archives, papers and property heretofore in my custody as Secretary of War, in care of Brevet Major General Townsend, the Senior Assistant Adjutant General, subject to your direction.

Leaving the War Office, Stanton retired to his Washington home. During the following year President Grant appointed him to the Supreme Court, but Old Mars was dead before the appointment could take effect.

During June of 1868 Thaddeus Stevens enjoyed a mild improvement in health, "a brief, deceptive Indian Summer," as one of his biographers has put it. What remained of his waning strength he invested in one last futile effort to depose Andrew Johnson. For the country as a whole impeachment was dead, but not for Thad Stevens. At his modest home on Capitol Hill he burned the midnight oil, framing new articles of impeachment.

It is easy to read into this terrible singleness of purpose nothing but hate for the person of Johnson and hate for the South. But to dispose of Stevens in this simple manner is to overlook the mainspring of his remarkable character. Stevens was an idealist, obsessed by a dream. The whole world was acquainted with his dream; he had often spelled it out in the House. To Stevens the outcome of the Civil War presented an opportunity that he believed must be seized now or perhaps be lost forever—the opportunity to write into law the stirring statement of the Declaration of Independence that all men are created equal. Yet like many idealists, he quite unidealistically failed to see that the ends do not justify the means. Whatever stood between Old Thad and his high goal must be swept aside, including even the government through which he was seeking to reach it. In his view he was striving only to put the finishing touches on the Founding Fathers' work.

On July 7 the House listened with respectful attention to what was to be his valedictory. It was the longest speech he had ever prepared, an amazing accomplishment. Old Thad did not have strength enough to say the words. The speech was read by the clerk. His new impeachment articles were there, all of them blatantly political. He did not press for their passage now; he signaled his intention to bring them up later. And his old dream was there.

"Providence has placed us here in an Eden," he began. "While nature has given us every advantage, man is still vile. But such large steps have lately been taken in the true direction, that the patriot has the right to take courage. My sands are nearly run, and I can only see with the eyes of faith . . . But you are promised length of days and a brilliant career. If you can . . . realize that every human being, however born . . . is your equal, that every inalienable right which belongs to you, belongs also to him, truth and righteousness will spread over the land, and you will look down . . . upon an empire of a hundred million happy people."

On July 27 Congress adjourned. The hot Washington summer was at hand. Ordinarily Old Thad would have headed for the cooler greenery of his farm in Adams County, Pennsylvania; but this summer his doctors would not hear of it. On August 11, his last day, his nephew, Thaddeus Stevens, and another relative, Simon Stevens, were on hand. He was unable to take nourishment but from time to time his housekeeper, Lydia Smith, pushed pieces of ice past his parched lips. Not far from Stevens' home was the Providence Hospital, a charitable institution which Stevens had helped to found and for which he had procured an appropriation of $30,000 from Congress. It was staffed by Negro Sisters of Charity, two of whose nuns, Sisters Lorette and Genevieve, were at the old man's bedside. At midnight Stevens breathed his last. For two days he lay in state in the rotunda of the Capitol. Then he was taken home to Lancaster, where approximately 20,000 people attended his funeral. He was buried in a Negro cemetery—his own choice—and the simple marker later erected carried the lines he himself had written:

> I repose in this quiet and secluded spot
> not from any natural preference for solitude,
> but finding other cemeteries
> limited by charter rules as to race,
> I have chosen this that I might illustrate in death
> the principles which I advocated through a long life,
> Equality of man before his Creator.

At the conclusion of the trial, only nine months remained of Andrew Johnson's administration. They were quiet months. In early July the President's eyes were on New York City. The Democratic National Convention was under way there. Johnson longed for the nomination. Not that he was eager to remain in the Presidency; he had quite enough of that. But he was human. To be named by his party under the circumstances, as Colonel Moore put it, would "have been a vindication such as no man had ever received." The President told Moore that he was being asked, "Why don't I join the Democratic party?" His answer: "Why don't they join me?" They didn't. On the initial ballot Johnson received 65 votes, the second largest number; but after many more ballots the Democratic ticket was Horatio Seymour of New York for President, Francis P. Blair, Jr., for Vice President.

Early in August the President was writing his letter to Ben Truman of which mention has been made. It was a discursive and revealing document:

Now I have been true to the Union and to my friends, [Johnson wrote] and have been generally temperate in all things. I may have erred in not carrying out Mr. Blair's request in putting into my

Cabinet Morton, Andrew and Greeley . . . Morton would have been a tower of strength . . . and so would Andrew. No Senator would have dared vote for my impeachment with those two men in my Cabinet.

Grant was untrue. He meant well for the first two years and much that I did that was denounced was through his advice. . . . But Grant saw the Radical handwriting on the wall, and heeded it. Grant did the proper thing to save Grant, but it pretty nearly ruined me. I might have done the same thing under the same circumstances . . . Grant . . . was the right man in the right place during the war, and no matter what his faults were or are, the whole world can never write him down—remember that.

[Sherman was] our greatest military genius . . . erratic and stubborn, but he don't know how to lie . . . The time will come when Sheridan will be looked upon by many distinguished military men as greater than Grant . . .

Mr. Lincoln is the greatest American that has ever lived. I do not mean by this to detract from the name of Washington, but Washington was an Englishman, you know . . .

Butler [was] the most daring and unscrupulous demagogue I have ever known. But his services for the Union during the war can never be over-estimated. I can never thoroughly despise him on that account . . .

I shall go to my grave with the firm belief that [Jefferson] Davis . . . and a few others of the arch-conspirators should have been tried, convicted and hanged for treason. There was too much precious blood spilled on both sides not to have held the leading traitors responsible . . . treason should be made odious and archtraitors should be punished.

The November elections were a Republican triumph all down the line. As inauguration day, March 4, 1869, approached, Grant let it be known that he would neither ride in the same carriage with Johnson nor speak to him. It was proposed that two carriages be used but Johnson quietly turned the suggestion down.

Ordinarily the retiring President spent the morning of inauguration day at the Capitol signing last-minute bills. Johnson chose to work in the council room of the White House, surrounded by his Cabinet. At precisely 12:30, according to Orville Browning, his tasks were finished. Then there were handshakes all around. Johnson and Colonel Moore preceded the little group down the stairs to the portico of the main entrance where the President got into his carriage and the Cabinet members into theirs and all "drove away, divested of official authorities."

The Johnsons did not leave the city immediately. As the ex-President told Ben Truman, who had traveled east to be with him, he hadn't got to Washington in a hurry and he saw no reason to leave it in one. For almost two weeks Johnson and his wife were guests at the home of John Coyle, publisher of the *Intelligencer,* while their daughter Martha and her family remained at the home of the Gideon Welleses.

On Wednesday, March 17, 1869, Welles wrote in his diary, "I this evening parted with ex-President Johnson and his family, who leave in the morning for Tennessee. No better persons have occupied the Executive Mansion. . . . Of the president, politically and officially, I need not here speak further than to say he has been faithful to the Constitution, although his administrative capabilities and management may not equal some of his predecessors. Of measures he was a good judge, but not always of men."

It was a just estimate: a man of admirable character, incorruptible and patriotic, Andrew Johnson was one of the best political philosophers and one of the poorest politicians ever to sit in the White House.

On the morning of March 18 there was a small crowd at the depot to see him off. No cheering, no speeches; but as his carriage appeared, the waiting men removed their hats and stood thus, silent, until his train pulled out of the station.

He would be back. It took him six years, and he met defeat and disappointment along the way, but in January of 1875 the state legislature of Tennessee sent him back to Washington as a member of the United States Senate.

On March 4, sixty-seven-year-old Andrew Johnson stepped into that chamber where seven years earlier he had stood by proxy before the bar of justice. Of the 35 men who had then pronounced him guilty of high crimes and misdemeanors, only 13 remained. One of them—Edmunds of Vermont—was addressing the chair. He glanced around as the gallery crowd, spotting Johnson, burst into thunderous applause. He forgot what he had risen to say, and made a sudden movement that sent a pile of books on his desk clattering to the floor and sat down.

By this time a score of Senators had advanced on Johnson with outstretched hands. When he reached his desk he found it covered with flowers. A little later, seeing that the demonstration in his honor was threatening to continue, he sought to stop it by fleeing to the cloakrooms. Many of the Senators followed, practically all of those who had not yet had a chance to welcome him. "I miss my old friends," he told one of them, ". . . Fessenden, Fowler, Trumbull, Grimes, Henderson, Ross, all gone." There were tears in his eyes.

The Congressional session was short. Toward the end of the month Johnson was en route home to spend most of the summer with his wife and his daughter, Martha, and her family in Greeneville. Late in July he paid a visit to his other daughter, Mrs. Mary Stover. It was noon of Thursday, July 29, when he arrived at Mrs. Stover's farm-home in Carter County, two miles from Elizabethton. Weary from his journey he went upstairs for a rest after lunch, accompanied by Lili Stover, his granddaughter. The young lady had just left his room when, hearing a thud behind her, she hurried back to find Johnson on the floor, the victim of a stroke.

Partly paralyzed but in full possession of his senses, he refused to have a doctor. For the next twenty-four hours he lay in bed, cheerful and alert, talking over old times with members of his family and visiting neighbors. Then at three o'clock Friday afternoon a second stroke induced a coma from which he never revived. At two-thirty the next morning, July 31, 1875, Andrew Johnson was dead.

Three Tennessee cities requested the privilege of providing his final resting place, but after consultation with the other members of the family Mrs. Johnson, who was to survive her husband by only six months, declined these offers with thanks. The decision was to bury the former President in a spot he himself had chosen, a conical-shaped hill only a mile and a half from his Main Street home in Greeneville.

On Monday, the day of the funeral, all business closed, all buildings were draped in black. Thousands of people poured into the little town. Some were dignitaries from Washington and elsewhere, but most were plain folks from the hills. The people of Tennessee knew the value of their man; other Americans would learn it in due time. For generations historians, following false leads, would tend to bestow on Johnson an appraisal only a little less harsh than that his enemies had given him during his lifetime. But other historians, coming along later, would redress this historial injustice. Digging into Johnson's papers as these accumulated, poring over the diaries and memoirs of his associates as these became available, conscientious scholars would put the picture right, making it possible for distant generations to join with Gideon Welles in hailing the seventeenth president as the Defender of the Constitution.

The funeral services were conducted by the Masonic Lodge, of which Johnson had been an active member. Care was taken to honor all requests he had made concerning his burial: his body was wrapped in an American flag, and his head was pillowed on one of his own thumb-worn copies of the Constitution of the United States.

BIBLIOGRAPHY

Manuscripts

Letters: Leonard J. Farwell to James Rood Doolittle, February 8, 1866; Doolittle to State Historical Society of Wisconsin, March 12, 1866. Originals in Doolittle Papers at State Historical Society, Madison, Wis.

James Rood Doolittle Papers. Library of Congress.

Sydney Howard Gay Papers. New York, Columbia University Libraries, Special Collections.

Joseph Holt Papers. Library of Congress.

Andrew Johnson Papers. Library of Congress.

Andrew Johnson-Miscellaneous Items. New York Historical Society.

William G. Moore Diary Transcript. In Johnson Papers. Library of Congress.

Samuel Holden Parsons Papers. Library of Congress.

Edwin McMasters Stanton Papers. Library of Congress.

Thaddeus Stevens Papers. Library of Congress.

Benjamin F. Wade Papers. Library of Congress.

Documents

U.S. Congress. *The Congressional Globe.*

——. *Official Congressional Directory.*

——. *House Report* 104. Committee on the Judiciary. Assassination of Lincoln. . . . 39th Congress, 1st session. July, 1866.

——. 39th Congress, 1st session. *House Report* No. 30. Report of the Joint Committee on Reconstruction . . . (in vol. 2 of House Reports, Set 1273).

U.S. Congress. *Senate Executive Documents,* 39th Congress, 1st Session. (Washington, 1866), I, No. 2. Reports of Carl Schurz and Ulysses S. Grant on conditions in South. (in vol. 1, Set No. 1237)

————. *Senate Executive Document* 43, 39th Congress, 1st Session. Dated April 9, 1866. (in vol. 2, Set 1238) Report of Benjamin F. Truman on conditions in South.

————. House judiciary committee on the impeachment investigation. Testimony taken before the . . . committee . . . in the investigation of the charges against Andrew Johnson. Second session, 39th Congress; 1st session, 40th Congress, 1867. 2 vols.

————. 40th Congress, 2d session. Report of the Select Committee on the New Orleans Riots, 1867.

————. 40th Congress, 2d session 1867-1868 Senate. Johnson, Andrew . . . defendant. *The Great Impeachment and Trial of Andrew Johnson* . . . Philadelphia: T. B. Peterson & Brothers, 1868.

————. 40th Congress, 2d session. *Trial of Andrew Johnson, President of the United States.* . . . 3 vols. 1868.

————. Serial No. 1315. *Senate Journal.* 40th Congress, 2nd session. Contains, as appendix, proceedings of Senate preliminary to impeachment trial of Andrew Johnson.

————. Senate (62nd Congress, 2d session). *Senate Document* 867 . . . Extracts from the Journal of the U.S. Senate in all cases of impeachment presented by the House . . . 1798-1904. Washington, 1912.

————. Joint committee on printing. *Biographical Directory of the American Congress.* 81st Congress, 2d session. House Document no. 607. Washington, 1950.

————. 84th Congress, 1st session. Document No. 121. "Our American Government. What Is It? How Does It Function?" Washington, 1955.

United States. *Ninth Census of the United States, 1870.* Population and Social Statistics.

United States. *War of the Rebellion: A Compilation of the Official Records of the Union and Confederate Armies.* 130 vols. Short title: *Official Records.* Washington, 1880-1901.

*Serial Sources**

Andrews, Rena Mazyck. "Johnson's Plan of Restoration in Relation to that of Lincoln." *Tennessee Historical Magazine,* Series 2, VI (1931), p. 168-181.

---

* Newspapers are not listed here, but those consulted are cited in the text.

Beale, Howard K. "On Rewriting Reconstruction History." *American Historical Review*, XLV (July, 1940), p. 807-827.

Binckley, J. W. "The Leader of the House." *Galaxy*, I (July 15, 1866), p. 493-500.

Boutwell, George S. "The Impeachment of Andrew Johnson from the Standpoint of One of the Managers of the Impeachment Trial." *McClure's Magazine*, XIV (1899-1900), p. 171-182.

Brogan, D. W. "The Crisis of American Federalism." *Glasgow University Publications*, LX (1944), p. 1-43.

Brown, Gilbert Patten. "The Unique Personality of Andrew Johnson." *Masonic Review*, XXIII (December, 1931), p. 16-19.

Brown, Wenzell. "The Fearless Andrew Johnson." *American Mercury*, LXX (1950), p. 608-17.

Brownlow, Walter P. "Defense and Vindication of Andrew Johnson." *The Taylor-Trotwood Magazine*, VII (September 1908), p. 491-503.

(Brownson, Orestes). "Stevens on Reconstruction." *Brownson's Quarterly Review*, Series I (1864—April issue), CLXVI, p. 166.

Brigance, William Norwood. "Jeremiah Black and Andrew Johnson." *Mississippi Valley Historical Review*, XIX (1932), p. 205-218.

Caskey, W. M. "First Administration of Governor Andrew Johnson." *East Tennessee Historical Society Publication*, No. 1 (1929), p. 43-59.

Chase, Salmon Portland. "Diary and Correspondence of Salmon Portland Chase." (American History Association, *Annual Report* for 1902, vol. 2)

Clark, Allen C. "Richard Wallach and the Times of His Mayoralty." *Records of the Columbia Historical Society*, Washington, D.C., XXI (1918), p. 195-245.

Donald, David. "Why They Impeached Andrew Johnson." *American Heritage*, VIII, No. 1 (December, 1956), p. 20-25-plus.

Doolittle, James Rood. "Andrew Johnson." *Harper's Weekly*, X (September 15, 1866), p. 582.

Dunning, William A. "More Light on Andrew Johnson." *American Historical Review*, XI, No. 3 (April 1906), p. 574-594.

Gerry, Margarita S. "The Real Andrew Johnson." *Century Magazine*, CXV (November, 1927), p. 54-56; (December, 1927), p. 218-230.

Gipson, Lawrence H. "The Statesmanship of President Johnson." *Mississippi Valley Historical Review*, II (1915-1916), p. 363-383.

Goodlett, A. G. "Andrew Johnson." (Letter to editor.) *Taylor-Trotwood Magazine*, VII (August, 1908), p. 479-480.

Hyman, Sidney. "What Is the President's True Role?" *New York Times Magazine.* (September 7, 1958), p. 108-109.

(Lowell, James Russell). "The Seward-Johnson Reaction." *North American Review,* CIII (October, 1866), p. 520-549.

―――. "The President's Message." *North American Review,* CII (January 1866), p. 250-260.

―――. "The President on the Stump." *North American Review,* CII (January-April 1866), p. 530-544.

McCall, S. W. "Washington During Reconstruction." *Atlantic Monthly,* LXXXVII (June, 1901), p. 817-826.

Nichols, Roy F. "A Great Party Which Might Have Been Born in Philadelphia." *Pennsylvania Magazine of History and Biography,* LVII (1933), p. 359-374.

Phifer, Gregg. "Andrew Johnson Argues a Case." *Tennessee Historical Quarterly,* XI, No. 2 (June, 1952), p. 148-170.

―――. "Andrew Johnson Loses His Battle." *Tennessee Historical Quarterly,* XI, No. 4 (December, 1952), p. 291-328.

―――. "Andrew Johnson Takes a Trip." *Tennessee Historical Quarterly,* XI, No. 1 (March 1952), p. 3-22.

―――. "Andrew Johnson Versus the Press in 1866." *The East Tennessee Historical Society's Publications. . . .* No. 25 (1953).

Purcell, Richard J. "The Misjudged Andrew Johnson." *Catholic Educational Review,* XXXI (1933), p. 587-600.

Raymond, Henry W., ed. "Extracts from the Journal of Henry J. Raymond." *Scribner's Monthly,* XX (1880), p. 227.

Sioussant, St. George Leakin, ed. "Notes of Colonel W. G. Moore, Private Secretary to President Johnson, 1866-1868." The *American Historical Review,* XIX (October 1913 to July 1914), p. 98-132.

―――. "Tennessee and National Political Parties 1850-1860." American Historical Association *Annual Report . . .* for the year 1914. Vol. 1, p. 243-258. Washington, 1916.

Smelser, Marshall. "The Dred Scott Case—Up to Now." *Interracial Review,* XIV, No. 9 (September, 1941), p. 134-36.

Stern, Philip Van Doren. "The President Came Forward and the Sun Burst Through the Clouds." *American Heritage,* IX, No. 2 (February, 1958), p. 10-15, 94-97.

Strong, Mary Katherine. "Post-War Congressional Elections." *Current History,* X (May, 1946), p. 435-441.

Thompson, Carol L. "Andrew Johnson and the Lost Cause." *Current History,* XIV (June, 1948), p. 336-341.

Truman, Benjamin F. "Anecdotes of Andrew Johnson." *Century Magazine*, LXXXV (January, 1913), p. 435-440.

Welles, Gideon. "Lincoln and Johnson: Their Plan of Reconstruction and the Resumption of National Authority." *Galaxy*, XIII (1872), p. 521, 663.

Witmer, T. Richard. "Some Hitherto Unpublished Correspondence of Thaddeus Stevens." Lancaster County Historical Society, Lancaster, Pa., *Historical Papers and Addresses*, XXXV (1931), p. (49)-68.

Special Sources

Ashley, Margaret. "An Ohio Congressman in Reconstruction." (Unpublished) Master's Thesis, Faculty of Political Science, Columbia University, 1916.

Bartlett, Mrs. Margaret Johnson Patterson, great-granddaughter of President Johnson. Correspondence with author.

(Conover, Sanford). Material on, in National Archives:
Criminal 4525, Supreme Court of District of Columbia. Record Group 21 Pardon Attorney Case File B576: United States vs. Sanford Conover alias Charles A. Dunham. Record Group 204.

Curtis, William H. *Ad Interim and Ad Outerim; or Confidential Disclosures of State Secrets. . . .*2d ed. Washington, 1868. (Pamphlet)

Locke, David Ross. *"Swinging Round the Cirkle": or Andy's Trip to the West, Together with a Life of Its Hero*. By Petroleum V. Nasby, a Dimicrat of Thirty Years standing, and who allus Tuck his liquor straight. New York, 1866. (Pamphlet)

Swinney, Everette. "Andrew Johnson's Swing Around the Circle: the Study of an Appeal to the People." (Unpublished) thesis . . . submitted in partial fulfillment of the requirements for the degree of Master of Arts, August, 1957. (The Pennsylvania State University, the Graduate School Department of History.)

Books

Adams, Francis A. *An Autobiography*. Boston, 1916.

Adams, Henry. *The Education of Henry Adams*. Boston, 1927.

Adams, John Quincy. *Massachusetts and South Carolina. Correspondence Between John Quincy Adams and Wade Hampton and Others of South Carolina*. Boston, 1868.

Albjerg, Esther Marguerite (Hall). *The New York Press and Andrew Johnson*. Durham (N.C.), 1927.

Allen, W. *Governor Chamberlain's Administration in South Carolina: A Chapter in Reconstruction in the Southern States.* New York, 1888.

Ames, Mary Clemmer. *Ten Years in Washington.* Hartford (Conn.), 1873.

Andrews, J. Cutler. *The North Reports the Civil War.* Pittsburgh, 1955.

Appleton's Annual Cyclopedia. New York, 1861-.

Avary, Myrta. *Dixie After the War.* Boston, 1937.

Bacon, George Washington. *Life and Speeches of President Andrew Johnson.* London, 1866.

Baker, Lafayette C. *History of the United States Secret Service.* Philadelphia, 1867.

Bancroft, Frederick. *The Life of William H. Seward.* 2 vols. New York, 1900.

Barnes, Thurlow Weed. *Memoir of Thurlow Weed.* 2 vols. Boston, 1884.

Battles and Leaders of the Civil War. Robert Underwood Johnson and Clarence Clough Buel, eds. 4 vols. New York, 1956.

Beale, Howard K. *The Critical Year: A Study of Andrew Johnson and Reconstruction.* New York, 1930. (Reprint, 1958.)

Beard, Charles A. *The Republic: Conversations on Fundamentals.* New York, 1943.

Belden, Thomas Graham and Marva Robins Belden. *So Fell the Angels.* Boston, 1956.

Bentley, George R. *A History of the Freedmen's Bureau.* Philadelphia, 1955.

Bill, Alfred Hoyt. *The Beleaguered City: Richmond 1861-65.* New York, 1946.

Binkley, Wilfred E. *American Political Parties.* 3rd. ed., rev. & enl. New York, 1958.

Blaine, James G. *Twenty Years of Congress: From Lincoln to Garfield. . . .* 2 vols. Norwich (Conn.), 1884.

Botume, Elizabeth Hyde. *First Days Amongst the Contrabands.* Boston, 1893.

Boutwell, George S. *Reminiscences of Sixty Years in Public Affairs.* 2 vols. New York, 1902.

Bowers, Claude G. *The Tragic Era: the Revolution After Lincoln.* New York, 1929.

Boykin, Edward C. *Congress and the Civil War.* New York, 1955.

Bradford, Gamaliel. *As God Made Them: Portraits of Some Nineteenth-Century Americans.* Boston, 1929.

———. *Wives.* New York, 1925.

Briggs, Emily Edson. *The Olivia Letters.* New York and Washington, 1906.

Brockett, L. P. *Men of Our Day.* St. Louis, 1872.

Brogan, D. W. *Government of the People: A Study in the American Political System.* New ed. New York, 1943.

Brooks, Noah. *Statesmen.* New York, 1893.

———. *Washington in Lincoln's Time.* New York, 1895.

Brooks, Van Wyck. *The Times of Melville and Whitman.* New York, 1947.

Brown, Stuart Gerry. *We Hold These Truths: Documents of American Democracy.* New York, 1941.

Browne, Albert Gallatin. *Sketch of the Official Life of John A. Andrew as Governor of Massachusetts* (with) *valedictory address by Governor Andrew* . . . January 5, 1866 . . . on reconstruction. New York, 1868.

Browne, Charles F. *The Complete Works of Artemus Ward.* New York, 1898.

Browning, Orville H. *The Diary of Orville Hickman Browning.* T. C. Pease and J. C. Randall, eds. 2 vols. Springfield (Ill.), 1925.

Buck, Paul H. *The Road to Reunion, 1865-1900.* Boston, 1937.

Bumgardner, Edward. *The Life of Edmund G. Ross: the Man Whose Vote Saved a President.* Kansas City, 1949.

Burton, Theodore E. *John Sherman.* Boston, 1906.

Butler, Benjamin F. *Butler's Book.* Boston, 1892.

———. *Private and Official Correspondence of General Benjamin F. Butler, During the Period of the Civil War.* 5 vols. Norwood (Mass.), 1917.

Cable, George Washington. *The Negro Question.* New York, 1958.

Carter, Hodding. *The Angry Scar.* New York, 1959.

Caskey, Willie Malvin. *Secession and Restoration of Louisiana.* University (La.), 1958.

Catton, Bruce. *This Hallowed Ground.* New York, 1956.

Chadsey, Charles Ernest. *The Struggle Between President Johnson and Congress over Reconstruction.* New York, 1896.

Chapman, John Jay. *The Selected Writings of John Jay Chapman.* Jacques Barzun, ed. New York, 1957.

Chase, Salmon Portland. *Inside Lincoln's Cabinet: the Civil War Diaries of Salmon P. Chase,* David Donald, ed., New York, 1954.

Chestnut, Mary Boykin. *A Diary from Dixie*. Isabella D. Martin and Myrta Lockett Avary, eds. New York, 1905.

Church, William Conant. *Ulysses S. Grant and the Period of National Preservation and Reconstruction*. New York, 1897.

Clark, Delbert. *Washington Dateline*. New York, 1941.

Clarke, Grace Julian. *George Washington Julian*. Indianapolis, 1923.

Conrad, Earl. *Mr. Seward for the Defense*. New York, 1956.

Coolidge, Louis A. *The Life of Ulysses S. Grant*. Boston, 1922.

Cole, Cyrenus. *Iowa Through the Years*. Iowa City, 1940.

Coulter, Ellis Merton. *The South During Reconstruction, 1865-77*. Baton Rouge, 1947.

———. *William G. Brownlow: Fighting Parson of the Southern Highlands*. Chapel Hill, 1937.

Cox, Samuel Sullivan. *Three Decades of Federal Legislation*. Providence, 1885.

Craven, John J. *Prison Life of Jefferson Davis*. New York, 1905.

Crenson, Gus Arthur. *Andrew Johnson and Edwin M. Stanton: A Study in Personalities, 1861-1868*. Washington, 1949.

Crook, W. H. *Memories of the White House: the Home Life of Our Presidents from Lincoln to Roosevelt*. Henry Rood, ed. Boston, 1911.

———. *Through Five Administrations*. New York, 1910.

Cumming, Kate. *A Journal of Hospital Life in the Confederate Army of Tennessee*. Louisville and New Orleans, 1866.

Current, Richard Nelson. *Old Thad Stevens, a Story of Ambition*. Madison, 1942.

Cowan, Frank. *Andrew Johnson, President of the United States: Reminiscences of His Private Life and Character. . . .* 2d ed. Greenesburgh, Pa., 1894.

Dabbs, James McBride. *The Southern Heritage*. New York, 1958.

Davis, Varina. *Jefferson Davis, Ex-President of the Confederate States of America*. 2 vols. New York, 1890.

DeWitt, David Miller. *Impeachment and Trial of Andrew Johnson*. New York, 1903.

———. *The Judicial Murder of Mary E. Surratt*. Baltimore, 1895.

Dorris, Jonathan Truman. *Pardon and Amnesty under Lincoln and Johnson: The Restoration of the Confederates to Their Rights and Privileges, 1861-1898*. Chapel Hill, 1953.

Dowdey, Clifford. *Experiment in Rebellion*. New York, 1946.

DuBois, W. E. Burghardt. *Black Reconstruction, an Essay Toward a*

History of the Part which Black Folk Played in the Attempt to Reconstruct Democracy in America, 1860-1880. New York, 1935.

Dunning, William Archibald. *Essays on the Civil War and Reconstruction and Related Topics.* New York, 1898.

———. *Reconstruction, Political and Economic, 1865-1877.* Vol. 22 in *The American Nation: A History,* ed. by Albert Bushnell Hart, 1907.

Dykeman, Wilma. *The French Broad* (Rivers of America). New York, 1955.

Fessenden, Francis. *Life and Public Services of William Pitt Fessenden.* . . . 2 vols. Boston, 1907.

Fiske, John. *The Mississippi Valley in the Civil War.* Boston, 1900.

Fleming, W. L. *Documentary History of Reconstruction.* 2 vols. Cleveland, 1906, 1907.

———. *The Sequel of Appomattox.* New Haven, 1919.

Forney, John W. *Anecdotes of Public Men.* 2 vols. New York, 1873, 1881.

Foulke, William Dudley. *Life of Oliver P. Morton.* 2 vols. Indianapolis, 1899.

Furman, Bess. *White House Profile.* Indianapolis, 1951.

Grayson, William J. *James Louis Petigru, A Biographical Sketch.* New York, 1866.

Greene, Lawrence, comp. *America Goes to Press: the News of Yesterday.* Indianapolis, 1936.

Hale, Edward Everett, Jr. *William H. Seward.* Philadelphia, 1910.

Hall, Clifton Rumery. *Andrew Johnson, Military Governor of Tennessee.* Princeton, 1916.

Hamilton, Peter J. *The Reconstruction Period.* Vol. 16 of *History of North America.* Philadelphia, 1905.

Hamilton, Joseph Gregoire de Roulhac. *Life of Andrew Johnson.* . . . Greeneville (Tenn.), 1930.

Hart, Albert Bushnell, ed. *American History Told by Contemporaries.* 4 vols. New York, 1932.

Haynes, George H. *Charles Sumner.* Philadelphia, 1909.

———. *The Senate of the United States.* 2 vols. Boston, 1938.

Hendrick, Burton J. *Bulwark of the Republic: a Biography of the Constitution.* Boston, 1938.

———. *Lincoln's War Cabinet.* Boston, 1946.

Henry, Robert Selph. *The Story of the Confederacy.* Rev. ed. Indianapolis, 1957.

————. *The Story of Reconstruction.* Indianapolis, 1938.

Herbert, Hilary Abner and others. *Why the Solid South?* Baltimore, 1890.

Hesseltine, William B. *Lincoln and the War Governors.* New York, 1948.

Hill, Frederick Trevor. *Decisive Battles of the Law.* New York, 1907.

Holzman, Robert S. *Stormy Ben Butler.* New York, 1954.

Horn, Stanley F. *The Decisive Battle of Nashville.* Baton Rouge, 1956.

Howe, Julia Ward. *Reminiscences: 1819-1899.* Boston, 1899.

Hoxie, Richard Leveridge. *Vinnie Ream: Printed for Private Distribution Only and to preserve a Few Souvenirs of Artistic Life from 1865 to 1878.* Washington, 1915.

Hurd, Charles. *Washington Cavalcade.* New York, 1948.

Isley, Jeter Allen. *Horace Greeley and the Republican Party, 1853-1861.* Princeton, 1947.

Johnson, Edgar. *Charles Dickens, His Tragedy and Triumph.* 2 vols. New York, 1952.

Jones, James S. *Life of Andrew Johnson.* Greeneville, 1901.

Josephson, Matthew. *The Robber Barons: the Great American Capitalists 1861-1901.* New York, 1934.

Julian, George W. *Political Recollections.* New York, 1884.

Kean, Edward Younger, ed. *Inside the Confederate Government: The Diary of Robert Garlick Hill Kean.* New York, 1957.

Keckley, Elizabeth Hobbs. *Behind the Scenes.* New York, 1868.

Kendrick, Benjamin B. *The Journal of the Joint Committee of Fifteen on Reconstruction: 39th Congress 1865-1867.* New York, 1914.

Kennedy, John F. *Profiles in Courage.* New York, 1956.

Kimmel, Stanley. *The Mad Booths of Baltimore.* Indianapolis, 1940.

King, Horatio. *Turning on the light: A Dispassionate Survey of President Buchanan's Administration from 1860 to Its Close.* Philadelphia, 1895.

Korngold, Ralph. *Thaddeus Stevens: A Being Darkly Wise and Rudely Great.* New York, 1955.

Laski, Harold J. *The American Presidency.* London, 1940.

Leech, Margaret. *Reveille in Washington.* New York, 1941.

Lewis, Lloyd. *Sherman: Fighting Prophet.* Rev. ed., New York, 1953.

Lichtenstein, Gaston. *Louis D. Wilson, Mexican War Martyr, Also Thomas H. Hall. Andrew Johnson as He Really Was. . . .* Richmond, 1911.

Lorant, Stefan. *Lincoln, a Picture Story of His Life.* Rev. and enl. ed. New York, 1957.

Lothrop, Thornton Kirkland. *William Henry Seward.* Boston, 1899.

Lowell, James Russell. *Political Essays.* Boston, 1889.

MacMahon, Arthur W., ed. *Federalism: Mature and Emergent.* New York, 1955.

McCarthy, Charles H. *Lincoln's Plan of Reconstruction.* New York, 1901.

McClure, Alexander Kelly. *Abraham Lincoln and Men of War-times: Some Personal Recollections.* . . . Philadelphia, 1892.

————. *Old Time Notes of Pennsylvania: A . . . record of the . . . inner history of all political movements since . . . 1838.* Autograph ed. 2 vols. Philadelphia, 1905.

————. *Our Presidents and How We Make Them.* New York, 1902.

McCulloch, Hugh. *Men and Measures of Half a Century.* New York, 1888.

McKitrick, Eric L. *Andrew Johnson and Reconstruction.* Chicago, 1960.

McPherson, Edward. *Political History of the United States During the Period of Reconstruction.* 2d ed. Washington, 1875.

Miller, Alphonse B. *Thaddeus Stevens, the Sinister Patriot.* New York, 1939.

Miers, Earl Schenck. *The General Who Marched to Hell: William Tecumseh Sherman and His March to Fame and Infamy.* New York, 1951.

Miller, John C. *Origins of the American Revolution.* Boston, 1943.

Milton, George Fort. *The Age of Hate.* New York, 1930.

Mitgang, Herbert, ed. *Lincoln as They Saw Him.* New York, 1956.

Moore, Frank. *Speeches of Andrew Johnson, President of the United States, with Biographical Introduction.* . . . Boston, 1865.

Morgan, James. *Our Presidents: Brief Biographies.* . . . New York, 1926.

Morgan, J. M. *Recollections of a Rebel Reefer.* Boston, 1917.

Morrow, Ralph E. *Northern Methodism and Reconstruction.* East Lansing (Mich.), 1956.

Mott, Frank Luther. *American Journalism: a History of Newspapers in the United States Through 250 Years: 1690 to 1950.* Rev. ed. New York, 1950.

————. *A History of American Magazines.* 4 vols. Cambridge, 1938-1957.

Myrdal, Gunnar and others. *An American Dilemma: the Negro Problem and Modern Democracy.* 2 vols. New York, 1944.

Nevins, Allan. *American Social History as Recorded by British Travelers.* New York, 1923.

———. *The Emergence of Lincoln.* 2 vols. New York, 1950.

———. *The Emergence of Modern America: 1865-1878.* New York, 1927.

———. *Ordeal of the Union.* 2 vols. New York, 1947.

Newell, Robert Henry. *The Orpheus C. Kerr Papers.* . . . New York, 1871.

Nicolay, John G. and John Hay. *Abraham Lincoln, a History.* 10 vols. New York, 1894-1905.

———. *Complete Works of Abraham Lincoln.* . . . New and enl. ed. 12 vols. New York, 1894-1905.

Nye, Russell B. *George Bancroft, Brahmin Rebel.* New York, 1944.

Oberholtzer, Ellis Paxson. *A History of the United States Since the Civil War.* 5 vols. New York, 1917.

O'Connor, Richard. *Sheridan, the Inevitable.* Indianapolis, 1953.

Old South Leaflets, vol. VIII. Boston, undated.

Phelps, Elizabeth Stuart and others. *Our Famous Women.* Hartford, 1888.

Pierce, Edward L. *Memoir and Letters of Charles Sumner.* 4 vols. Boston, 1893.

Pittman, Ben. *The Assassination of President Lincoln and the Trial of the Conspirators.* . . . New York, 1865.

Poore, Ben: Perley, ed. *The Conspiracy Trial for the Murder of the President.* 3 vols. Boston, 1865.

———. *Perley's Reminiscences of 60 Years in the National Metropolis.* Tecumseh (Mich.), 1886.

Pound, Roscoe and others. *Federalism as a Democratic Process* . . . New Brunswick (N.J.), 1942.

Pratt, Fletcher. *Stanton, Lincoln's Secretary of War.* New York, 1953.

Quarles, Benjamin. *The Negro in the Civil War.* Boston, 1953.

Randall, James Garfield. *The Civil War and Reconstruction.* New York, 1937, 1953.

———. *Lincoln the President.* 4 vols. (Vol. IV completed by Richard Nelson Current from Professor Randall's notes.) New York, 1946-1955.

Randall, Ruth Painter. *Mary Lincoln: Biography of a Marriage.* Boston, 1953.

Redding, Saunders. *The Lonesome Road: The Story of the Negro's Part in America.* New York, 1958.

Rhodes, James Ford. *History of the United States from the Compromise of 1850.* 7 vols. New York, 1893-1906.

Richardson, James D. *Messages and Papers of the Presidents, 1789-1897.* Vol. VI, "Abraham Lincoln and Andrew Johnson." Washington, 1899.

Riddle, Albert Gallatin. *The Life of Benjamin F. Wade.* Cleveland, 1886.

Ross, Edmund Gibson. *History of the Impeachment of Andrew Johnson.* Santa Fe, 1896.

Ross, Ishbel. *First Lady of the South: the Life of Mrs. Jefferson Davis.* New York, 1958.

————. *Proud Kate.* New York, 1953.

Russell, William Howard. *My Diary North and South.* New York, 1954.

Salmon, Lucy Maynard. *The Newspaper and the Historian.* New York, 1923.

Sandburg, Carl. *Abraham Lincoln: the War Years.* 4 vols. New York, 1939.

Savage, John. *The Life and Public Services of Andrew Johnson . . . Including His State Papers, Speeches and Addresses.* New York, 1866.

Schlesinger, Arthur Meier, Jr. *The Age of Jackson.* Boston, 1945.

Schouler, James. *History of the Reconstruction Period: 1865-1877.* Vol. VII of *History of the United States of America Under the Constitution.* New York, 1913.

Schurz, Carl. *The Reminiscences of Carl Schurz.* 3 vols. New York, 1907.

Scott, Eben Greenough. *Reconstruction During the Civil War in the United States.* Boston, 1895.

Sheridan, Philip Henry. *Personal Memoirs. . . .* 2 vols. New York, 1904.

Sherman, John. *Recollections of Forty Years in the House, Senate and Cabinet.* 2 vols. New York, 1895.

Sherman, William T. *Memoirs of General William T. Sherman.* New ed. Bloomington (Ind.), 1957.

Smith, William Ernest. *The Francis Preston Blair Family in Politics.* 2 vols. New York, 1933.

Stern, Philip Van Doren. *An End to Valor: the Last Days of the Civil War.* Boston, 1958.

Stewart, William Morris. *Reminiscences of Senator William Morris*

Stewart of Nevada. George Rothwell Brown, ed. New York and Washington, 1908.

Stoddard, William Osborn. *The Lives of the Presidents,* vol. VII. New York, 1888.

Strode, Hudson. *Jefferson Davis, American Patriot, 1808-1861.* New York, 1955.

Strong, George Templeton. *The Diary of George Templeton Strong.* Allan Nevins and Milton Halsey Thomas, eds. 3 vols. New York, 1952.

Stryker, Lloyd Paul. *Andrew Johnson: A Study in Courage.* New York, 1929.

Sumner, Charles. *Works.* (Statesmen ed.) 20 vols. Boston, 1910.

Swanberg, W. A. *First Blood: the Story of Fort Sumter.* New York 1957.

————. *Sickles the Incredible.* New York, 1956.

Tappan, George L. *Andrew Johnson—Not Guilty.* New York, 1954.

Taylor, Richard. *Destruction and Reconstruction. . . . Personal Experiences.* New York, 1955.

Temple, Oliver Perry. *Notable Men of Tennessee from 1833 to 1875.* New York, 1912.

Trefousse, Hans L. *Ben Butler: the South Called Him Beast!* New York, 1957.

Trowbridge, John Townsend. *Picture of the Desolated States . . . 1865-1868.* Hartford, 1868.

Van Deusen, Glyndon G. *Horace Greeley: Nineteenth-Century Crusader.* Philadelphia, 1953.

Warden, W. W. *The Private Life and Public Services of Salmon P. Chase.* Cincinnati, 1874.

Weisberger, Bernard A. *Reporters for the Union.* Boston, 1953.

Welles, Gideon. *Diary of Gideon Welles.* 3 vols. Boston, 1911.

White, Horace. *The Life of Lyman Trumbull.* Boston, 1913.

White, Laura. *Robert Barnwell Rhett: Father of Secession.* New York, 1931.

White, Leonard D. *The Republican Era.* New York, 1958.

Whyte, James. *The Uncivil War: Washington During the Reconstruction.* New York, 1958.

Wilson, Forrest. *Crusader in Crinoline: the Life of Harriet Beecher Stowe.* New York, 1941.

Wiltse, Charles M. *John C. Calhoun: Sectionalist, 1840-1850.* Indianapolis, 1951.

Winston, Robert Watson. *Andrew Johnson, Plebian and Patriot.* New York, 1928.

Winston, Robert Watson. *High Stakes and Hair Trigger: the Life of Jefferson Davis.* New York, 1930.

Williams, Kenneth P. *Lincoln Finds a General: A Military Study of the Civil War,* vol. IV. New York, 1956.

Williams, Thomas Harry. *Lincoln and the Radicals.* Madison (Wis.), 1941.

Woodward, Comer Vann. *Reunion and Reaction: the Compromise of 1877 and the End of Reconstruction.* New York, 1951.

Woodward, W. E. *Meet General Grant.* New York, 1928.

Works Progress Administration. *A Guide to the Nation's Capital.* New York, 1942.

Books (Fiction)

Crabb, Alfred Leland. *Lodging at the Saint Cloud: A Tale of Occupied Nashville.* Indianapolis, 1946.

McSpadden, Joseph Walker. *Storm Center: A Novel about Andy Johnson.* . . . New York, 1947.

Tourgee, Albion. *A Fool's Errand* (a Story of Reconstruction). New York, 1879.

ACKNOWLEDGMENTS

Since much of the factual material of this book was obtained from primary sources, the assistance of many individuals and institutions was sought and in every case generously and courteously given. In this connection I am greatly indebted to Dr. C. Percy Powell and others of the Library of Congress, to Mr. John Maddox of the National Archives, to Mr. Kenneth Lohf of the Special Collections reading-room at the library of Columbia University, to Mr. W. R. Leech of the New York Historical Society, and to the staffs of New York Public Library, New York University Library, Yale University Library and the public libraries of Bridgeport, Danbury, Southport, Fairfield and Westport, Connecticut.

I would also like to express my gratitude for permission to make use of material found in unpublished theses, diaries and manuscripts in the holdings of Columbia University and the State Historical Society of Wisconsin.

In addition my warm private thanks are due to Mrs. Margaret Johnson Patterson Bartlett of Greeneville, Tennessee, great-granddaughter of President Johnson; to my friend, Raymond J. Neville, many of whose suggestions for treatment have been incorporated in the book; to Professor Allan Nevins; to Professor LeRoy P. Graf of the University of Tennessee; to Mr. Bruce Catton; to Mr. Everette Swinney and Mr. Frank Evans of Pennsylvania State University; to Captain Scarritt Adams, U.S.N.; and to my patient and knowing mentor, Mr. Robert Giroux, editor-in-chief of Farrar, Straus and Cudahy.

[365]

The numerous contemporary newspapers consulted are not listed in the Bibliography, but those used are cited in the text. The decision to confine references to an occasional footnote has been made under the impression that most readers are not interested in this information, together with the fact that many of the sources used are indicated in a general way in the book itself.

INDEX

(The abbreviation AJ stands for Andrew Johnson)

[367]

THE SENATE AS A COURT OF IMPEACHMENT FOR THE TRIAL OF ANDREW JOHNSON